The Addictions

Multidisciplinary Perspectives and Treatments

Edited by

Harvey B. Milkman
Metropolitan State College

Howard J. Shaffer
Harvard Medical School

Lexington Books
D.C. Heath and Company/Lexington, Massachusetts/Toronto

Dedicated to our loving parents
Sid and Lee Milkman
Milton and Ruth Shaffer

Library of Congress Cataloging in Publication Data

Main entry under title:

The Addictions: multidisciplinary perspectives and treatment.

   Based on the proceedings of a national conference entitled: The addictions: an interdisciplinary synthesis of concepts and treatments, held in Denver, Colo., Oct. 28–29, 1983.
   Includes bibliographies and index.
   1. Substance abuse—Congresses. I. Milkman, Harvey, 1944–   . II. Shaffer, Howard, 1948–   . [DNLM: 1. Substance Dependence—prevention & control—congresses. 2. Substance Dependence—therapy—congresses. WM 270 A2244 1983]
   RC564.A293   1985   616.86   84–47871
   ISBN 0–669–08739–4 (alk. paper)

Second printing, October 1985

Published simultaneously in Canada

Printed in the United States of America on acid-free paper

International Standard Book Number: 0–669–08739–4

Library of Congress Catalog Card Number: 84–47871

Contents

Part II Treatment Perspectives 85

Part III Epilogue 183

Figures and Tables

Figures

Tables

Preface

Harvey B. Milkman

This book evolved from a series of conversations between Stanley Sunderwirth, an organic chemist, and me, a clinical psychologist. Each of us held radically different views regarding the etiology of mental disorders.

In the spring of 1980 I assumed responsibility for developing a course offering on schizophrenia. I set out to meet the dual objectives of educating families and friends of patients, and creating a meaningful learning experience for students. It soon became apparent that a comprehensive approach to the topic should include multiple disciplines. Speakers were recruited from the diverse fields of genetics, biochemistry, psychology, psychiatry, and social work. Upon completion of the course, class evaluations revealed an overwhelming enthusiasm for the interdisciplinary experience.

My own comprehension of schizophrenia took a quantum leap. Whereas I was previously impressed with the importance of symbolism and metaphor in psychotic communications, I gained a new appreciation for the role of neurochemistry in thought disorders.

During the same period I began to consider that, in the field of addiction, *experience* may be perceived as the protagonist and the user's drugs of choice merely as supporting actors, that is, pharmacologic defense mechanisms. Sunderwirth became intrigued with this formulation from a biochemical standpoint. He postulated that similar neurochemical consequences might be involved in compulsive risk taking as well as in the abuse of stimulant drugs. Similarly, he hypothesized that experiences that promoted sensations of tranquility and somnolence might have neurochemical similarities to repetitive opiate ingestion. The Milkman and Sunderwirth collaboration resulted in publication of "Addictive Processes" (1982). Since that time we have continued developing a multidisciplinary model for the addictions.

In the summer of 1982, Howard Shaffer and I began to discuss the importance of a multidisciplinary approach to addictive disorders. Shaffer was impressed with the necessity for developing a solid philosophical and scientific base in the addiction field. We both saw the need for movement from the medical concentration on biochemically based theory and treatment to a model which includes psychological and social mechanisms as well. Consequently we collaboratively developed a national conference, *The Addictions: An Interdisciplinary Synthesis of Concepts and Treatments*, held in Denver, Colorado, from October 28 to 29, 1983. This book, based largely on the presentations at the Addictions Conference, represents yet another phase in the interdisciplinary evolution of a more comprehensive understanding of addictive phenomena.

We are deeply grateful to the many authors who have entrusted their clinical, research, and theoretical expertise to this publication. In addition to the aforementioned crucial collaborations with Howard Shaffer and Stanley Sunderwirth, I am especially thankful to William A. Frosch, David E. Smith, and Lloyd Sederer for their contributions and continued support during the past two decades.

I would like to thank Richard Fontera, President of Metropolitan State College, for offering his leadership in the development of the Addictions Conference. The following individuals were also instrumental in actualizing this event: Douglas Jacobs, Director, and Bonnie Cummins, Assistant Director, Continuing Education Division, Department of Psychiatry, The Cambridge Hospital; Carolyn Dyer and the staff of the North Charles Institute for the Addictions; Andrew Breckel III, Assistant Vice-President for Off-Campus Programs, Metropolitan State College; Skip Ackler, Director, and the staff of the Department of Conferences and Seminars, Metropolitan State College. I would also like to thank Edward W. Karnes, Chairperson, and Jack Hesson, Professor, Department of Psychology, Metropolitan State College, for their friendship and encouragement throughout this entire sequence of events.

Reference

Milkman, H. & Sunderwirth, S. (1982). Addictive processes. *The Journal of Psychoactive Drugs, 14* (3), 177–192.

Introduction: Crisis and Conflict in the Addictions

Howard J. Shaffer
Harvey B. Milkman

> Even though it's not your idea . . . it still might be a good idea.
> William A. Frosch

The multiplicity of phenomena collectively known as the addictive behaviors has a long and rich social history. The field that has developed as a result of the study of these phenomena is of much more recent vintage. As a result of its youth, this field suffers through energy, naivete, unbounded curiosity, and conflicting explanations of its identity and purpose. It is difficult to gain perspective on a field as diverse and complex as the addictions. This is a field rooted historically in a variety of disciplines that include medicine, psychology, physiology, sociology, social work, biology, chemistry, politics, and witchcraft, to name only a few. The addictive behaviors seem to defy classification and explanation. For example, the documented history of intoxicant abuse is at least five thousand years old; narcotics became controlled substances in 1914 with the passage of the Harrison Act; however, addictive behaviors have been considered a diagnostic category only since 1934 (Szasz, 1974). Five thousand years of use and only twenty years have passed between government intervention and drug abuse becoming the target of medical/clinical intervention!

The Addictions: A Problem of Disciplinary Identity

Identity problems in young sciences are not uncommon. Neither are the theoretical and clinical controversies that are stimulated by the constituents of these disciplines. Recently, Shaffer and his associates have suggested that the addiction field is in a preparadigm stage of scientific development (Burglass & Shaffer, 1983; Gambino & Shaffer,

1979; Khantzian & Shaffer, 1981; Shaffer, 1982, 1983a, 1983b; Shaffer & Burglass, 1981; Shaffer & Gambino, 1979; Shaffer & Gambino, 1983; Shaffer & Kauffman, in press). A paradigm, according to Kuhn (1962), is essentially the framework or perspective that defines the rules and standards of practice for a particular community of workers (that is, physicists, psychiatrists, psychologists, etc.). Individuals working in the field of addictions do not share a unitary set of rules or standards for the treatment of dependence disorders; in fact, there is controversy as to whether or not these disorders are multi- or unidimensional. For example, as clinicians who treat addictive disorders debate the efficacy and morality of drug versus drug-free treatment and whether or not psychotherapy can proceed or be useful while a patient is using a particular substance, others argue the utility of abstinence or controlled use as a treatment outcome.

Similarly, there is little agreement as to the etiology of addictive disorders. For example, pharmacologists understand the addictions as a set of pharmacologic problems involving such pharmacologic categories as drugs, tolerance, or binding sites. Similarly, psychologists and psychiatrists are typically willing to read into the phenomenon of addiction those problems of learning, compulsion, or ego function. Physiologists posit problems of withdrawal, metabolism, or target organ effects. Sociologists see processes of social regulation, peer pressure, and/or environmental forces. Politicians, lawyers, and law enforcement agents view addiction problems as involving controlled substances, criminals, and/or deterrence. At present, no single theory dominates thinking in the field of addictive behaviors or outlines clinical interventions comprehensively. "Nonetheless, current theory and practice, despite the extreme diversity and often strident discord in the field, reflect a growing consensus on the importance of using scientific methods in both research and practice, and on modeling the older, established scientific disciplines" (Burglass & Shaffer, 1981, p. xxi).

Scientific Development and the Addictions: A Preparadigm Stage

The diversity of models and explanatory mechanisms postulated as responsible for the development of the addictive disorders and the wide range of competing theories offered to guide the course of treatment compete for scientific and clinical popularity (for example, Lettieri, Sayers & Pearson, 1980). When a theory gains support—and the consequent momentary ascendancy to popularity that accompanies such explanatory power—without an integrative perspective with which to judge its efficacy, the field gradually loses interest and the model loses popularity. These debates over legitimate methods, problems, and standards of solution serve to define competing schools of thought rather than to facilitate agreements among constituents of these parties. Such debates characterize and are hallmarks of a preparadigm period (Kuhn, 1962). Though the concept of paradigm was applied primarily to the physical sciences, it is applicable to the current state of affairs in the addictions.

In the absence of a paradigm, it is difficult to agree on what the important parameters of addictive disorders are. Furthermore, the evidence intended to support the constructs of dependence, tolerance, neuroadaptation, character disorder, etc., is often clouded because experts have difficulty agreeing on the important data. "In the absence of a paradigm all of the facts that could possibly pertain to the development of a given science are likely to seem equally relevant" (Kuhn, 1962, p. 15). During a preparadigm period, controversy continues without a forseeable end. More importantly, without an operative paradigm, the psychiatric community does not have any generally agreed upon standards for determining the utility of one approach versus another or the efficacy of any theory to explain the observed phenomena. Thus, without such guidelines, it is no wonder that clinicians do not energetically endorse the findings generated by researchers. Furthermore, these conditions impede our understanding of the nature of the field and serve to block efforts at teaching and training in the human services in general and the addictions in particular.

Crisis of Categories

The conflict inherent in a preparadigm stage of scientific development has created a crisis of categories in the addictions (Burglass & Shaffer, 1981). This crisis was precipitated by questions and concerns regarding the adequacy of existing categories of explanation for the present stage of research in the addictions field. Progress in any scientific field takes place when the explanatory categories employed are capable of clarifying, explaining, and generating an understanding of the phenomenon under investigation; typically, these categories are validated by the research that follows. However, new ideas emerge from the research that was stimulated by existing categories. These new concepts question the earlier generative categories and the postulates on which they rest. The outcome is a crisis of categories. In the mature sciences, this crisis is rapidly resolved by referring to the set of rules of method and practice that serve to guide the field—an operative paradigm.

It is precisely because the addictions lack an accepted paradigm that the field is in crisis "with regard to the basic categories by which it gathers data and assembles ideas into theory. Thus, the various discipline-specific ideas and theories can neither disprove nor invalidate one another. These perspectives simply coexist; each has its loyal adherents; each pursues its particular version of truth about the addictions in its own way" (Burglass & Shaffer, 1981, p. xxii).

Reductionism and the Addictions

Humans love to classify. Most of us spend a lifetime classifying things in our environment in order to make sense of and understand our lives. This tendency has been responsible (since Aristotle) for the trend of reductionism in science. For example, scientists often explain things at one level by describing things at a more micro-level of analysis: psychologists often defer explanations of the mysteries of the mind to physiologists, who defer to biologists, who defer to chemists, who defer to physicists. Paradoxically, physicists often explain complex and confusing physical events by deferring to psychologists and their explanations of perception and the mind.

In the addictions, the trend of reductionism, paralleled by advancing technology, can be illustrated by the wide range of models offered to explain addictive behavior during the last one hundred years. These explanations have included, for example, weak will, moral deprivation, ego deficits, social impoverishment, interactive psychosocial factors, behavioral and social learning, metabolic deficiencies, endorphin and other central nervous system imbalances. Although these explanations have been reductionistic and categorical, these models have been useful in helping us to understand the specifics of a great many different areas; currently, addictive behaviors are among those that seem to defy satisfactory explanation in spite of our capacity for classification.

It is no longer useful to consider only the narrow and categorical elements of our society that distress us. Drugs are a part of the social landscape; the psychoactive use of chemicals interacts with every part of our social sphere (Freedman, 1972). Though we may want to deny, repress, or change it, drug use and drug-seeking behavior are here to stay. We may propose to limit the use of these substances to situations where appropriate indications exist or to make greater efforts to ensure their safety but we should be aware that the proliferation of chemicals will likely continue. Furthermore, Peele (1979) (Peele & Brodsky, 1975) has demonstrated that addictive behaviors need not be limited to behavior patterns that depend on the intake of exogenous chemicals. More recently,

Milkman and Sunderwirth (1982) have articulated an integration of the biological, psychological, and social factors that may be responsible for the variety of behavior patterns that have come to be described as addictive. According to these views, experience is the protagonist and drugs of choice are merely auxiliary, supporting actors. This broadened perspective opens a Pandora's box of potential vehicles for the addictive disorders: Consider the current fascination with music videos (for example, M-TV), cult ceremonial practices, video games, computers, risk-taking stunts, and even the fascination and compulsive attraction of some to nuclear weapons and war (Vonnegut, 1984; Vosseler, 1984).

During the present period of research and practice without an operative paradigm, the multidimensional considerations of biological, psychological, sociological, and behavioral heuristics (for example, Lazare, 1976, 1979) are natural partners in any serious attempt to describe and understand the complexities of progressive behavior patterns that are characterized by a subjective compulsion to continue, loss or reduction of personal control, evidence of neuroadaptation (for example, Milkman & Sunderwirth, 1982), the salience of the destructive behavior pattern relative to other activities, and the tendency for rapid reinstatement of the behavior pattern following a period of abstinence (Burglass & Shaffer, 1983).

The Addictions: Multidisciplinary Perspectives and Treatments brings together disparate clinical observations, research findings, and theoretical formulations in order to promote a higher level synthesis of fundamental and apparently related human problems. This book is designed to ease the crisis of categories in the addictions by presenting a variety of contemporary perspectives that both challenge and complement each other—clashes that may bring us closer to a unified perspective. It is also an attempt to reduce the trend of unidimensional reductionism and simplistic explanation in a field beset by complexity. Finally, this collection is an attempt to confront directly the contemporary controversies in the addiction field. The volume is organized around two central yet overlapping themes: theory and treatment. Each theoretical position is derived from a synthesis of pertinent research studies and conceptual formulations within major discipline subcategories. The treatment section describes contemporary applications of these addiction theories in clinical practice.

Theoretical Perspectives

In the biological arena theoretical positions are presented from the subdisciplines of genetics, neurochemistry, and biopharmacology. In "Inheriting

Addictions: A Genetic Perspective with Emphasis on Alcohol and Nicotine," Collins reviews data from family studies, twin studies, and twins-reared-apart studies which indicate that addictions have a genetic basis. Although both alcoholism and smoking are clearly influenced by genetic factors, environmental factors are also important and a genotype-by-environment interaction is postulated as critical for understanding the development of alcohol and nicotine compulsions. Milkman and Sunderwirth (1983) have defined addiction as "self-induced changes in neurotransmission which result in problem behaviors." In "Biological Mechanisms: Neurotransmission and Addiction," Sunderwirth describes how neuroadaptation may account for increasing drug hunger or craving for certain nondrug-oriented activities, (for example, risk taking, meditation) which may have neurochemical consequences similar to the ingestion of psychoactive substances. The final, biologically based, chapter by Freedman, "Biopharmacologic Factors in Drug Abuse," describes effects of the long-term sensitization of various neuronal systems involved in chronic use of stimulants such as amphetamines or cocaine. Freedman also describes how alcohol withdrawal in a subgroup of alcoholic patients leads to an irritable hypomanic state which may be related to the effects of alcohol on adrenergic systems.

Although there are many psychological theories which attempt to explain addictive phenomena, behavioral and psychoanalytic formulations comprise the mainstream of psychological thought. Frosch's "An Analytic Overview of Addictions" indicates how the evolution of psychoanalytic understanding of addiction recapitulates the history of psychoanalytic theory. While early interest focused on orality and other libidinal drives, recent interest centers on ego defect and the control of punitive rage. In "Trends in Behavioral Psychology and the Addictions," Shaffer and Schneider review the behavioral approaches to human problems and illustrate them with examples from the fields of substance abuse and excessive behaviors. The current trend toward cognitive-behaviorism is examined along with changes in treatment practices, which parallel modifications in behavioral theory. After a period of radical behaviorism, detached from cognitive processes, contemporary behavioral models display a strong and decisive trend toward the inclusion of internal events which have been the perennial concentration of psychoanalytic thought.

Although psychological and biological factors are critically important in comprehending what impels someone to use an intoxicant and how the intoxicant affects the user, the influence of physical and social setting, within which the use occurs, must also be considered. In "The Social Psychology of Intoxicant Use: The Interaction of Personality and

Social Setting," Zinberg and Shaffer explore how social changes influence the process of social learning, which, in turn, changes the average expectable environment. These events lead to the development of social mores, rules, sanctions, and rituals which determine the informal social controls that limit intoxicant use and abuse.

In the absence of effective informal social controls, law represents the formal social controls placed on individuals to restrict addictive behaviors. In "Addictive Behavior and the Justice System," Hunter and Pudim explore the legislative debate about whether or not addicts should be allowed clemency because of diminished capacity resultant from addictive disease. The authors explain the informal social influences which underlie the current judicial trend toward a verdict of "guilty, but mentally ill."

Treatment Perspectives

Effective treatment is dependent on accurate diagnosis, thus the diagnostic process represents the initiation of treatment. Ongoing evaluation of the patient's condition and progress allows for further and even more specific treatment (Menninger, 1963). In "Testing Hypotheses: An Approach for the Assessment of Addictive Behaviors," Shaffer and Neuhaus describe an efficient means of organizing and verifying clinical information, thus making the assessment procedure both manageable and teachable. In concert with the Theoretical Perspectives section of this book, Shaffer and Neuhaus review clinical assessment hypotheses which have emerged from consideration of the various disciplines represented, that is, biological, psychodynamic, behavioral, and sociological. Guidelines are provided for gathering and ordering information which supports or contraindicates the viability of further inquiry and/or intervention.

In "A Biobehavioral Approach to the Origins and Treatment of Substance Abuse," Crowley describes treatment based on the interplay between variables that promote or inhibit addictive behaviors. Substance and social influences which tend to facilitate drug abuse are availability, social acceptability, and pharmacologic reinforcing effect. Person or set variables which increase the probability of use are risk-taking orientation, prior drug use experience, genetic predisposition, and sex; males predominate among drug abusers. Counteracting these influences are potent, immediate, and certain social or pharmacologic punishments, positive social modeling, and reinforcement of drug-incompatible behaviors.

The contemporary array of reinforcements and punishments which surround the use and abuse of cocaine illustrate a dynamic interplay of the influences described above. In "The Use of Marijuana and Alcohol by Regular Users of Cocaine: Patterns of Use and Style of Control," Burglass provides a preliminary discussion of the elements of successful controlled substance use. Although cocaine provides a frame of reference for the work, the primary interest is not cocaine per se. Rather it is learning how ways of using one drug might modify the use and control of another, thereby exploring the dimensions and elements of successful substance use.

Psychodynamically oriented clinicians have long argued that behavioral approaches to addiction do not adequately address the specific intrapsychic meaning of the addictive substance or activity. In "Addiction, Adaptation, and the 'Drug-of-Choice' Phenomenon: Clinical Perspectives," Khantzian and Schneider describe how specific drugs may be used, in an adaptive manner, to provide relief from distress and to help people cope with their internal emotional life and external reality. In this view, the drug-of-choice serves as a pharmacologic defense mechanism. Individuals who have experimented with different classes of drugs, yet show distinct drug preferences, are understood as medicating themselves for underlying psychiatric problems and for painful, unbearable affective states.

A primary example of the critical function of social setting in the addictions is provided by the hospital environment. In this milieu, the abuse of narcotic drugs by both nurses and physicians far exceeds that of the general population and is considered by some as "an occupational hazard." In "Treatment of the Chemically Dependent Health Professional," Buxton, Jessup, and Landry describe alcohol and drug addiction among professionals who work in a medical setting. A model for peer intervention is provided, as well as specific guidelines for the evaluation of treatment efficacy.

The majority of contemporary treatments for alcoholism center around the concept that it is a progressive disease which, if left untreated, may lead to increasing biological, psychological, or social dysfunction and probable death. In "Addictive Disease: Concept and Controversy," Smith, Milkman, and Sunderwirth discuss the implications of applying the disease model to the compulsive and continued use of a wide spectrum of psychoactive drugs, including the popular stimulant cocaine. A critique of the model, based on diminished attention to personal and social responsibility, is also presented.

In "Cognitive-Behavioral Treatment for Problem Drinking," Emrick, Hansen, and Maytag discuss the most potent treatment alternative to the disease model for addiction. Depending on many factors, an alcohol-dependent individual may be treated with either the goal of total, permanent abstinence from alcohol or the goal of moderate, nonproblem, drinking. These treatments begin with a differential assessment of the particular nature and etiological factors involved in an individual's dependence on alcohol. A number of behavioral and cognitive procedures are then employed to help an individual achieve his or her drinking goal. These include self-monitoring of drinking behavior, functional analysis of drinking behavior, self-concept development, alteration of thinking responses to excessive drinking, and alteration of the cognitive and behavioral responses of significant others that activate or reinforce excessive drinking behavior.

In recognition of the variety of effective models for understanding and treating a wide spectrum of compulsive problem behaviors, in a large number of individuals, Frye presents "A Multimodality Approach to the Treatment of Addiction." From a sociobiological perspective, humans have developed the ability to alter consciousness as a survival device under circumstances in which application of usual reality testing functions may be sufficiently demoralizing to mean the difference between life and death. A void is created when the individual is asked to give up his or her addictive resources, which have their origins in survival mechanisms. The multimodality approach seeks to provide individually designed treatment compensation for the lost addictive resources. Traditional and innovative addiction treatment methods are reviewed in this context.

In the epilogue, Sederer discusses several implications of the interdisciplinary synthesis presented in this book. As we increasingly recognize the crucial importance of biological, psychological, and social variables in the determination and treatment of addiction, we repeatedly confront uncertainty about the legitimate turf of our professional endeavors. We discover that we have no hierarchy of causation and no prescribed sequence for intervention. What guides our next step—according to Sederer—must be the social, moral, and ethical implications of the science of addictions.

References

Burglass, M.E. & Shaffer, H. (1983). Diagnosis in the addictions: Conceptual problems. *Advances in Alcohol and Substance Abuse*, 3 (½), 19–34.

Burglass, M.E. & Shaffer, H. (1981). The natural history of ideas in the treatment of addictions. In H. Shaffer & M.E. Burglass (Eds.), *Classic contributions in the addictions*. New York: Brunner/Mazel.

Freedman, A.M. (1972). Drugs and society: An ecological approach. *Comprehensive Psychiatry*, 13, 411–420.

Gambino, B. & Shaffer, H. (1979). The concept of paradigm and the treatment of addiction. *Professional Psychology*, 10, 207–223.

Khantzian, E.J. & Shaffer, H. (1981). A contemporary psychoanalytic view of addiction theory and treatment. In J. Lowinson & P. Ruiz (Eds.), *Substance abuse: Clinical problems and perspectives* (p. 465–475). Baltimore: Williams & Wilkins.

Kuhn, T.S. (1962). *The structure of scientific revolutions.* Chicago: University of Chicago Press.

Lazare, A. (1976). The psychiatric examination in the walk-in clinic. *Archives of General Psychiatry, 33,* 96–102.

Lazare, A. (1979). Hypothesis testing in the clinical overview. In A. Lazare (Ed.), *Outpatient psychiatry: Diagnosis and treatment.* Baltimore: Williams & Wilkins.

Lettieri, D.J., Sayers, M. & Pearson, H.W. (Eds.) (1980). *Theories on drug abuse: Selected contemporary perspectives.* (National Institute on Drug Abuse Research Monograph 30; DHHS Publication No. (ADM)80-967). Washington, D.C.: U.S. Government Printing Office.

Menninger, K. (1963). *The vital balance: The life process in mental health and illness.* New York: Viking Press.

Milkman, H. & Sunderwirth, S. (1983, October). The chemistry of craving. *Psychology Today,* pp. 36–44.

Milkman, H. & Sunderwirth, S. (1982). Addictive processes. *Journal of Psychoactive Drugs, 14*(3), 177–192.

Peele, S. (1979). Redefining addiction II. The meaning of addiction in our lives. *Journal of Psychedelic Drugs, 11,* 289–297.

Peele, S. & Brodsky, A. (1975). *Love and addiction.* New York: Signet.

Shaffer, H. (1982). How did addictive behavior become the object of clinical assessment? From natural history to clinical practice. *Bulletin of Psychologists in Substance Abuse, 1,* 159–162.

Shaffer, H. (1983a). Integrating theory, research and clinical practice: A perspective for the treatment of the addictions. *Bulletin of Psychologists in Substance Abuse, 2,* 34–41.

Shaffer, H. (1983b). The natural history and social ecology of addictive behaviors. *Advances in Alcohol and Substance Abuse, 3*(½), 1–6.

Shaffer, H. & Burglass, M.E. (Eds.) (1981). *Classic contributions in the addictions.* New York: Brunner/Mazel.

Shaffer, H. Gambino, B. (1979). Addiction paradigms II: Theory, research, and practice. *Journal of Psychedelic Drugs, 11,* 207–223.

Shaffer, H. & Gambino, B. (1983). Addiction paradigms III: From theory-research to practice and back. *Advances in Alcohol and Substance Abuse, 3*(½), 135–152.

Shaffer, H. & Kauffman, J. (in press). The clinical assessment and diagnosis of addiction I: Hypotheses testing. In T. Bratter & G. Forrest (Eds.), *Alcoholism and substance abuse: Strategies for intervention.* New York: Free Press.

Szasz, T. (1974). *Ceremonial chemistry: The ritual persecution of drugs, addicts, and pushers.* New York: Anchor Press.

Vonnegut, K. (1984, February 1). The worst addict of them all. *The Valley Advocate,* p. 1.

Vossler, M. (1984). Nuclear addiction. *Report of International Physicians for the Prevention of Nuclear War, Inc., 2,* 6.

Part I
Theoretical Perspectives

1
Inheriting Addictions: A Genetic Perspective with Emphasis on Alcohol and Nicotine

Allan C. Collins

The issue of whether genetic factors contribute to the development of addictions is intimately related to the often emotional issue of whether genetic factors contribute to behavior in general. The science that attempts to resolve this issue is called behavior genetics, a rapidly growing field of scientific endeavor. Behavior geneticists have been studying the genetic basis for such things as schizophrenia, manic-depression, specific cognitive abilities and certain aspects of personality (Plomin, DeFries & McClearn, 1980). These forms of behavior, and virtually all others that have been studied, appear to be influenced by both genetic and environmental factors. It is not nature *or* nurture, rather nature *and* nurture that seem to influence many behavioral traits. This review will cite some of the data that indicate this is also the case for addiction to alcohol and tobacco.

Research Strategies

Establishing whether a particular trait or, in the words of the geneticist, phenotype, is influenced by heritable factors (genetics) is generally accomplished by the use of one or more of several research strategies. These are family studies, adoption studies, twin studies, and twins-reared-apart studies.

Family studies involve ascertaining whether a particular phenotype runs in families. Not all traits that run in families have a genetic basis.

The work of the author cited in this review was supported, in part, by Public Health Services grants AA-03527 and DA-03194.

The assistance of Sharon Huntoon in preparation of the manuscript is appreciated.

For example, speaking Polish, eating pizza, and playing softball seem to run in families, but these probably do not have a heritable basis. Rather, it may be argued that such traits are likely to be determined almost exclusively by environment. Other traits, such as height, clearly seem to run in families. Does this mean that height is influenced only by genetic factors? Probably not. For example, it is well known that we are considerably taller than were our great-grandparents (Genoves, 1970). Presumably, the better nutrition of today's Americans contributed to the growth. Thus, environmental factors influence the genetic factors—a genotype-by-environment interaction. Since members of the same family presumably have similar environments, family studies only suggest a heritable basis.

Adoption studies have been carried out to avoid the "similar environment in families" issue. It has been argued that if a trait is expressed in an adoptee to the same degree or extent as was the trait in the adoptee's biological parents, the trait is influenced by genetic factors. If, however, the adoptee resembles his or her adopted parents, the trait is likely to be environmentally influenced. The degree to which the adoptee differs from both biological and adoptive parents is a measure of the genotype-by-environment interaction.

Twin studies are perhaps the most powerful of the geneticist's tools. Two types of twins exist—monozygotic (MZ, identical) and dizygotic (DZ, fraternal). The MZ twins have exactly the same genetic configuration at all genetic loci, whereas the DZ twins are no more similar than are normal brothers and sisters. DZ twins do, however, have a more uniform environment than do normal brothers and sisters. Twin studies usually measure concordance; if one twin exhibits a particular trait, does the other twin also exhibit this trait? Concordance values, which range between 0 (no genetic influence) and 1 (absolute genetic influence) are usually higher in MZ twins than they are in DZ twins, and this difference (MZ twin concordance minus DZ twin concordance) is a measure of the genetic influence on a trait.

Twins-reared-apart offer the most powerful tool for studying the genetic influences on a trait. It has been argued that MZ twins have a very similar environment in addition to their identical genotype. Twins-reared-apart, that is, adopted twins reared in separate families, often can be used to more fully assess genetic influences. If MZ twins reared in different environments are concordant for a specific trait, the likelihood that this trait is genetically determined is enhanced. If the twins reared apart differ, environmental influences are implied. Only recently have researchers started to use this powerful tool for alcohol studies.

Alcohol Genetic Studies

Virtually all of the methods described above have been used to ascertain whether genetic factors influence the development of alcoholism. Nearly all of these studies clearly indicate that genetic factors influence the development of this disease. However, the studies frequently differ in their estimate of the degree of genetic influence. This is probably the case because of differences in methodologies. For example, the definition of alcoholism used is frequently different. Of more importance, none of the studies indicate that the development of alcoholism is one-hundred percent inherited. Environmental factors contribute to the development of this disease. Additional research is needed in order to increase our understanding of precisely what kind of environmental factors interact with precisely which genes to influence the development of alcoholism.

The study of genetic factors on alcohol consumption and alcoholism has received considerable attention. This review will not attempt to summarize all of the available literature. The reader is referred to the excellent reviews of Goodwin (1979) and Murray, Clifford, & Gurling (1983) for a more complete discussion of the genetics and alcohol literature.

Family Studies

In a recent review, Cotton (1979) cited more than 140 studies that indicated an increased incidence of alcoholism in families where one or more members had been diagnosed as alcoholics. Both male and female first-degree relatives of alcoholics show an increased incidence of alcoholism. In general, these studies indicate that the progeny of an alcoholic father or mother have two to four times the probability of becoming alcoholic than is the population norm.

Adoption Studies

As mentioned previously, family studies are the least informative of the methods used to assess genetic bases. Adoption studies are more informative. The basic premise of these studies is, if offspring resemble biological more than adoptive parents, a heritable basis is probable. The most conclusive of these studies are those of Goodwin and coworkers (1973, 1974, 1977). In the first of these studies (Goodwin et al., 1973), fifty-five male adult adoptees with an alcoholic biologic parent were compared with seventy-eight adoptees with nonalcoholic parents. The incidence of alcoholism was nearly four times greater in the adoptees with an alcoholic biological parent. A later study (Goodwin et al., 1974) compared the indicence of alcoholism in adopted-away sons of alcoholics with their biological brothers who had been raised by the alcoholic parent. The incidence of alcoholism was virtually identical in the two groups. Goodwin and coworkers (1977) suggest that genetic factors may not be nearly as important in determining the development of alcoholism in females.

Schuckit, Goodwin, & Winokur (1972) studied 164 half-siblings of 69 alcoholic parents. The children were raised by one biological parent and one adoptive parent. Of these half-sibs, 46 had one alcoholic parent and 118 did not. Only fourteen percent of those without an alcoholic parent became alcoholic themselves, whereas fifty percent of those with an alcoholic biological parent became alcoholic.

These adoption studies clearly indicate that genetic factors influence the development of alcoholism. They also indicate, particularly for females, that environment also plays a critical role.

Twin Studies

The majority of the twin studies have been carried out in Scandinavia. This has occurred because the Scandinavian countries maintain an active twin registry, which allows easy access to large numbers of twins.

The first twin study specifically concerned with alcohol abuse was that of Kaij (1960), who studied 174 male twin pairs; one or both of the twins had been reported to the local temperance board. The twins were classified according to drinking patterns into five different groups. Concordance for drinking pattern (same group) was 53.5 percent for MZ (identical) twins and 28.3 percent for DZ twins. When only probands with chronic alcoholism were considered, 71.4 percent of the fourteen co-twins of alcoholic MZ probands were also alcoholic compared with 32.3 percent of cotwins of alcoholic DZ probands.

Hrubec and Omenn (1981) reviewed the medical records of 15,924 male twins between fifty-one and sixty-one years of age who had been listed in the files of the Veterans Administration as suffering from an alcohol-related disorder. The concordance for alcoholism was 26.3 percent in MZ twins and 11.9 percent in DZ twins. Similarly, 21.1 percent of MZ twins were concordant for alcoholic psychosis, while only 6.0 percent of DZ twins had received this diagnosis. For liver cirrhosis, 14.6 percent of MZ twins and 5.4 percent of DZ twins were concordant.

Vesell, Page, and Passanti (1971) have assessed alcohol elimination rates in MZ and DZ twins. Each of the MZ twins pairs had virtually identical alcohol elimination rates, whereas the DZ twins pairs usually differed significantly from one another. Thus, metabolic factors appear to be one site of genetic control of alcohol response.

Twins-Reared-Apart

The use of twins-reared-apart to study genetic influences is, as pointed out previously, the most powerful tool available to behavior geneticists. Unfortunately, this tool has not been used to a significant extent in alcohol-related research. Farber (1981) noted in her review of the twins-reared-apart literature that only nineteen sets of MZ twins-reared-apart have been analyzed for alcohol consumption. Both twins were non-drinkers in seven sets, both were heavy drinkers in three sets and both were moderate to light drinkers in six sets. A modest discordance was seen in three sets where one twin was assessed as being a moderate to light drinker while the other was a nondrinker. Further research with these twin pairs should prove invaluable in assessing genetic roles in drinking, but the data support the argument that alcohol consumption is influenced by genetic factors.

Animal Studies

While the human genetic studies have argued that genetic factors play a role in alcoholism, they have done little to define exactly what that role might be. Do genetic factors influence tolerance to alcohol, addictability, or even whether people like the taste of alcohol? Such studies have not been done, but animal studies indicate a clear role for genetic factors. (See Deitrich and Collins [1977] and Collins [1979].) Genetic factors influence preference for alcohol (Collins, 1979), initial sensitivity to alcohol (McLearn & Kakihana, 1981; Riley, Worsham, Lester & Freed, 1977; Randall, Carpenter, Lester & Friedman, 1975), and severity of alcohol withdrawal (McClearn, Wilson, Petersen & Allen, 1982). Such studies indicate that both metabolism of alcohol and central nervous system sensitivity to alcohol are influenced by genetic factors.

Genetics and Smoking

Compared to alcohol, very little has been done to study the potential role of genetic factors in influencing tobacco use. Those studies that have attempted such assessments have obtained data that support the notion that smoking is influenced by genetics, but the degree of influence is not as great as is the influence of genetics on alcohol consumption or alcoholism.

Human Studies

Fisher (1958) was the first to suggest that genetic factors may contribute to smoking. He used the twin method to estimate the influence of heredity on smoking. Of fifty-seven pairs of adult, male MZ twins, thirty-three were concordant (nine pairs nonsmokers, twenty-two pairs cigarette smokers, and two pairs cigar smokers) with respect to smoking behavior. Of thirty-one pairs of adult, male DZ twins, only eleven pairs were concordant. This degree of concordance is considerably lower than that seen for alcohol consumption and alcoholism, suggesting that environmental factors are of greater importance in controlling smoking than is the case for alcoholism.

Shields (1962) investigated the smoking behavior of DZ and MZ twins; some of the MZ twins were reared apart. Of eighteen DZ twin pairs, nine were concordant for smoking and nine were discordant. A much greater degree of concordance was seen among the MZ twins, and rearing condition had little influence. For those reared together, twenty-one pairs were concordant and five were discordant. A similar finding was obtained with those reared apart (twenty-three pairs concordant, four pairs discordant). Other studies using different methodologies (for example, Cederlof, Friberg & Lundman, 1977; Crumpacker et al., 1979) serve to support the notion that genetic factors influence smoking behavior, but this influence is not as strong as the genetic influence on alcoholism.

Animal Studies

A major emphasis of the research done by the author of this review is on analysis of the genetic influences on the response of mice to nicotine. Nicotine, the major active component of tobacco, has numerous effects. Virtually all of these effects are influenced by genetic factors in the mouse (Marks, Burch & Collins, 1983). Interestingly, this genetic influence is not via nicotine metabolism (Hatchell & Collins, 1980). Rather, differential central nervous system sensitivity, probably involving differences in the brain receptors for nicotine (Marks et al., 1983), underlie these genetically influenced differences in nicotine effects. Clearly, additional work is needed to precisely define the role of nicotine receptors in genetically influenced response to nicotine in mice and genetically influenced smoking in humans.

Conclusion

The data that indicate genetic factors influence alcoholism are considerable. Although fewer studies have been made and the degree of influence appears to be less, the same conclusion can be made for smoking. Does this mean that a fatalistic approach should be taken to smoking and alcoholism? This would seem foolhardy. Neither alcoholism nor smoking appears to be influenced solely by genetic factors. Significant environmental influences seem to exist. An important area of research is to identify the environmental factors that can reduce these addictions in genetically susceptible people.

Another research strategy that holds promise involves a biochemical approach. Genes seem to work by controlling the amount or activity of proteins. Many proteins are enzymes. Presumably, an identification of those enzymes that are involved in the genetic influence on alcoholism would allow the development of a strategy, for example, to supplement the body with the product of this enzyme.

The complexity of the genetic control in alcoholism and smoking makes it highly probable that more than one gene, perhaps many, control these behaviors. This may be consistent with the notion that people drink to excess or smoke for many reasons, and that alcoholism is actually a family of diseases. Considerable additional research will be needed to identify the genes involved in these addictions and to suggest how these genes or gene products (enzymes) can be modified to affect a rational treatment for alcoholism or smoking.

References

Cederlof, R., Friberg, L. & Lundman, T. (1977). The interactions of smoking, environment, and heredity and their implications for disease etiology. *Acta Medica Scandinavica Supplementum, 612.*

Collins, A.C. (1979). Genetics of ethanol preference: Role of neurotransmitters. In E. Majchrowicz (Ed.), *Biochemistry and pharmacology of ethanol* (Vol. 2, pp. 207–221). New York: Plenum Press.

Cotton, N. (1979). The familial incidence of alcoholism: A review. *Journal of Studies on Alcohol, 40,* 89–116.

Crumpacker, D.W., Cederlof, R., Friberg, L., Kimberling, W.J., Sorenson, S., Vandenberg, S.G., Williams, J.S., McClean, G.E., Grever, B., Iyer, H., Krier, M.J., Pederson, N.L., Price, R.A. & Roulette, I. (1979). A twin methodology for the study of genetic and environmental control of variation in human smoking behavior. *Acta Genetica Medica Gemellologiae, 28,* 173–195.

Deitrich, R.A. & Collins, A.C. (1977). Pharmacogenetics of alcoholism. In K. Blum (Ed.), *Alcohol and opiates* (pp. 141–154). San Francisco: Academic Press.

Farber, S.L. (1981). *Identical twins reared apart.* New York: Basic Books.

Fisher, R.A. (1958). Cancer and smoking. *Nature, 182,* 596.

Genoves, S. (1970). De nuevo el aumento secular: Una revision general muestra que existen muchas didas e interrogantes. *Anales de Antropologia, 7,* 25–42.

Goodwin, D.W. (19079). Alcoholism and heredity: A review and hypothesis. *Archives of General Psychiatry, 36,* 57–61.

Goodwin, D.W., Schulsinger, F., Hermansen, L., Guzes, S.B. & Winokur, G. (1973). Alcohol problems in adoptees raised apart from alcoholic biological parents. *Archives of General Psychiatry, 28,* 238–243.

Goodwin, D.W., Schulsinger, F., Knop, J., Mednick, S. & Guze, S. (1977). Alcoholism and depression in adopted-out daughters of alcoholics. *Archives of General Psychiatry, 34,* 751–755.

Goodwin, D.W., Schulsinger, F., Moller, N., Hermansen, L., Winokur, G. & Guze, S. (1974). Drinking problems in adopted and nonadopted sons of alcoholics. *Archives of General Psychiatry, 31,* 164–169.

Hatchell, P.C. & Collins, A.C. (1980). The influence of genotype and sex on behavioral sensitivity to nicotine in mice. *Psychopharmacology, 71,* 45–49.

Hrubec, Z. & Omenn, G.S. (1981). Evidence of genetic predisposition to alcoholic cirrhosis and psychosis. *Alcoholism: Clinical and Experimental Research, 5,* 207–215.

Kaij, L. (1960). *Alcoholism in twins.* Stockholm: Almquist and Wiksell.

McClearn, G.E. & Kakihana, R. (1981). Selective breeding for ethanol sensitivity: Short-sleep and long-sleep mice. In G.E. McClearn, R.A. Deitrich & V.G. Erwin (Eds.), *Development of animal models as pharmacogenetic tools* (DHHS Publication No. (ADM) 81-1133, pp. 147–159). Washington, D.C.: U.S. Government Printing Office.

McClearn, G.E., Wilson, J.R., Petersen, D.R. & Allen, D.L. (1982). Selective breeding in mice for severity of the ethanol withdrawal syndrome. *Substance and Alcohol Actions/Misuse, 3,* 135–143.

Marks, M.J., Burch, J.B. & Collins, A.C. (1983). Genetics of nicotine response in four inbred strains of mice. *Journal of Pharmacology and Experimental Therapeutics, 226,* 291–302.

Murray, R.M., Clifford, C.A. & Gurling, H.M.D. (1983). Twin and adoption studies: How good is the evidence for a genetic role. *Recent Developments in Alcoholism, 1,* 25–48.

Plomin, R., DeFries, J.C. & McClearn, G.E. (1980). *Behavioral genetics: A primer.* San Francisco: Freeman.

Randall, C.L., Carpenter, J.A., Lester, D. & Friedman, H.J. (1975). Ethanol-induced mouse strain differences in locomotor activity. *Pharmacology, Biochemistry, and Behavior, 3,* 533–535.

Riley, E.P., Worsham, E.D., Lester, D. & Freed, E.X. (1977). Selective breeding of rates for differences in reactivity to alcohol. *Journal of Studies on Alcohol, 38,* 1705–1717.

Schuckit, M.A., Goodwin, D.W. & Winokur, G. (1972). A study of alcoholism in half siblings. *American Journal of Psychiatry, 128,* 1132–1136.

Shield, J. (1962). *Monozygotic twins brought up apart or brought up together.* London: Oxford University Press.

Vesell, E.S., Page, J.G. & Passanti, G.T. (1971). Genetic and environmental factors affecting ethanol metabolism in man. *Clinical Pharmacology and Therapeutics, 12,* 192–201.

2
Biological Mechanisms: Neurotransmission and Addiction

Stanley G. Sunderwirth

Addiction has been defined as "self-induced changes in neurotransmission that result in social problem behaviors" (Milkman & Sunderwirth, 1983, p. 36). This definition encompasses the psychological, biochemical, and social aspects of addictive processes. It differs from those concepts which stress only the biological aspects of addiction, such as Milam and Ketcham's (1981) genetic emphasis with regard to alcoholism. The definition also differs from Peele's (1976) emphasis on the psychological aspect of addiction while downplaying the chemical factors involved in addictive behavior. The definition that Milkman and I have proposed describes a unified model of addiction which encompasses the role of the set, setting, and substance. David Smith (personal communication, 1983) feels that the concept of self-induced is not a good descriptor for the disease model. Our definition does not contradict the disease model. Certainly, any individual who is engulfed in the agony of destructive addictive behavior has a disease, or at least the addiction should be treated as a disease. We prefer our definition because it includes some personal responsibility for behavior and implies that individuals have some control over their life at some point in the addictive process.

The model that we describe including the psychological, biochemical, and social aspects of addiction is not limited to substance abuse. It encompasses any activity characterized by compulsion, loss of control, and continuation in spite of harmful consequences. This characterization has been a landmark in identifying addictive behaviors. As indicated in an earlier study, Milkman and Frosch (1977) showed that individuals ingest drugs which elicit a mood or level of arousal consistent with their characteristic mode of dealing with stress. That is, those individuals who characteristically deal with stress by active confrontation with their environment choose stimulant drugs. On the other hand, those individuals who prefer to withdraw from an active confrontation with their environment, choose opiate or satiation-type drugs. In addition, certain individuals choose activities related to imagery or fantasy in order to deal with stress. These individuals select hallucinogenic drugs as their drugs of choice. Therefore, we believe that the desired feeling differs among addicted individuals, and this desired feeling determines the activity or substance which individuals choose to abuse.

It might be useful at this point to define neurotransmission as the mechanism by which signals or impulses are sent from one nerve cell (neuron) to the other. It should also be noted that the more rapid the neurotransmission in certain pathways of the central nervous system, the more intense will be the feeling or state of arousal. Therefore, the arousal-type person seeks activities or substances which would increase the rate of neurotransmission in the part of the brain responsible for mood. Such activities could include gambling, sky diving, promiscuity, crime, hang-gliding or any other kind of risk-taking activity. The drug of choice of these individuals would be amphetamines. On the other hand, the satiation-type person would choose activities or substances which decrease the rate of neurotransmission. Such activities would include excessive involvement in television or music, meditation, and overeating.

Regardless of whether the change in neurotransmission is brought about by an activity or a substance, the brain attempts to reestablish the rate of neurotransmission which was present before the activity or substance ingestion commenced. Once the brain has reestablished the rate of neurotransmission, the individual becomes tolerant to the original level of substance intake or activity and must increase these activities in order to achieve the desired state of arousal brought about by a change in the rate of neurotransmission. At this point, there is an altered response of the individual to the drug. Withdrawal of the activity or agent may result in withdrawal symptoms because of the altered brain chemistry that was established during the period of abuse to compensate for the stress placed on the central nervous system by the activity or substance.

In order to understand the relationship between neurotransmission and addiction, it is necessary to understand the basic elements of neurotransmission. Goldstein (1982) has said that the language of the brain is chemistry, and chemistry is indeed a language. In order to understand the concept of neurotransmission associated with addiction, some basic chemistry of the brain must be understood. The central nervous system (CNS) is composed of the brain and the spinal cord. The communication system of the CNS is composed of many billions of neurons or nerve cells. These neurons are made up of three basic parts: the soma, or cell body; the axon; and the dendrites. The soma is the "brain" of the nerve cell and determines when the neuron will send an impulse on to the next neuron. The soma must make this decision very quickly, based on hundreds of inputs—both inhibitory and excitatory. Should the soma make the decision to fire, the impulse travels down the axon to another neuron. The central nervous system is not hard-wired, and therefore there must be a mechanism for conveying the impulse from one nerve cell to the other. The electrical flashes between nerve cells, as seen in one of the episodes of Cosmos, is not a true picture of what happens.

As has been mentioned earlier, the language of the brain is chemistry, and therefore the transmission across the synaptic junction between two neurons is chemical. When the impulse arrives at the presynaptic terminal (figure 2–1), small molecules known as neurotransmitters are released into the synaptic junction. These neurotransmitters cross the synapse and attach themselves to receptor sites on the postsynaptic terminal. It is important to realize that the relationship between neurotransmitter and receptor is very much like a lock and key. Only certain shapes of keys will fit into the lock. If a sufficient number of neurotransmitters attach themselves to receptor sites, a depolarization of the postsynaptic membrane occurs, which results in the impulse being transmitted on to the next neuron.

The concept of the lock and key is an extremely interesting one. For example, it is possible to have molecules that are similar to neurotransmitters attach themselves to receptor sites on the postsynaptic terminal. However, often these phony neurotransmitters will not permit the membrane to be depolarized. It is very much like putting a Vega key in a Camaro ignition. The key will fit but will not turn on the motor. However, the Vega key in the Camaro ignition does prevent a Camaro key, which would turn on the engine, from being inserted. This is the basis for the Haldol treatment for schizophrenia. Haldol occupies the receptor sites normally occupied by the neurotransmitter dopamine. However, the Haldol does not cause the membrane to be depolarized and, therefore, the impulse will not be transmitted down to the next neuron. This blocking of the dopamine receptor sites inhibits the overactive neurotransmission that is often associated with schizophrenia.

Once the neurotransmitter has been released from the receptor site, it may be reabsorbed into the presynaptic terminal and stored in the synaptic vesicles within the presynaptic terminal. However, there are a number of things that can happen to the neurotransmitter before it reaches the safe hiding place of the synaptic vesicle. If cocaine is being ingested, this will tend to prevent the neurotransmitter from being reabsorbed into the presynaptic terminal, resulting in an excess of the neurotransmitter in the synapse. Since more neurotransmitter is therefore available for attachment to receptor sites, there will be an increase in the rate of neurotransmission, with the resulting increase in the state of arousal. This is, of course, why the individual was taking cocaine in the first place.

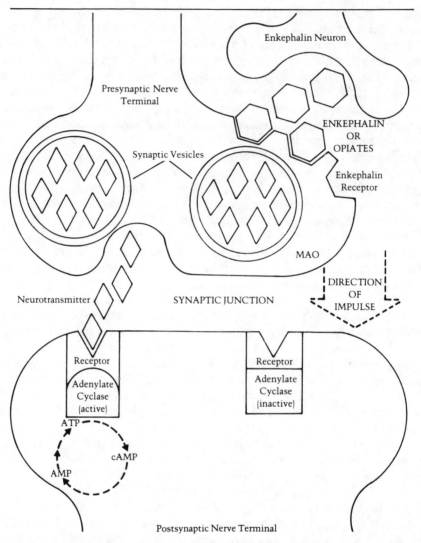

Enkephalin Neuron

Presynaptic Nerve
Terminal

Synaptic Vesicles

ENKEPHALIN
OR
OPIATES

Enkephalin
Receptor

MAO

Neurotransmitter

SYNAPTIC JUNCTION

DIRECTION
OF
IMPULSE

Receptor

Adenylate
Cyclase
(active)

Receptor

Adenylate
Cyclase
(inactive)

ATP

cAMP

AMP

Postsynaptic Nerve Terminal

Note: Modified from H. Milkman & S. Sunderwirth (1982). Addictive processes. *Journal of Psychoactive Drugs, 14*(3), 177–192.

Figure 2–1. Chemical Transmission of a Nerve Impulse

Another obstacle which the neurotransmitter faces before reaching the synaptic vesicle is enzymatic attack once it enters the presynaptic terminal. Inside the presynaptic terminals are monoamine oxidases (MAO), which degrade catecholamines such as dopamine and norepinephrine. In the normal individual, the amount of monoamine oxidase is regulated so that there will be an adequate supply of neurotransmitter. However, in certain individuals there is too much monoamine oxidase, and this will result in a lowered level of the neurotransmitter, thus bringing about a state of depression in that individual. Since enzymes are proteins and may be considered as being under genetic control, it is easy to see how certain disturbances of the central nervous system may be inherited.

Another important aspect of neurotransmission occurs within the postsynaptic terminal. The enzyme adenylate cyclase is activated within this terminal if it makes contact with a receptor site occupied by a neurotransmitter (figure 2–1). This activated adenylate cyclase then has the ability to convert adenosine triphosphate (ATP) to cyclic adenosine monophosphate (cAMP). Cyclic adenosine monophosphate has the effect of increasing membrane sensitivity and thereby increasing neurotransmission (Greengard, 1975). A generalization is that an increase in the level of cAMP would result in an increase in the state of arousal (Milkman & Sunderwirth, 1982). Therefore, any activity which brings about an increase in the release of neurotransmitters results in an increase in the level of cAMP characterized by an increase in the state of arousal. However, as indicated earlier, the brain attempts to counter the effects of activities which result in a change in neurotransmission. Using the adenylate cyclase model, we would say that this opposing effect of the brain is accomplished by changing the level of this enzyme. Figure 2–2 is used to explain this model. Therefore, an initial increase in cAMP brought about by an increase in neurotransmission is countered by a decrease in the level of adenylate cyclase. When this occurs, the desired state of arousal or mood can only be achieved by increased activity or increased substance ingestion. At this point, the individual has become tolerant to the original level of activity or substance intake and must, therefore, increase these activities in order to achieve the desired state of arousal. Withdrawal of the activity or agent results in a greatly decreased production of cAMP with the resultant crash which accompanies forced inactivity or substance abstinence. This model of addiction is based on the enzyme expansion model of Goldstein and Goldstein (1968).

Although the adenylate cyclase model is a useful one in explaining addictions, it is probably not the only enzymatic system which is affected by self-induced changes in neurotransmission. It is quite possible that the enzymes (MAO) responsible for the destruction of the neurotransmitters also change. For example, an individual engaged in arousal activities or amphetamine ingestion may bring about an increase in the amount of MAO present in the presynaptic terminal. This would result in a decrease in the amount of neurotransmitter available for release

Phase of Involvement	Neurochemical Consequences of Activity (A, B, C, D, E)	Level of neurotransmitter	Level of adenylate cyclase	Level of cAMP	Level of Arousal
I. Baseline, i.e, no arousal activity or amphetamine ingestion	(diagrams)	baseline	baseline	baseline	baseline
II. Initial amphetamine ingestion or arousal activity	(diagrams)	elevated	baseline	elevated	elevated
III. Chronic amphetamine ingestion or arousal activity	(diagrams)	elevated	lowered	lower in than activity II (tolerance)	seeking arousal
IV. Cessation amphetamines or arousal activities	(diagrams)	baseline	remains low	lower than baseline	significant craving

— neurotransmitter

— postsynaptic receptor (with neurotransmitter)

— postsynaptic receptor (without neurotransmitter)

— adenylate cyclase—active

— adenylate cyclase—inactive

Neurochemical Basis for Addiction to Amphetamine or Arousal Activities

into the synaptic junction, resulting in a decrease in neurotransmission. In all probability, several enzyme systems are affected.

In the case of a satiation-type personality, the individual seeks activities or substances which will decrease the rate of neurotransmission. Such substances would be the various opiates. In addition, it is believed that satiation-type activities bring about a release of enkephalins or endorphins which act as the body's own opiates. Opiates or enkephalins attach themselves to receptor sites on the presynaptic terminal. (See figure 2–1.) This results in a decrease in the release of the neurotransmitter. It is this decrease in the release of the neurotransmitters which results in a decreased rate of neurotransmission, which is the desired effect of the satiation-prone individual. The body then counters these effects by changing enzyme levels in order to bring the rate of neurotransmission back to a normal state. This could be done by increasing the level of adenylate cyclase which would result in an increase in the level of cAMP so that the person would be tolerant to the initial level of opiate ingestion or satiation activities. One way of representing this alteration in brain chemistry may be seen in figure 2–3 (Goldstein & Goldstein, 1968). In this case, the actual size of the letters corresponds to the level of those substances in the neurons. There could also be a change in the level of enkephalinase, the enzyme responsible for the splitting of the enkephalin molecule (Goldstein, 1979). Thus, the long-term effect of satiation activities or opiate ingestion might be an increase in the level of enkephalinase. Upon withdrawal from the satiation activity or opiate ingestion, there would be an excess of enkephalinase which would bring about a decrease in enkephalin and therefore an increase in the rate of neurotransmission. This increased rate of neurotransmission would result in a state of agitation for the person withdrawing from opiate ingestion or satiation activities.

Until now we have discussed arousal activities and satiation activities and have only touched on fantasy-type activities. However, fantasy plays an important part in the lives of many individuals. Many individuals deal with the stress in their life through imagery, which is sometimes enhanced by the use of hallucinogenic drugs. In many religions of the world, visions or experiences with divinities have formed the basis of those religions. While not as well understood as the effect of stimulants or opiates, the effects of hallucinogens is obviously an interference in the normal mechanism of neurotransmission in certain parts of the central nervous system. There is a very close relationship between the structure of the neurotransmitter serotonin and various hallucinogenic compounds such as LSD, psilocin, and DMT.

Since we have indicated that addiction is based on changes in the level of enzymes, it is very clear that certain individuals would be more

Phase of Involvement	NEUROCHEMICAL CONSEQUENCES OF ACTIVITY	Level of Neurotransmitter	Level of adenylate cyclase (AC)	Level of cAMP	Level of Arousal
I. Baseline, i.e., no opiates or "satiation" activities	ATP → AC → cAMP	baseline	baseline	baseline	baseline
II. Initial opiate ingestion or "satiation" activities (X)	ATP → AC ⤙X⤚ cAMP	lowered	baseline	lowered	satiated
III. Chronic opiate ingestion ore "satiation" activities	ATP → AC ⤙X⤚ cAMP	lowered (same as in Activity II)	increased	somewhat lowered (nearly baseline)	"satiation" seeking
IV. Cessation of opiates or "satiation" activities	ATP → AC → cAMP	baseline (same as in Activity I)	increased	increased	significant craving (withdrawal symptoms)

Figure 2–3. Neurochemical Basis for Addiction to Opiates or Satiation Activities

prone to these enzymatic changes than other individuals. It appears that persons who have a propensity to alter their enzyme levels more rapidly than others would be more prone to addiction. Since changes in enzyme levels and indeed the presence or absence of enzymes themselves have been shown to be linked to genetics, it is very probable that addictive disease has a genetic basis. However, we maintain that the concept of self-induced changes in neurotransmission that result in social problem behaviors is a sound definition of addiction. As indicated earlier, this definition indicates some measure of control over our lives. In the Hindu religion, individuals are born into this world with certain characteristics (karma) carried over from a previous life. We might consider karma to be our genetic makeup, since this comes from our ancestors, which in some respects represent our previous lives. However, Hindus also believe that they need not be completely dominated by their karma. There is another concept in Hindu philosophy called dharma, which is the free will. The Hindu's believe that bad karma may be overcome by good dharma. If we consider that dharma is our free will as exemplified by our cerebral cortex and that karma is represented by our limbic system, in modern terms, we would say let your cerebral cortex dominate your limbic system.

References

Goldstein, A. (1979). High on research. *Journal of Drug and Alcohol Dependence,* 3(3), 6–9.

Goldstein, A. (1982). Presentation at the 6th Annual Summer Institute on Drug Dependence.

Goldstein, A. & Goldstein, D.B. (1968). Enzyme expansion theory of drug tolerance and physical dependence. *Association for Research in Nervous and Mental Disease, 46*, 265–267.

Greengard, P. (1975). Cyclic nucleotides, protein phosphorylation and neuronal function. In G.I. Drummond, P. Greengard & G. Robinson, (Eds.), *Proceedings of the 2nd International Conference on Cyclic AMP. Advances in Cyclic Nucleotide Research* (Vol.5, pp. 585–601). New York: Raven Press.

Milam, J.R. & Ketcham, K. (1981). *Under the influence.* Seattle: Madrona.

Milkman, H. & Frosch, W. (1977). The drug of choice. *Journal of Psychedelic Drugs, 9*(1), 11–24.

Milkman, H. & Sunderwirth, S. (1982). Addictive processes. *Journal of Psychoactive Drugs, 14*(3), 177–192.

Milkman, H. & Sunderwirth, S. (1983, October). The chemistry of craving. *Psychology Today,* pp. 36–44.

Peele, S. (1976). *Love and addiction.* New York: New American Library.

3
Biopharmacologic Factors in Drug Abuse

Robert Freedman

Drug abuse is a multifactor biomedical and psychosocial disorder. One of the objects of our research has been to examine the response of the nervous system to chronic administration of various abused substances. It is our hypothesis that the response of the nervous system to drugs of abuse may be part of the physiological reason for the continued problems which drug abusers face. Many of these problems may be totally unrelated to the reasons for which the drugs were abused in the first place. We also hypothesize that many of these problems can be better understood through the use of an animal model. By examining in some detail the alterations in brain function produced by the chronic administration of drugs, a biological model may predict aspects of abusive behavior. Two examples are given in this chapter. Both have to do with the effects of abused substances on noradrenergic neurotransmission in the central nervous system, as studied in the pathway from the nucleus locus coeruleus to the cerebellar Purkinje cell in laboratory rats.

The two classes of drugs of abuse which will be examined are stimulant drugs, such as amphetamine and phencyclidine, and alcohol. We will attempt to show, through a biological model, the possibility of a physiological basis for paranoid psychoses during both acute and chronic stimulant administration and, in particular, we will show a physiological basis for a prolonged psychosis following cessation of stimulant use. In the second section of the chapter, we will show how activation of noradrenergic neurotransmission during alcohol withdrawal may account for some of the behavioral abnormalities seen in recently detoxified alcoholics.

Supported by USPHS Grant DA-02429 and funds from the Veterans Administration Innovative Alcohol Program.

Chronic Stimulant Administration and Psychosis

Stimulant drugs have long been known to cause psychotic illnesses, both with acute and with chronic usage. The mechanism for amphetamine-induced psychosis is probably stimulation of central catecholaminergic neurotransmission, which is mediated both by noradrenergic and dopaminergic pathways. Our studies have shown that both amphetamine and phencyclidine can mimic central adrenergic neurotransmission through a mechanism of action that involves release of endogenous catecholamine from nerve terminals. We measure this release by its effect on the firing rate of cerebellar Purkinje neurons, which are known to receive noradrenergic synapses from the nucleus locus coeruleus. Since norepinephrine is an inhibitory neurotransmitter in the cerebellum, activation of these pathways results in a decrease in firing rate of the Purkinje neuron. Purkinje neurons have a statistically predictable firing rate in anesthetized animals, which is most significantly controlled by norepinephrine. Thus, measurement of Purkinje cell discharge rate can provide a measure of noradrenergic neurotransmission which takes into account both presynaptic and postsynaptic changes induced by a particular drug. Since the firing rate is predictable from animal to animal, chronically treated animals can be compared with saline-treated controls.

Using this model, we have found that acute administration of amphetamine or phencyclidine both cause a decrease in the firing rate of cerebellar Purkinje neurons consistent with their putative effects on norepinephrine release. Chronic administration results in increased effectiveness of the drug (Freedman & Marwaha, 1980). Figure 3–1 compares animals who are naive to amphetamine with those who have been treated chronically for twenty-one days. There is a marked decrease in both basal firing rate and in firing rate in response to amphetamine administration in the chronically treated animals. This increased effectiveness of amphetamine may well correlate with the clinical observation that humans taking chronic, moderate to low doses of stimulant drugs begin to experience supersensitivity or *reverse tolerance* to the stimulant. They become increasingly likely to have complications such as movement disorder or psychosis, which may be related to increased catecholaminergic neurotransmission in various areas of the brain. This increased sensitivity to the drug is in contradistinction to the tolerance developed to the euphoriant aspects of the drug. Since the drug is most commonly taken for its euphoriant effects, an individual taking the drug for these purposes would, even while developing tolerance to the desired effect, increase his risk for psychosis.

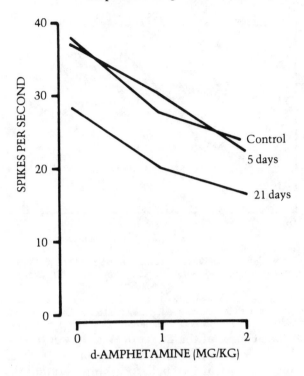

Source: Freedman, R. & Marwaha, J. (1980). Effects of acute and chronic amphetamine treatment on Purkinje neuron discharge in rat cerebellum. *Journal of Pharmacology and Experimental Therapeutics, 212,* pp. 390–396. © 1980, American Society for Pharmacology and Experimental Therapeutics.

Note: Control animals were not treated before recording. One group of six animals was treated daily for 5 days, another for 21 days. Each point represents the mean of all animals in the treatment group.

Figure 3–1. Graph of Mean Discharge Rate (Spikes per Second) versus Dosage of d-Amphetamine for Animals Treated with 2 mg/kg/day

The effects of chronic amphetamine administration on basal firing rate of the Purkinje neuron actually increase upon drug withdrawal (Sorensen, Johnson & Freedman, 1982). Figure 3–2 shows a curve of mean firing rate of cerebellar Purkinje neurons in animals withdrawing from chronic treatment with low-dose (2 mg/kg) amphetamine. Note that animals chronically treated with saline have a basal firing rate of approximately 38 Hz. These animals do not begin to approach that firing rate until after seven weeks of withdrawal, despite the relatively short period (three weeks). This finding suggests that withdrawal from stimulant use

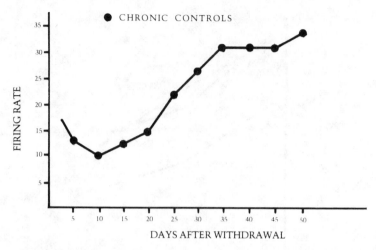

DAYS AFTER WITHDRAWAL

Source: Sorenson, S., Johnson, S.W. & Freedman, R. (1982). Persistent effects of amphetamine on Purkinje neurons following chronic administration. *Brain Research, 247,* 365–371.

Note: Each point on the line is the mean (± SEM) of 6–30 neurons recorded from 1–5 rats. Rats were treated daily with amphetamine (2mg/kg, i.p.) for 21 days. The "chronic controls" indicates value obtained from 6 rats treated daily with saline (1 ml/kg, i.p.) for 21 days.

Figure 3–2. Time-course of the Effect of Withdrawal from Chronic Treatment with d-Amphetamine on the Rate of Spontaneous Activity of Cerebellar Purkinje Neurons

is long-lived, even after relatively brief periods of administration. It is our hypothesis that this long-term withdrawal may account for the persistent psychoticlike effects, particularly paranoia, seen after chronic stimulant abuse. A similar long-term withdrawal has been noted using dopaminergic model systems, so that it would seem to apply to both major catecholamine systems in the brain. Several cases have recently been reported of patients who have chronically abused stimulant drugs at low doses and have developed psychosis several days after withdrawal. The dip in our curve during the first week of withdrawal would seem to correspond in time course to this clinical phenomenon, and therefore may explain why these patients became psychotic when off the drug when they had never been psychotic on the drug (Johnson, Freedman & Sorensen, 1983).

Thus, an animal model may explain the phenomenon of increasing likelihood of psychosis in patients who chronically abuse stimulant drugs as well as the persistent psychotic effects of chronic stimulant abuse. Psychosis is not generally a desired effect during stimulant abuse, but may rather be a consequence of the effects of chronic drug administration on central nervous pathways.

Effects of Alcohol Withdrawal on Noradrenergic Neurotransmission

Unlike stimulants, which are complex molecules and have specific actions, alcohol is a drug which affects many parts of the nervous system because of its simple molecular structure. Although any animal model can never fully explain the effects of drugs on human behavior, the examination of a single neuronal system, when studying alcohol administration, is perhaps even more risky. Nonetheless, a study of particular neuronal systems does allow the formation of very precise hypotheses. It is our wish in this section to demonstrate which hypotheses about norepinephrine may have some clinical relevance to understanding phenomena in alcohol withdrawal.

Acute administration of low doses of alcohol produce a brief increase in cerebellar Purkinje neuron firing (Sorensen, Carter, Marwaha, Baker & Freedman, 1981). In examining reasons for this increase, we were interested to see if it represented a specific blockade of noradrenergic input to the cerebellum. Since noradrenergic input is inhibitory, blockade of this input would result in the increase in firing observed. The increase in firing is prevented if cerebellar noradrenergic circuitry is removed by previous treatment with the neurotoxin, 6-hydroxydopamine (6-OHDA) or if noradrenergic neurotransmission is blocked by pretreatment with propranolol, a beta-adrenergic blocking agent. It is surprising, however, that alcohol even transiently should have such a specific effect on noradrenergic neurotransmission since alcohol applied directly to Purkinje neurons by various micropressure ejection techniques depresses cell firing.

The answer for alcohol specificity lies not in the molecular structure but in its route of administration. Alcohol given intraperitoneally travels to the brain along capillaries. Locus coeruleus has a unique capillary supply reflecting its origin in the neural crest rather than in the neural tube. Locus coeruleus neurons are individually surrounded by capillaries, as opposed to Purkinje neurons and most other brain neurons in which there is some distance between the blood supply and individual neurons. Thus, this unique capillary supply takes alcohol preferentially from the bloodstream to locus coeruleus neurons more quickly than it can reach Purkinje neurons; there is a brief period of blockade of noradrenergic neurotransmission as alcohol first reaches and anesthetizes locus coeruleus neurons. Subsequently, as alcohol reaches all areas of the brain, there is a general depression of all neuronal responses.

Studies of chronic alcohol administration and withdrawal suggest that during withdrawal there is a rebound activation of noradrenergic neurons with an increase in noradrenergic metabolites, suggesting that there is increased neurotransmission. Increases in noradrenergic neurotransmission have generally been associated with mania rather than depression, although the general clinical impression is that most patients who have been recently detoxified from alcohol have a depressed mood. In surveying recently detoxified alcoholics, that is, alcoholics who have been off alcohol from between one to three weeks, we have found that many of them show signs of mild degrees of hypomania (Lubman, Emrick, Mosimann & Freedman, 1983). While they have depressed mood, they also have signs of irritability, grandiosity, normal to increased levels of activity, and normal to increased sex drives. While none of these is a textbook picture of the euphoriant manic, many of them represent mildly depressed and irritable characters with slightly increased psychomotor activity. Alcoholics who have been detoxified for longer periods of time and are medical inpatients do not show similarly increased symptoms of mania. We have been able to document this mild degree of hypomania using both Minnesota Multiphasic Personality Inventory (MMPI) rating scales and the Manic State Rating Scale.

This syndrome is not found in all recently detoxified alcoholics but is present in a subset. A biological concomitant in some of the patients is an increased excretion of urinary MHPG (3-methoxy-4-hydroxy-phenethylene glycol), which is a metabolite of norepinephrine. One self-medication for the alcoholic who finds himself discharged from a brief treatment setting would be to return to drinking, as alcohol is an effective way to anesthetize temporarily the nucleus locus coeruleus and therefore decrease noradrenergic neurotransmission. Thus, the alcoholic who drinks to calm himself following detoxification may well be simply trying to regulate neurotransmission mediated by norepinephrine. Better treatments may be to prolong the detoxification period in patients who are clinically hypomanic following alcohol withdrawal or to treat these patients briefly with lithium carbonate, which has had some success as a preventive agent for a return to drinking.

It is obvious that a biological model based on the consideration of only one neurotransmitter system is particularly inadequate to explain the many effects of a simple molecule such as ethanol, and also neglects many psychosocial factors. Certainly not all withdrawing patients show signs of hypomania; our findings may only be applicable to a small subset of patients. However, this biological model may stimulate an examination in more detail of the affective syndromes present in alcoholics about to be discharged from brief detoxification programs and may serve to identify patients who are at biological risk for a return to drinking.

References

Freedman, R. & Marwaha, J. (1980). Effects of acute and chronic amphetamine treatment on Purkinje neuron discharge in rat cerebellum. *Journal of Pharmacology and Experimental Therapeutics, 212,* 390–396.

Johnson, S.W., Freedman, R. & Sorensen, S. (1983). Effects of d-amphetamine withdrawal in rats and man [Letter to the editor]. *American Journal of Psychiatry, 140,* 953–954.

Lubman, A., Emrick, C., Mosimann, W.F. & Freedman, R. (1983). Altered mood and norepinephrine metabolism following withdrawal from alcohol. *Drug and Alcohol Dependence, 12,* 3–13.

Sorensen, S., Carter, D., Marwaha, J., Baker, R. & Freedman, R. (1981). Disinhibition of cerebellar Purkinje neurons from noradrenergic inhibition during the rising phase of blood ethanol. *Journal of Studies on Alcohol, 42,* 908–917.

Sorensen, S., Johnson, S. & Freedman, R. (1982). Persistent effects of amphetamine on Purkinje neurons following chronic administration. *Brain Research, 247,* 365–371.

4
An Analytic Overview
of Addictions

William A. Frosch

Psychoanalytic interest in problems of drug abuse and of other addictions is as old as psychoanalysis. Freud (1954) wrote to Fliess in 1897 that "masturbation is the one great habit that is a 'primary addiction' and that the other addictions, for alcohol, morphine, tobacco, etc., only enter into life as a substitute and replacement for it." With the development of increased analytic understanding of earlier phases of development, attempts to understand drug use and habituation shifted to oral libidinal strivings, both primary and defensive, and somewhat later to aggression.

Libidinal Strivings

In 1905, Freud (1962) attributed smoking and drinking to oral eroticism—a reinforcement of constitutional lip eroticism. Brill (1922) agreed that smoking was genetically derived from thumb-sucking. It was seen as a continuation of autoerotic activity and a manifestation of exhibitionism. Narcissistic and sadomasochistic components may also be recognized in Brill's case material.

The importance of orality in determining drug abuse continued to be stressed by later authors. They wrote, for example, "any tension is felt as tension was felt by the infant, that is, as a threat to [his] very existence." In 1932 Glover pointed out that the emphasis placed by the drug users themselves on oral elements must be discounted. He suggested that these elements were often emphasized by such patients in defense against primitive excretory sadism.

Affect, Ego, and Defenses

In 1926 attention turned from exclusively libidinal considerations to the development of affect, ego, and defenses. Rado (1926) suggested that drug use results in an undermining of genital potency and a turning away from real object love. The drug may become the only love; pharmacogenic orgasm may be substituted for genital orgasm.

In 1928, Glover formulated three main factors in the etiology of alcoholism. First, partial fixation of the libido at oral and anal sadistic levels of development; second, a marked tendency to regress to a narcissistic stage of ego organization which sets into action a primitive ego mechanism of projection; third, a disordered and severe primitive conscience leading to fruitless exploitation of the same mechanism of projection. More recently, the increasing interest in the role of ego defect and the role of alterations in ego functioning may be seen in the work of Savitt (1954, 1963). He states that "the vicissitudes of early ego development and later ego maturation which facilitate fixation and encourage regression appear to play a dominant role in predisposing an individual to the development of a crippling morbid craving" (Savitt, 1963, p. 56).

Hartmann (1969) reported some results of a study group of the American Association for Child Psychoanalysis formed to investigate the use of drugs by adolescents. They studied twelve adolescent patients and their parents. In both parent and child, they examined libido, aggression, and superego development, as well as the relationship of parent to child. The patient's ego functioning, affect, and object relationships before and after experience with drugs were also examined. It was hoped to compare the drug experiences in terms of onset, conscious and unconscious motivation, and genetic determinant, as well as the course of the drugs in relation to treatment and to the patient's other symptoms.

Hartmann (1969) concluded,

If we look at these findings one by one, . . . none of them could be called pathognomonic for drug users or drug addicts. Neurotic patients, whether or not they take drugs, certainly also have infantile mothers. A mother's seductive behavior may lead to a boy's passivity, sexual disturbances, learning difficulties, and neurotic symptoms either in combination with or without drug taking. The same thing can be said about adolescents who show oral fixations and regressions. These factors are not specific to drug taking, but are also found in neuroses, depressions, delinquencies, and even psychoses. Early traumata such as severe illness and operations, or the loss of a parent during childhood, can be found as causative factors in disturbed adolescents, drugs or no drugs. Low frustration tolerance, depression, and difficulties in establishing mature object relationships are characteristics and symptoms we see frequently during this period of life, drugs or no drugs . . . these considerations make it clear that none of the aforementioned data on symptoms, character structures, childhood experiences, background, etc., can by themselves explain the wish or the imperative need for drugs . . . (p. 391)

Hartmann (1969) suggested that some of the points that Rado (1933) made over thirty-five years ago seem to apply also to the current drug-using population:

1. There is a basic depressive character with early wounds to narcissism and defeats in ego development.
2. There is an intolerance for frustration and pain with a constant need to change a "low" into a "high." This may come from an early lack of satisfying object relations.
3. There is an attempt to overcome the lack of affectionate and meaningful object relations through the pseudocloseness and fusion with other drug takers during their common experience.
4. The artificial technique of maintaining self-regard and satisfaction with drugs, of avoiding painful affects, and alleviating symptoms results in a change from a reality-oriented to a pharmacothymic-oriented regimen. This leads to severely disturbed ego functions and ultimately to conflict with reality. Eventually, the drug taking becomes a way of life.

Krystal and Raskin (1970) have described, primarily in alcoholics, a developmental problem in differentiation of affect resulting in dedifferentiation, resomatization, and deverbalization. Feelings become overwhelming and out of control, anxiety and anger indistinguishable from each other or from other affects. Wurmser (1977) also notes a defect in heroin addicts in affect defense which leads to the use of external substances or behaviors to manage feeling states; a thing (drugs, food, gambling, video games) is invested with magical power and control. Similarly, Treece and Khantzian (1977) emphasized problems in affect tolerance and suggested that drug craving may represent defensive transformation and displacement of distressful internal states. Khantzian (1977) has proposed a defect in the ego function of self-care resulting from failures in internalization of vital functions which in turn leaves the individual at risk for disease, accident, and violence. The addict appears not to have learned from parents to recognize, evaluate, and appropriately respond to danger.

These more recent descriptions by psychoanalysts of individuals with addictive behavior show considerable agreement both with each other and with descriptions derived from other methods of data collection and theoretical stance (Lang, 1983). These may be characterized as impulsivity, difficulty tolerating feelings and delaying gratification, and an antisocial personality style. A disposition to sensation seeking, perhaps the behavioral equivalent of Khantzian's (1977) ego defect in self-care, is also commonly reported.

Greenspan (1977) has suggested that these observations can best be organized in a psychoanalytic matrix consistent with the principle of multiple determination. "Thus, for a given individual, using an addictive drug might incorporate at the same time, the satisfaction of certain primitive impulses and needs, a structural defect in one of the ego's substructures dealing with impulse or affect regulation, and an adaptation to an extraordinarily stressful environment" (Greenspan, 1977, p. 73).

Developmental Perspective

Psychoanalysis views children as born preadapted to an average expectable environment. With an adequately empathic, nuturant mother, they go through a complex development, facing and mastering a series of frustrations and successes. These have traditionally been summarized by psychoanalysts under the shorthand labels of oral, anal, phallic, and genital stages. From another point of view, Erikson (1963) has described a linked series of stages in ego development.

Greenspan (1977) has summarized the developmental perspective necessary to the matrix he suggests. The following highlights some of the pitfalls which are postulated to play a role in addictive behaviors. The infant's failure to achieve beginning regulation of internal experience in a context of maternal attachment can result from environmental trauma, unusual constitutional sensitivity of the infant, absence of a pleasurable maternal object, or problems in the mother-infant interaction. Drugs may facilitate homeostatic regulation or later substitute for human attachment.

The infant who fails toward the end of the first year to consolidate a separate image of self from mother may as an adult use drugs to help do so. In the second year, separation individuation requires experimentation in the presence of a permissive but protecting figure. Failure to achieve this mastery may interfere with the capacity to experience and channel aggression and may lead to the use of drugs for a safe merging with an omnipotent object. Both Piaget (1954) and Mahler (1967) point out that from twelve to eighteen months the infant repeats and reworks earlier issues. If nurturant support is not available during this rapprochement phase, anxiety may lead to a fragmented self, impairment of self-esteem, impulsivity, depression, and other serious characterologic difficulties with strong masochistic components. Drugs can simultaneously represent the ambivalently held object and provide a sense of satisfaction and an outlet for sadistic and masochistic components of unresolved rage.

Around the age of three, the child achieves object constancy, a continuing internal image of both self and important others, as well as of the delineated boundary between self and others. This forms the basis of such ego functions as reality testing, impulse control, and the development of a synthesized view of the world. To do so, the child must relinquish the dependent attachment to mother and experience the expected sadness and mourn. Some, however, cling to the partner and defend against depression, in part supporting this defense against the specific feelings or experiences, such as separation or loss, with drugs.

As Greenspan (1977) notes, life is rarely so neatly structured. "Behavioral patterns become organized around multiple determinants from multiple developmental levels. In addition . . . one must also consider dynamic, structural and adaptive components of that pattern" (p. 79). Despite complexity, one of the implications of this developmental view is that, in addition to the commonalities we see across groups of drugs and behaviors, there will be distinctive meanings for particular drugs or behaviors. Drugs, for example, produce not only distinctive changes in physiology but also specific and distinct alterations in states of consciousness and specific alterations of a variety of ego functions. These alterations may be progressive as well as regressive.

The individual patterns of drug-induced alteration of ego functions are related to the drug ingested, the dose and the social context, as well as to the individual's predrug ego structure. Having once experienced the particular drug-induced pattern of ego function, the user may seek it out again for either defensive purposes as a solution to conflict or as a substitute for defective ego structure or for primary delight. This may result in preferential choice of drug. This idea was presaged by Schilder in the 1920s: "The psychic effect of every intoxication is a specific effect. It is a great problem of the future to determine which psychic systems are affected by the different poisons . . . the psychic system . . . is affected in a specific manner by narcotic drugs and differently by different drugs" (Schilder, 1951, p. 170).

In 1932 Glover suggested that "different types of drug addiction represent variations in the amount of original erotogenic sources of libido (and consequently different fusions of sadism): hence that they represent variations not only in the structure of the primitive ego, but in the type of mechanism employed to control excitation . . . my view is that the addict exploits the action of the drug in terms of an infantile system of thinking" (p. 201).

Psychodynamic Meaning of Drugs

More recently, Wieder and Kaplan (1969) have echoed this theme.

> Any drug's influence is mediated through its psychodynamic meaning or "placebo effect," and, if it possesses them, pharmacologic properties.

Symbolic importance is attached not only to the *agent* itself, which may represent object or part object; or to the *act* of using it, which may be in the service of fulfilling wishes to control, attack or influence the object or self; but also to the *physiological concomitants,* which stimulate fantasies, or are secondarily incorporated into them—i.e., what we called the *pharmacogenic effect.* It represents diffuse, direct and indirect alterations in cellular physiology and biochemistry, whose ultimate psychic expression appears as a modification of the energy equilibrium of the personality structure or as cathectic shifts. It is the pharmacogenic effect which, we feel, has not been sufficiently studied." (p. 400)

Unfortunately, however, clinical reality is rarely so simple. Combinations of the same drug and same individual often produce different effects. Obviously, dose, route of administration, environmental setting at the moment of drug use, and the specific intrapsychic state of the user at the time of taking the drug are important factors. For example, alcohol as used by the alcoholic in high doses is sedative. In lower doses, the more obvious result may be disinhibition or impulse control, either primary or secondary to a reduction of anxiety. The latter is more typical of social use of alcohol. Similarly, the active principles in marijuana are sedative in low doses and hallucinogenic in high doses. Thus, although the induced ego state is related to the specific drug, we must still keep these other factors in mind as we attempt to understand the psychodynamics of the individual in each case. As Fenichel (1945) said, "The problem of addiction reduces itself to the question of the nature of the specific gratification which persons of this type receive or try to receive from their chemically induced sedation or stimulation, and the conditions that determine the origin of the wish for such gratification" (p. 376).

It has been suggested that the main groups of psychoactive agents each tend to produce specific alterations in ego state which might be termed satiation, fantasy, or arousal, for example. These may recapitulate a series of such experiences, the originals of which appear to lie in specific phases of early child development. A particular drug thus may facilitate a particular regressive or progressive solution to conflict or defect, and may, therefore, be preferentially chosen. Studies by Milkman and Frosch (1973, 1977) lend support to this suggestion. Use of opiates tended to bolster withdrawal and repression by inducing a state of decreased motor activity, underresponsiveness to external situations, and reduction of perceptual intake. In contrast, amphetamines elevated scores on autonomous functioning and sense of confidence; there was a feeling of heightened perceptual and motor abilities accompanied by a stronger sense of potency and self-regard. A consistent finding was that ego structures were more adaptive in the amphetamine user than in the heroin user, suggesting they suffered from either less defect or less regression.

It is important to emphasize that the nature of these observations and studies makes it impossible to establish causal relationships. Are the personalities observed antecedent to drug use, concomitant, or resultant? Zinberg (1975) has suggested that many of the similarities observed come about from immersion in the drug culture and exclusion from the usual world and that labeling plays a role in the behaviors. Studies by Kandel (1978) and by Smith and Fogg (1978), however, suggest that some of these features are antecedent to immersion within the drug culture. Clearly, the data also suggest that these antecedents are modified as one moves from initial use to continuing use, to the transition from use to abuse, to cessation or control of abuse, and all too often to relapse. As Lang (1983) points out

> if we look at personality as a contributor, a predispositional component to or concurrent dimension of substance use and abuse . . . different personality characteristics or styles may make different contributions depending upon the type, frequency, time, consequences, and stage of substance involvement under consideration . . . individual perceptions, attitudes and values and personal traits or styles can explain why given comparable environments people vary in their substance use. (p. 218)

Despite our difficulties demonstrating more than some generalities about the personality of addictive behaviors, the construct of addictive personality may be "theoretically necessary, logically defensible and empirically supportable" (Sadava, 1978, p. 199). Without such a construct, which includes the symbolic meaning of the experience (while recognizing that this may be a post hoc rationalization), it will be difficult to explain the variation in drug use between individuals with apparently comparable life experience.

Psychoanalysis is a psychology of conflict, of how an individual finds the best possible solutions in life, of the path to psychological homeostasis, and of the ways we learn to seek compensation and comfort for our hurts. For a variety of reasons, some we all share and some idiosyncratic, many of us use drugs in this process, at times with maladaptive consequences. It is important to study the details of this psychological pathway so that we may learn to avoid the pitfalls.

References

Brill, A.A. (1922). Tobacco and the individual. *International Journal of Psychoanalysis, 3,* 430–444.

Erikson, E.H. (1963). *Childhood and society* (2nd ed.). New York: W.W. Norton.

Fenichel, O. (1945). *The psychoanalytic theory of neurosis.* New York: W.W. Norton.

Freud, S. (1954). Letter to Fliess. In M. Bonaparte, A. Freud & E. Kris (Eds.), *The origins of psychoanalysis: Letters to Wilhelm Fliess:* Drafts and notes, 1887–1902. New York: Basic Books.

Freud, S. (1962). *Three essays on the theory of sexuality.* New York: Basic Books.

Glover, E. (1932). On the aetiology of drug addiction. *International Journal of Psychoanalysis, 13,* 298–328. [Reprinted in Glover, E. (1956). *Selected papers of psychoanalysis. Vol. I: On the early development of the mind.* New York: International Universities Press.]

Greenspan, S.I. (1977). Substance abuse: An understanding from psychoanalytic, developmental and learning perspectives. In J.D. Blaine & D.A. Julius (Eds.), *Psychodynamics of drug dependence* (NIDA Research Monograph No. 12; DHEW Publication No. ADM 77–470) (pp. 73–87). Washington, D.C.: U.S. Government Printing Office.

Hartmann, D. (1969). A study of drug-taking adolescents. *Psychoanalytic Study of the Child, 24,* 384–398. Reprinted from *Psychoanalytic Study of the Child,* by permission of International Universities Press, Inc. Copyright © 1969 by International Universities Press, Inc.

Kandel, D.B. (1978). Convergences in prospective longitudinal surveys of drug use in normal populations. In D.B. Kandel (Ed.), *Longitudinal research on drug abuse: Empirical findings and methodological issues* (pp. 3–38). Washington, D.C.: Hemisphere Publishing.

Khantzian, E.J. (1977). The ego, the self, and opiate addiction: Theoretical and treatment considerations. In J.D. Blaine & D.A. Julius (Eds.), *Psychodynamics of drug dependence* (NIDA Research Monograph No. 12; DHEW Publication No. ADM 77–470) (pp. 101–117). Washington, D.C.: U.S. Government Printing Office.

Krystal, H. & Raskin, H.A. (1970). *Drug dependence: Aspects of ego function.* Detroit: Wayne State University Press.

Lang, A.R. (1983). Addictive personality: A viable construct? In P.K. Levinson, D.R. Gerstein, & D.R. Maloff (Eds.), *Commonalities in substance abuse and habitual behavior* (pp. 157–235). Lexington, MA: Lexington Books.

Mahler, M. (1967). On human symbiosis and the vicissitudes of individuation. *Journal of the American Psychoanalytic Association, 15,* 740–760.

Milkman, H. & Frosch, W.A. (1973). On the preferential abuse of heroin and amphetamine. *Journal of Nervous and Mental Disease, 156(4),* 242–248.

Milkman, H. & Frosch, W.A. (1977). The drug of choice. *Journal of Psychedelic Drugs, 9(1),* 11–24.

Piaget, J. (1954). *The construction of reality in the child.* New York: Basic Books.

Rado, S. (1926). The psychic effects of intoxicants: An attempt to evolve a psychoanalytical theory of morbid cravings. *International Journal of Psychoanalysis, 7,* 396–413.

Rado, S. (1933). The psychoanalysis of pharmacothymia. *Psychoanalytic Quarterly, 2,* 1–23.

Sadava, S.W. (1978). Etiology, personality and alcoholism. *Canadian Psychological Review, 19,* 198–214.

Savitt, R.A. (1954). Clinical communications: Extramural psychoanalytic treatment of a case of narcotic addiction. *Journal of the American Psychoanalytic Association, 2,* 494–502.

Savitt, R.A. (1963). Psychoanalytic studies of addiction: Ego structure in narcotic addiction. *Psychoanalytic Quarterly, 32,* 43–57.

Schilder, P. (1951). *Introduction to a psychoanalytic psychiatry.* (Nervous and mental disease monograph series no. 50). (Translator, B. Glueck). New York: International Universities Press.

Smith, G.M. & Fogg, C.P. (1978). Psychological predictors of early youth, late youth, and nonuse of marihuana among teenage students. In D.B. Kandel (Ed.), *Longitudinal research on drug use: Empirical findings and methodological issues* (pp. 101–113). Washington, D.C.: Hemisphere Publishing.

Treece, C.J. & Khantzian, E.J. (1977). Psychodynamics of drug dependence: An overview. In J.D. Blaine & D.A. Julius (Eds.), *Psychodynamics of drug dependence* (NIDA Research Monograph No. 12; DHEW Publication No. ADM 77–470) (pp. 73–87). Washington, D.C.: U.S. Government Printing Office.

Wieder, H. & Kaplan, E.H. (1969). Drug use in adolescents: Psychodynamic meaning and pharmacogenic effect. *Psychoanalytic Study of the Child, 24,* 399–431. Reprinted from *Psychoanalytic Study of the Child,* by permission of International Universities Press, Inc. Copyright © 1969 by International Universities Press, Inc.

Wurmser, L. (1977). Mr. Pecksniff's horse? In J.D. Blaine & D.A. Julius (Eds), *Psychodynamics of drug dependence* (NIDA Research Monograph No. 12; DHEW Publication No. ADM 77–470) (pp. 73–87). Washington, D.C.: U.S. Government Printing Office.

Zinberg, N.E. (1975). Addiction and ego function. *Psychoanalytic Study of the Child, 30,* 567–588.

5
Trends in Behavioral Psychology and the Addictions

Howard J. Shaffer
Robert J. Schneider

The purpose of this chapter is to provide an overview of the behavioral approaches and trends that have influenced the treatment of addictive behaviors. It is in the spirit of exploration and discovery that we examine the behavioral view as an important ingredient in the development of a practice theory in the addictions. Since a comprehensive review of behavioral psychology and behavioral approaches to the addictions is beyond the scope of this book, we will briefly examine the history and development of behavioral psychology and then illustrate these ideas with theoretical and clinical material from the field of substance abuse. This discussion will conclude with a contemporary integration of these approaches and, finally, a consideration of the directions and trends that behavioral approaches may take in the future.

The Behavioral Perspective and Behavior Therapy

Behavior therapy means many different things to different people. Behavior therapy is not, nor was it ever, a monolithic concept or treatment approach (Wilson, 1978a, 1978b). Nonetheless, current behavioral theory and practice, despite extreme diversity and often strident discord among adherents, reflect agreement regarding the importance of using scientific methods in both research, assessment, and practice in the field of addictive behaviors.

The development of the behavioral approaches came about as a result of dissatisfaction during the 1950s with psychoanalytic models and the failure of this approach to explain and solve the riddle of addiction. Consequently, approaches that boasted a more solid empirical and scientific base were widely adopted, though not without concurrent controversy among competing theoretical camps. These behavioral theories were generated from paradigms provided by the models of learning developed by Ivan Pavlov and B.F. Skinner; these paradigms were popularly known as classical (or respondent) and operant conditioning, respectively.

These approaches generated the view that psychopathology is a learned set of dysfunctional behaviors rather than the result of deep-seated psychological trauma or physical illness. Thus, the disorders of thinking, feeling, and acting were conceptualized as maladaptive responses to environmental events which, once learned by the individual, are maintained in the present by reinforcing contingencies.

Behavior thereapy is based on the philosophical assumption that the individual and the environment are an interacting system of events and that the developing person reacts from birth to external conditions in both the physical and social environment; therefore, individual behavior is influenced, that is, altered or maintained, in predictable ways. On the basis of this experience with the external world, the organism acquires consistent patterns of reacting to new conditions as it develops through the life cycle. Finally, according to behavioral theory, individual behavior, modified and/or maintained by experience, is the major focus and subject matter of scientific and clinical inquiry.

Scientific Methods and the Behavioral Approach

The approach of applying scientific methods to the study of human behavior is one (if not the) identifying characteristic of the behavioral approaches. The scientific method is based on the principle that only objectively observable and verifiable data can be included in a science of human behavior. All interactions between individuals and their respective environments should be observable and quantifiable and, therefore, measurable. The natural course of inquiry into the meaning of human behavior requires, according to the behaviorists, adherence to the rules of the scientific method. These rules include two major characteristics: (1) the formulation of a theory about the cause/effect relationship between systems of interacting variables that include the individuals and their environments; and (2) the development of hypotheses that lend themselves to experimental verification through empirical testing. The adherence to these rules has been responsible for the development of behavioral methods such as applied behavior analysis, which we will discuss later.

Pavlov and Skinner: An Experimental Approach. Pavlov and Skinner have taken the experimental, empirical, scientific approach to the study of human behavior. Their theories of respondent and operant conditioning are based on the principle of association initially formulated by

Aristotle. Aristotle noted that the organisms in the environment were an interacting system of events, that connections of associations are bonded in the interaction, and that these associations constitute the reservoir of experiences which form the basis for reactions to future environmental events. Interestingly, for Aristotle, the soul or the mind of an individual was its function, that is, behavior was not separable from the body. When Aristotle talked about behavior he referred to thinking, feeling, and motor behavior.

During the past decade, many of Skinner's disciples have taken the radical position that internal events are nonexistent; however, Skinner (1953, 1971) had indicated many years before that these events, internal to the individual, were natural events that were difficult to quantify and therefore not useful in a behavioral analysis. He did not question the existence of these events. New advances in measurement technique have yielded many internal and previously unquantifiable behaviors distinctly measurable and therefore appropriate targets of behavioral assessment and intervention. In fact, these new approaches have, in part, been responsible for the rapid acceptance of the cognitive behavioral approaches that are currently quite popular and in widespread use. For example, during a recent case conference, a psychoanalyst asked a patient just how anxious he was feeling at that point relative to other situations. The patient, displaying evaluation apprehension, responded, "pretty anxious." The psychoanalyst, unknowingly, was practicing a form of behavioral assessment. Instead of accepting a vague "pretty anxious," a common behavioral measurement technique could have been utilized. This tactic—which yields more reliable and useful data than the approach above—would be to ask patients to rate their present anxiety on a scale of 0 to 100, where 0 represented as relaxed a feeling as they have ever experienced and 100 represented as anxious a feeling as they have ever experienced. The data obtained with this technique is generated on a ratio scale that permits useful comparisons to other ratings taken over time. Such a technique, albeit a behavioral tactic, can be readily integrated into most clinical approaches without disrupting the essential meaning of these nonbehavioral approaches. We will consider more of these issues later.

The Conditioning Theories of Abraham Wikler

In 1965, the late Abraham Wikler published a chapter on conditioning factors in opiate addiction and relapse. This chapter was the first to consider the roles that instrumental and classical conditioning play in the addiction process. Wikler's thinking predated contemporary cognitive-behavior modification theorists and practitioners by analyzing the relationship between cognitive and behavioral phenomena. This view considered the drug user as an active, self-determining individual who was not simply a victim of circumstance or conditioning. Addicts were human beings with feelings, thoughts, motives, and ideas, all of which were considered to come into play during the acquisition, maintenance, and extinction of addictive behavior. Wikler's two stage approach (for example, 1965, 1973) to substance abuse perhaps best illustrates the application of classical behavior theory to an understanding and treatment of addictive behavior (see table 5–1).

The theoretical motivation for the use of Naltrexone and Antabuse as clinical interventions is largely based on this two stage model as well as the pragmatic experience of outpatient treatment providers. Their experience indicated that typical substance abusers continue to spend a great deal of time in the environments that had previously been associated with substance use. Naltrexone treatment, therefore, was utilized to extinguish the bond between conditioned stimuli and conditioned responses. Naltrexone's action, that of a narcotic antagonist, essentially eliminates the unconditioned reinforcing properties of narcotics by blocking their action. Conversely, Antabuse punishes the use of alcohol by inducing a noxious syndrome; this syndrome—according to behavioral theory—should reduce the use of alcohol because the aversive consequences of such use replace the previous consequences, which were positively reinforcing. It should be readily apparent to both supporters and critics of behavioral theory that these interventions, like other treatments, work on some occasions while on others, they do not.

Table 5–1
Wikler's Simplified Two Stage Model of Conditioned Dependence

Stage One: Acquisition
(classical conditioning)

1. Conditioned stimuli (for example, works, room, thoughts, feelings)
2. Unconditioned stimulus (for example, narcotic)
3. Unconditioned response (for example, narcotic euphoria, "rush," nausea)
4. Soon tolerance develops and the UCS no longer elicits the UCR

Stage Two: Maintenance
(operant conditioning)

1. Withdrawal syndrome (for example, unpleasant effects of narcotic abstinence)
2. Application of narcotics (for example, "shooting up")
3. Negative reinforcement (for example, cessation of withdrawal syndrome)

Current Behavioral Treatment Approaches

Behavior therapists today engage in very different activities from their counterparts just ten to fifteen years ago. The full scope of the techniques practiced by contemporary behavior therapists is beyond the purview of this discussion. However, one of the trends that is dramatically revealed by a survey of contemporary behavioral practices is the shift in focus from solely external, observable behaviors to behaviors that are more cognitive and, hence, internal (Gochman, Allgood & Geer, 1982). In his classic book on freedom and dignity, Skinner (1971) commented that "a person does not act upon the world, the world acts upon him" (p. 211). Although many of his followers interpreted Skinner's statement to mean that overt behavior alone is accepted as the proper subject matter of scientific investigation, Skinner has stated that the study of subjective events should not be dismissed a priori simply because these are private events; in fact, he indicated that these events were not useful in a functional analysis. This position is very different from radical behaviorists who do not consider the existence of internal cognitive states as the proper targets of behavioral assessment and intervention. Gochman et al. (1982) demonstrated this cognitive trend during a recent survey of the American Association of Behavior Therapists. They reported that sixty-three percent of the respondents were somewhat eclectic in their practices and only twenty-seven percent were strictly behavioral. In addition, this study found that, of the behavior therapists surveyed, eighty-four percent utilized systematic desensitization and eighty-four percent utilized cognitive restructuring as techniques in their practices. These were the most popular procedures reported by the behaviorist. Not so long ago, only desensitization would have been reported as the most frequently used behavioral technique. Finally, and perhaps more surprising, seventy-six percent of the respondents were using contingency contracting, while only seventy-three percent and seventy-one percent were using modeling and shaping, respectively. Only a few years ago, it would have been heresy to even consider that these techniques might dominate the practice of behavior therapy.

Applied Behavior Analysis

As we have already described, behavioral approaches rest heavily on the notion of applied behavior analysis; specifically, this technique refers to the experimental analysis of behavior problems. In fact, this technique can be applied to the analysis of any pattern of behavior. Simply put, this is a behavior counting technique. However, if it was called counting, some of the magic and mystery of science would be missing. Hence, it remains applied behavior analysis.

According to the behavioral perspective, it is necessary to establish baseline levels of target behavior in order to empirically judge the efficacy of our clinical interventions. In addition, this technique permits continual monitoring of the target behavior so that we can determine if our treatment plan is influencing the behavior in the desired direction or, perhaps more importantly, so that we can adjust our treatment plan if the frequency or intensity of the undesired behavior increases. The following clinical case (Bernard, Dennehy & Keefauver, 1981) illustrates the concept of applied behavior analysis and its usefulness for the treatment of a high base rate pattern of excessive behavior: excessive coffee and tea drinking (see figure 5–1). In addition, this study illustrates the use of contingency contracting, since the patient contributed five dollars to charity for the first cup of coffee over the daily maximum (which was negotiated and changed regularly), and two dollars for each cup thereafter; the patient also received social praise for successfully reaching target levels of consumption. As this case study illustrates, the technique of applied behavior analysis engenders two characteristics that are associated with behavioral approaches. The first is the in-

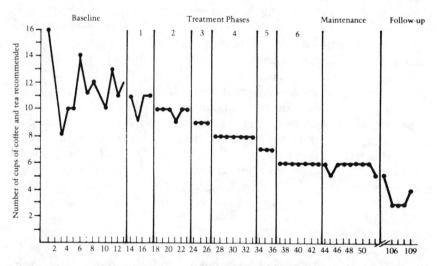

Source: M.E. Bernard, S. Dennehy, and L.W. Keefauver, Behavioral treatment of excessive coffee and tea drinking: A case study and partial replication. *Behavior Therapy* 12, 547. Copyright © 1981, Association for Advancement of Behavior Therapy; reprinted with permission.

Note: The criterion level for each treatment phase was one cup less than the previous treatment phase.

Figure 5–1. Subject's Daily Coffee and Tea Intake during Baseline, Treatment, Maintenance, and Follow-up

sistence on the study of individuals rather than groups. Though there are some exceptions to this principle, the majority of behaviorists tend to study individual, not group, behavior. Second, behavioral treatment is based on the principle of reinforcement, that is, positive reinforcement, negative reinforcement, and punishment.

Contemporary Behavioral Models

Neoclassical S-R Model: A Mediational Approach

The neoclassical approaches are based on the principles of conditioning, with particular emphasis on classical and counterconditioning models for the treatment of abnormal behavior. This work derives from the pioneering contributions of Eysenk, Rachman, and Wolpe, who sought to base their practice on the conditioning and learning principles generated by Pavlov, Guthrie, and Hull (Wilson, 1978a). The hallmark of this neoclassical period in behavior therapy is the centrality ascribed to various internal constructs of dysphoria. For example, anxiety, craving, and the fear associated with withdrawal are constructs central to the treatment techniques of systematic desensitization, reciprocal inhibition, and flooding that are most closely associated with this framework. Essentially direct derivations of conditioning and learning theory, these techniques are intended to extinguish the underlying dysphoria that is assumed to maintain certain dysfunctional patterns of behavior. The application of these methods rests squarely on the assumption that covert processes follow the same laws of learning that establish and maintain overt behaviors.

Neoclassical models consider unobservable, internal events such as the internal representations of anxiety as intervening events that are anchored to antecedent and consequent reference points that are observable. Thus, this point of view accepts cognitive and other internal emotional states as appropriate targets for the study, assessment, and treatment of behavioral approaches. Wilson (1982) has noted that conditioning concepts contributed a great deal more to behavior therapy than just the introduction of particular treatment techniques.

A more fundamental benefit was the conceptual and methodological emphasis that the study and application of conditioning principles brought to clinical research and practice. The detailed specification of therapeutic techniques, the focus on behavior per se in assessment, treatment, and evaluation of therapy outcome, and the advances in measurement and methodology were all directly associated with the methodological behaviorism that characterized the conditioning approach. (Wilson, 1982, p. 294)

Social Learning Theory

Social learning theory is a comprehensive behavioral approach to human functioning which assumes that both deviant and prosocial behavior patterns are developed and maintained on the basis of three distinct regulatory systems (Wilson, 1978a). First, social learning theorists assume that some behavior patterns are primarily under the control of external stimulus events and are affected largely by classical conditioning processes. Second, reinforcement processes—the main focus of operant conditioning—are considered as another major form of behavior control. Third, and perhaps the most important system of regulatory influence for the social learning school, is the role of cognitive mediational processes. Social learning theorists, unlike traditional operant and classical conditioning theorists, view human behavior as an active rather than a passive event. Individuals are not passive respondents to contingencies that exist in their environment, but rather are active participants in determining their reinforcement and interpreting the relevance of such contingencies.

A social learning analysis considers the influence of environmental events on the acquisition and regulation of behavior as largely determined by cognitive processes. These internal mental events determine what environmental influences are attended to, how these are perceived, and whether these might affect the future behavior of the individual. Modeling, one of the best known and widely used social learning methods, provides an excellent example of cognitive learning. In operant conditioning, in order for learning to occur, a response must be performed and followed by reinforcement or punishment. However, complex human behavior would rarely be acquired unless learning also occurred through observation alone without the need for direct reinforcement of specific behaviors. This is the essence of modeling. We are reminded of the research that has demonstrated the need for individuals to learn how to interpret the effects of various psychoactive drugs in order to enjoy rather than be sickened by the experience (for example, Becker, 1953).

Another distinguishing characteristic of social learning theory is that psychological functioning involves a reciprocal interaction between a person's behavior and the environment. Though this may sound similar, Albert Bandura (1977a, p. 203) interpreted these interactions in a new light

> environments have causes, as do behaviors. It is true that behavior is regulated by its contingencies, but the contingencies are partly of a person's own making. By their action, people play an active role in producing the reinforcing contingencies that impinge upon them. . . . Behavior partly creates the environment, and the environment influences the behavior in a reciprocal fashion. To the often repeated dictum, change

the contingencies and you change behavior, should be added the reciprocal side, change behavior and you change contingencies.

Thus, according to Bandura—the founder of modern social learning theory—a person is neither driven by internal forces nor victimized by external pressures; rather, individuals are both the agents as well as the objects of environmental influence.

Social learning theory is also identified by the position its adherents take with respect to the causal influence that cognitions play in determining human behavior. Social learning theory vanguards the human capacity for self-directed behavior change. Thus, in addition to the acquisition and maintenance of behavior, activation and persistence of behavior is considered to be based mainly on cognitive mechanisms. For example, consider a patient who has received job-interview training after successful detoxification and psychotherapy. On his first interview the patient is offered the job but later loses it due strictly to economic conditions that have nothing to do with his performance. The future behavior of this patient will be powerfully influenced by his appraisal of the outcome of the first interview—success—and his loss of employment—failure. The patient may conclude that because the personnel director was extremely busy at the time of the interview, getting the job was really due to luck, that is, there was not enough time for proper questioning that would surely have revealed the patient unqualified for the position. Consequently, this individual might reduce his effort to seek employment or, even worse, stop trying to maintain his new pattern of behavior since it does not seem to be helping. From this brief vignette we can see the point of the social learning theorists: our cognitive explanations of behavior change will predict, in part, how lasting the effects of treatment will be and serve to activate or deactivate future patterns of activity.

Bandura (1977b) suggests that all therapeutic change techniques are effective to the extent that clients' *efficacy expectations* are improved. Efficacy expectations refer to the belief of clients that they are capable of performing actions which will be to their benefit. These are distinguished from *outcome expectations*, which are defined as a person's expectations that a given behavior will indeed produce certain outcomes. Thus, individuals can give up a certain behavior because they see their attempts as inadequate, or they can feel quite confident of their own abilities but frustrated by an unresponsive or punitive environment. This distinction is important because the helplessness experienced in each instance has a different source and different remedial implications. To alter helplessness arising from internal feelings of inadequacy (an efficacy expectation) requires the development of skills, competencies, and expectations of personal effectiveness. However, changing futility based on the results of one's behavior (an outcome expectancy) might necessitate changes in the environment to restore one's belief in the system.

These mechanisms by which human behavior is acquired and regulated (efficacy and outcome expectancies) are clearly formulated in terms of cognitive processes. Furthermore, these cognitive processes are not the result of immediate or momentary consequences. Rather, consequences "processed in the aggregate" (that is, many consequences over a considerable time period) serve as "unarticulated" ways of informing performers when they are effective as well as what they must do to improve effectiveness (Bandura, 1977b, p. 192). Thus, environmental stimuli are seen as predictive cues as well as behavioral determinants (classical conditioning). This shifts "the locus of the regulation of behavior from the stimulus to the individual" (Bandura, 1977b, p. 292). Similarly, the causal connection between behavior and aggregate consequences is contrary to the common view that behavior is controlled by its immediate consequences (operant conditioning).

Cognitive Behavior Therapy

The most recent discernible development within behavior therapy is the emergence of what has been loosely described as the cognitive connection. It is difficult to categorize the chaotic mixture of principles and procedures that comprise cognitive behavior therapy. However, Mahoney and Arnkoff (1978) have identified three major commonalities among the various therapies that have been considered cognitive. First, humans are considered to develop adaptive and maladaptive affective behavior via cognitive processes, for example, selective attention and symbolic coding. Second, these cognitive processes are functionally activated by systems that are considered to be identical to those that have been observed in the human learning laboratory and therefore are subject to the influence of reinforcement processes. Third, the task of the therapist is that of a diagnostician-educator who assesses maladaptive cognitive processes and subsequently arranges learning experiences which will alter cognitions and, in turn, the behavior-affect patterns to which these cognitions correlate.

Thus, like the neoclassical and social learning models, the cognitive approach to behavior therapy considers the multiplicity of internal events as the proper focus of behavioral interventions. (The interested reader should see Foreyt and Rathjen (1978) for a relevant examination of these issues.) In addition, the cognitive approach reiterates two important characteristics of the behavioral perspective: First, the importance of studying individuals rather than groups, and second, the essential role that reinforcement processes play in the development and treatment of abnormal patterns of behavior.

Recently, Wilson (1982) succinctly summarized the cognitive view of clinical disorders and the associated treatment interventions. This behavioral model serves as a "guide to the most efficient and effective use of planned behavioral interventions; preparing clients for the intended learning experiences; directing their attention, encoding, and retrieval processes along the proper channels during the planned encounter; and, subsequently, ensuring that they draw the appropriate conclusion from the experience" (Wilson, 1982, p. 296). The cognitive therapy of depression developed by Beck (for example, Beck, Rush, Shaw & Emery, 1979) demonstrates the integration of a variety of "behavioral procedures and cognitive restructuring strategies that are directly tied to performance-based experience, [and] provides an explicit illustration of the recommended cognitive behavioral mix" (Wilson, 1982, p. 296).

Rather than make artificial attempts to categorize and classify the multiplicity of heterogenous cognitive behavioral interventions, we would like to briefly introduce a multidimensional, cognitive behavioral intervention program that is prototypical of an integrated intervention program. This prevention program is based on the theory of psychological inoculation formulated by McGuire (1964) and is presently labeled smoking inoculation.

Prevention: An Opportunity to Integrate Contemporary Behavioral Approaches

Smoking inoculation (for example, Shaffer, Beck & Boothroyd, 1983) provides the opportunity to examine an applied primary prevention technique that illustrates a wide variety of behavioral, cognitive-behavioral, and social learning concepts. Specifically, the inoculation approach is based on the idea that we expect individuals to encounter the cultural analogue of germs, that is, social pressures toward the adoption of a behavior that is detrimental to their health; we can prevent infection if we expose persons to weak doses of such germs in a way that facilitates the development of antibodies, that is, skills for resisting the social pressures. The inoculation procedure that was used in a recently published study (Shaffer et al., 1983), was comprised of three components: cognitive preparation, skill acquisition, and rehearsal. The purpose of these procedures was to accomplish a variety of different objectives. The preparation phase provided subjects the opportunity to:

1. Identify the feelings, people, and places that elicit the desire to smoke
2. Recognize that one has the desire to smoke
3. Understand the cognitive, psychological, situational, and behavioral determinants of the desire to smoke

4. Emphasize the self-statements that contribute to lowering the level of the desire to smoke
5. Recognize the signs of arousal and personal tension early
6. Establish the inoculation approach as a viable coping/prevention strategy

The skill acquisition and rehearsal phases provided subjects the opportunity to:

1. Learn cognitive, affective, and behavioral skills that effectively permitted them to resist the pressure to smoke, for example, maintaining a task orientation toward resisting pressure and developing alternative behaviors that improve the capacity to cope with day-to-day anxieties
2. Learning new responses to media pressure (for example, not being liberated if dependent on cigarettes and recognizing the media's portrayal of smoking as distorted)
3 Learning to recognize affective discomfort that might influence decision making so that a more appropriate response can be made (for example, relaxation, or cognitive reframing)

These three phases of intervention provide a theoretically integrated technique based on behavioral models. It can be applied to a variety of disorders that previously fell between the cracks of clinical services. In fact, the smoking inoculation model was developed as a result of inoculation interventions that focused on stress (Jaremko, 1979; Meichenbaum, 1977; Meichenbaum & Turk, 1976), pain (Horan, Hacket, Buchanan, Stone & Demchik-Stone, 1977; Turk, 1978), and anger (Novaco, 1976, 1977).

Practicing Behavior Therapy

As a result of the multiplicity of behavioral approaches that we have discussed—even though we have only described representative contemporary models—one may be curious about the characteristics of a practicing behavior therapist's case load. In addition, for our purposes, it is interesting and informative to note the reported frequency of character and, the often concurrent, substance abuse disorders among those treated by behavior therapists. In a recent survey of the American Association of Behavior Therapists, Gochman et al. (1982) obtained this data. They found that ninety-three percent of the respondents reported treating adults while only forty-one percent and thirty-one percent indicated that they treated adolescents and children, respectively. The following list summarizes the disorders that were treated by the responding behavior therapists and the percentage of therapists that treated each disorder (based on Gochman et al., 1982). In descending order, from most treated to least, the treated disorders were: adjustment disorders (85%); neuroses (83%); phobias (46%); psychosomatic disorders (42%); mixed other disorders (38%); character disorders (37%); affective psychotic disorders (20%); schizoprenia (17%).

Conclusion

Though we have only touched the surface of the plethora of issues that surround behavior therapy, specific themes are manifest that until only recently remained implicit. First, behavioral models and interventions display a strong and decisive trend toward the inclusion of internal events, for example, cognitive processes, in the study of human behavior. Secondly, the techniques that once heavily dominated the clinical practice of behavior therapists are now beginning to wane in popularity, application, and efficacy—if these approaches were ever more than only mixed in effectiveness. For example, aversive conditioning approaches like electric shock, chemical aversion, rapid smoking, and covert sensitization are less popular now than ever (Callner, 1975; Gochman et al., 1982); perhaps this is a result of the mixed efficacy of these techniques, or more likely, because of the ethical and medical risks that are inherent considerations in their application. Conversely, the social learning approaches—such as contingency management, controlled use, inoculation prevention programs, and multidimensional component treatment programs—appear to be the direction to take, given the encouraging results (Krasnegor, 1980).

Thorenson and Coates (1978 p. 15) examined social learning theory and recognized the value of a "conceptual model sufficiently comprehensive to handle the reciprocal and interrelated cognitive, affective, behavioral, and environmental processes involved" in human learning. Though behavior therapy has evolved beyond the stimulus response model of classical conditioning, there is still the need and opportunity for further development and integration with other clinical approaches—including psychodynamic and analytic (Wachtel, 1973). Considering the evolution and development of behavioral approaches, Wilson (1982) may have accurately described the crossroads of contemporary behavior therapy when he speculated that "This is not the end. It is not even the beginning of the end. But it is, perhaps, the end of the beginning" (p. 305).

During a critical examination of the meaning of behavior therapy and behavior therapists, Kegan (1978) applauded the expansion of behaviorism to include cognition, that is, the meaning behind our behaviors, values, and investments. He expressed concern, however, with behaviorism's lack of a developmental framework that describes normative processes of change and growth for human organisms. Without some understanding of a person's built-in curriculum, Kegan suggests, behavioral therapists have no theoretical justification for intervention. In a sense, they arrive at human development too late, for example, when there is a problem. Their theories and skills are exclusively directed toward removal of current problems or the avoidance of potential problems.

Though Kegan has accurately identified several important issues that represent problems for the future of behavioral approaches, there are some points essential to Kegan's view with which we disagree. Certainly, an understanding of human development, complete with inherent values and judgments, is indispensable in the treatment of human beings. Behavioral perspectives have never denied or avoided this issue. Rather, behavioral approaches have presented us with a set of tactics to assist us in securing the objectives designated by an overall plan or applied strategy. In addition, behavioral psychology has offered a set of templates by which one can reasonably explain complex and difficult to comprehend patterns of human behavior; when appropriate, this understanding permits clinicians the opportunity to invoke a viable treatment strategy. The development and implementation of these strategies has not been the specific focus of behavioral psychology. The domain of clinical behavior therapy has focused on the development of specific intervention procedures that predict the direction of reactions to particular clinical procedures; similarly, the development of methods for measuring these responses has been the focus of behavioral psychology.

Interestingly, clinical psychologists already subscribe to a great variety of human developmental strategies. Some of these clinicians readily articulate the models that affect their practice while others remain more obscure; in either case, practitioners apply a clinical strategy (Shaffer & Gambino, 1979; Shaffer & Gambino, in press). Gochman et al. (1982) described the choices behavior therapists made when they selected a psychotherapeutic experience for themselves; seventy-three percent of the respondents in this study reported personal therapies that were either psychoanalytic or psychodynamic in nature. Alternatively, only eleven percent of those surveyed had entered behavioral therapy. These findings provide additional evidence in support of our position that diverse theoretical loyalties are represented among behavior therapists.

Regardless of a clinician's particular theoretical bias, all such influences affect not only the choice of clinical strategies and/or tactics but also the clinician's effectiveness in applying the selected interventions (Havens, 1982). Just as normal science and psychoanalysis are ways of conducting the business of science and psychoanalysis, respectively, these are also disciplines of substantive information. Kegan (1978) has criticized behavioral psychology for its substance; regardless of how accurate he may be, we should not lose site of the process (that is, the practice) that behaviorism has offered for the conduct of inquiry and treatment of the human condition.

Acknowledging and responding to these complex influences are important challenges to the practice of behavioral psychology. Rather than produce the feared dissolution of behavioral solidarity, we believe this dialogue highlights the enormous value that the behavioral approach offers and encourages all psychotherapists—including psychoanalysts—to consider the utility of these techniques, prescriptively, within their clinical practice.

Finally, during a recent interview, B.F. Skinner (1983) highlighted the relationship between scientists and compulsive gamblers.

> All scientific work pays off on a variable ratio schedule. So do hunting, fishing, exploring, prospecting, and so on. You never can tell when you are going to be reinforced, but reinforcements do keep turning up. The dedicated scientist is exactly like a pathological gambler. He's been hooked by a system, but in a way which is profitable for everyone. The scientist is fascinated by what he does, just as the gambler is, but nobody is taking his shirt. He's getting something out of it, and so is society. (p. 39)

According to Skinner, this vast array of interacting variable ratio reinforcement schedules can influence the behavior of treatment providers and recipients. Since many reinforcement schedules lie outside of conscious awareness, these influences can insidiously confuse clinicians and scientists alike. Nevertheless, the power of these contingencies can also provide valuable insight and direction for future areas of treatment and scientific inquiry. Presently, however, there are many strategies, tactics, and techniques that behavioral psychology has to offer both behavioral believers and those therapists who are simply in need of a wider range of therapeutic interventions.

References

Bandura, A. (1977a). *Social learning theory*. Englewood Cliffs, NJ: Prentice-Hall.

Bandura, A. (1977b). Self-efficacy: Towards a unifying theory of behavior change. *Psychological Review, 84,* 191–215.

Beck, A.T., Rush, A.J., Shaw, B.F. & Emery, G. (1979). *Cognitive therapy of depression.* New York: Guilford Press.

Becker, H.S. (1953) Becoming a marihuana user. *American Journal of Sociology, 59,* 235–243.

Bernard, M.E., Dennehy, S. & Keefauver, L.W. (1981). Behavioral treatment of excessive coffee and tea drinking: A case study and partial replication. *Behavior Therapy, 12,* 543–548.

Callner, D.A. (1975). Behavioral treatment approaches to drug abuse: A critical review of the research. *Psychological Bulletin, 82,* 143–164.

Foreyt, J.P. & Rathjen, D.P. (Eds.). (1978). *Cognitive behavior therapy.* New York: Plenum Press.

Gochman, S.I., Allgood, B.A. & Geer, C.R. (1982). A look at today's behavior therapists. *Professional Psychology, 13,* 605–609.

Havens, L. (1982). The choice of clinical methods. *Contemporary Psychoanalysis, 18,* 16–42.

Horan, J.J., Hacket, C., Buchanan, J.D., Stone, C.I. & Deachik-Stone, D. (1977). Coping with pain: A component analysis of stress inoculation. *Cognitive Therapy and Research, 1,* 211–221.

Jaremko, M.E. (1979). A component analysis of stress inoculation: Review and prospectus. *Cognitive Therapy and Research, 3,* 35–48.

Kegan, R. (1978). Can there be a meaning to being a behavior therapist?: A reply. *Counseling Psychologist,* 30–32.

Krasnegor, N.A. (1980). Analysis and modification of substance abuse: A behavioral overview. *Behavior Modification, 4,* 35–56.

Mahoney, M.J. & Arnkoff, D. (1978). Cognitive and self-control therapies. In S.L. Garfield & A.E. Begin (Eds.), *Handbook of psychotherapy and behavior change* (2d ed.). New York: Wiley.

McGuire, W.J. (1964). Inducing resistance to persuasion: Some contemporary approaches. In L. Berkowitz (Ed.), *Advances in experimental social psychology.* New York: Academic Press.

Meichenbaum, D. (1977). *Cognitive behavior modification.* New York: Plenum Press.

Meichenbaum, D. & Turk, D. (1976). The cognitive-behavioral management of anxiety, anger and pain. In P.O. Davidson (Ed.), *The behavioral management of anxiety, depression and pain.* New York: Brunner/Mazel.

Novaco, R.W. (1976). Treatment of chronic anger through cognitive and relaxation controls. *Journal of Consulting and Clinical Psychology, 44,* 681.

Novaco, R.W. (1977). Stress inoculation: A cognitive therapy for anger and its application to a case of depression. *Journal of Consulting and Clinical Psychology, 45,* 600–608.

Shaffer, H., Beck, J. & Boothroyd, P. (1983). The primary prevention of smoking onset: An inoculation approach. *Journal of Psychoactive Drugs, 5* 177–184.

Shaffer, H. & Gambino, B. (1979). Addiction paradigms II: Theory, research, and practice. *Journal of Psychedelic Drugs, 11,* 207–223.

Shaffer, H. & Gambino, B. (in press). Addiction paradigms III: From theory-research to practice and back. *Advances in Alcohol and Substance Abuse.*

Skinner, B.F. (1953). *Science and human behavior.* New York: Macmillan.

Skinner, B.F. (1971). *Beyond freedom and dignity.* New York: Alfred Knopf.

Skinner, B.F. (1983, August). [Interview with B. F. Skinner]. *APA Monitor,* p. 39.

Thorenson, C. & Coates, T. (1978). What does it mean to be a behavior therapist? *Counseling Psychologist,* 7(3), 3–21.

Turk, D. (1978). Cognitive behavioral techniques in the management of pain. In J.P. Foreyt & D.P. Rathjen (Eds.), *Cognitive behavior therapy.* New York: Plenum Press.

Wachtel, P.L. (1973). *Psychoanalysis and behavior therapy: Toward an integration.* New York: Basic Books.

Wikler, A. (1973). Dynamics of drug dependence: Implications of a conditioning Wilner & G.G. Kassebaum (Eds.), *Narcotics* (pp. 85–100). New York: McGraw-Hill.

Wilker, A. (1973). Dynamics of drug dependence: Implications of a conditioning theory for research and treatment. *Archives of General Psychiatry, 28,* 611–616.

Wilson, G.T. (1978a). Cognitive behavior therapy: Paradigm shift of passing phase? In J.P. Foreyt & D. P. Rathjen (Eds.), *Cognitive behavior therapy.* New York: Plenum Press.

Wilson, G.T. (1978b). On the much discussed nature of the term, "behavior therapy". *Behavior Therapy, 9,* 89–98.

Wilson, G.T. (1982). Psychotherapy process and procedure: The behavioral mandate. *Behavior Therapy, 13,* 291–312.

6

The Social Psychology of Intoxicant Use: The Interaction of Personality and Social Setting

Norman E. Zinberg
Howard J. Shaffer

I n order to study drug-induced states, and patterns of intoxicant use in particular, it is necessary to consider drug, set, and setting as a whole. *Set* refers to the personality structure of drug users, including their attitudes toward the experience and any values that might be associated with the activity. *Setting* is considered to be the influence of the physical and social environment within which the drug use takes place. "In order to understand an individual's decision to use a drug and his response to the experience at any effective dose below toxic levels, one must consider the drug-set-setting interaction since these factors affect the drug experience directly" (Zinberg, 1974; 1981, p. 242). In this chapter we will utilize this conceptual model to (1) clarify a variety of confusing issues associated with the study of intoxicant use, (2) suggest that the role of social setting has been underemphasized during the study of intoxicant use, and (3) examine the relationship between social setting and personality.

The relationships among drug, personality, and social structure, or drug, set, and setting, seem straightforward initially. Most observers of human behavior know that psychic states vary greatly, are influenced by the environment, and, of course, that drugs make an impact on these states. These relationships are easy to grasp in the abstract; surprisingly, however, these issues are very difficult to understand and accept in practice. Most of us are so accustomed to thinking of drugs in a medical context—medicines used for the treatment of specific conditions—that we assume the effect of a drug to (1) be the same for everyone and (2) remain relatively constant for anyone. Physicians are not eager to dispel this belief. In order to maximize the therapeutic effect of the drug prescribed, physicians avoid reminding the patient that it may have different effects on different patients with the same condition and, further, that its effects on the same patient may vary over time.

In spite of the medical/medicinal aura surrounding drugs, most drug experts have accepted the important influence of set and setting in determining drug effects. For those not experienced or accepting of the drug-set-setting interaction, consider the effects of alcohol. Almost everyone must be aware, either from observing his or her own behavior or the behavior of others, that the effects of alcohol vary from person to person and over time. We all have seen happy drinkers, morose drinkers, belligerent drinkers, and flirtatious drinkers. Sometimes alcohol can be a relaxant (for example, the martini after a hard day at the office), and sometimes it can be a stimulant (for example, the first drink at a party). At times alcohol releases inhibitions, and at other times those who have already put aside their inhibitions will take a drink or two to provide themselves with a socially acceptable alibi.

Often, alcohol is a mood accelerator, deepening depression or heightening elation, depending on the preexisting conditions. From the pharmacologic perspective, alcohol suppresses the action of certain inhibiting centers in the brain and can have no result inconsistent with this action. Yet the range of actual effects observed, both behavioral and psychic state changes, is extremely wide. It may be precisely this wide range of possibilities that makes alcohol such a popular drug. The multidimensional effects of alcohol serve to emphasize the importance of the interaction of drug, set, and setting.

The Impact of Social Setting on the Use and Users of Intoxicants

As a result of the changes in the social setting during the 1960s, people quite different from their earlier drug-using counterparts began to use illicit drugs. Weil, Zinberg, and Nelson (1968) chronicled this change in the first controlled examination of marijuana use. In this study, the chronic users, those that began using prior to 1965, were observed to be more anxious, more antisocial, and more likely to be dysfunctional than were the naive subjects who were just beginning to use marijuana in 1968. Thus, these early users were closer in spirit to the few disenchanted musicians, bohemians, blacks, and browns who had used marijuana before the drug revolution of the 1960s. By the late 1960s, drug use was being experienced as a more normative choice than it had been before 1965. Later, in the early 1970s, controlled marijuana users could not possibly have been described as individuals driven to drug use by deep-seated, self-destructive, unconscious motives.

The situation with heroin was more complicated. Since the 1920s, most heroin users had been low-skilled members of the working class who came from poor backgrounds and precarious family situations. Operationally and methodologically, any studies of these drug users were by definition examinations of the adverse impact of social and economic conditions on early personality development. While these studies attempted to demonstrate that such social conditions were, or were not, causally responsible for drug problems, in fact, the immediate objects of these investigations were the bitter personalities that had come from deprived backgrounds. Even now, the findings from this early research are being used to demonstrate a direct relationship between certain kinds of severe personality disturbances and drug use.

The Relationship between Personality and Drug Use: A Psychodynamic Perspective on the Addictive Personality

The viewpoint that drug use can be explained primarily as a consequence of personality is founded in one or another of the theories of early personality development. Although it is very difficult to distinguish between genetic predispositions and early postnatal influences when examining early development, dynamic personality theorists postulate that some people find it more difficult than others to cope with certain powerful, primitive impulses. This difficulty arises and becomes disruptive during the developmental process. The histories of many compulsive opiate users were prototypical of what has been called an addictive personality. These individuals often had trouble in school, began to smoke cigarettes heavily before the age of twelve, and had consistent and vicious struggles with parents or other family members; sometimes they became runaways or had obesity problems at an early age. Often these individuals were observed to have problems with the police during their early teens; this was also a period when they began to use alcohol and/or any other intoxicating substances that were available. In fact, they often used intoxicants to the extreme. This pattern of behavior led to other difficulties that indicated lack of control, for example, auto accidents, expulsion from school, loss of jobs, or fighting. Finally, these alleged addictive personalities concentrated on one drug, usually heroin but sometimes a barbiturate, and used it often and compulsively.

When looking at people with histories such as those described above—users who actually comprise only one segment of compulsive users—it is easy to see why clinicians or theorists often concluded that drug use was related, perhaps isomorphically, to the user's disordered personality. Furthermore, post hoc examinations of a compulsive user readily yielded a personal history that indicated varying degrees of early trauma which might have been responsible for the observed addictive disorder. For example, an obvious trauma would be the loss of a mother or father, or the breakup of the family structure (perhaps through death, desertion, mental illness, or some form of addiction). Failing to display overt evidence of early trauma, the compulsive user might reveal a deep sense of being unloved and rejected, usually by the mother but at times by various significant others. Such powerful, unfulfilled longings for love, acceptance as a worthwhile and lovable human being, and a sense of basic trust in another or in one's self can lead to overwhelming feelings of desolation and rage; these are the emotional forces over which drug-using individuals have been unable to develop reliable internal controls.

Some personality theorists (for example, Knight, 1937; Rado, 1958; Rosenfeld, 1965; Wishnie, 1974) assume that intoxicant use can help individuals with these debilitating conflicts by providing the surcease from frustration that was not provided by the absent or unloving mother. From this perspective, the users' impulses to take heroin, alcohol, or other drugs is considered to be a translation of those unfulfilled early longings or needs.

Other theorists (Kaplan & Weider, 1974; Khantzian, 1975; Khantzian, Mack & Schatzberg, 1974; Krystal & Raskin, 1970) have suggested that intoxicants, especially heroin, are used as anodynes to the rage that has resulted from so much frustration. In other words, if internal controls over these feelings are poor or nonexistent, the drug will act as a tranquilizer or pharmacologic defense mechanism. When this is the case, the decision to use drugs is viewed as an attempt at self-medication. This attempt at pharmacologic control is typically a misguided effort to adapt to the stresses of life and reduce the destructive consequences of these poorly controlled feelings since, in part, the use of illicit drugs breeds a host of new and different stresses that require more demanding and mature defense mechanisms than are readily available under such adverse conditions.

The Changing Psychoanalytic Perspectives

While the early psychoanalytic writers drew a fairly simple picture of the relationship between unrelieved impulses leading to intoxicant use, contemporary writers have presented a thesis that is far more complex. Consequently, while attempting to explain how unrelieved impulses may lead to disorganized and poorly functioning internal psychic structure, a poor self-image, and lack of self-esteem, contemporary analysts have emphasized the process of identification, or lack of it, with reasonable parental figures. Their observation, made particularly with regard to alcoholics, that families with significant addicted members breed more addicts has led them to theorize that unrelieved desires for acceptance and closeness can be expressed by attempting to be like the desired person or object. It is as if unconsciously choosing to be like the object will ensure being liked by the object.

Since this drama is usually played out entirely within the unconscious intrapsychic realm, and therefore not recognized by the individual, the very suggestion that he is drinking in order to be close to an alcoholic father he now hates would be an anathema to him. Nevertheless, most personality theorists attach great importance to the enormous guilt that arises in individuals, particularly addicts, because of the raw and uncontrolled quality of their impulses. These theorists view the addict's sense of guilt as the cause—not the consequence—of much self-destructiveness and difficulty with self-care.

Throughout the history of the study of addictive behaviors, personality theorists have used a variety of models and concepts to explain the phenomena under investigation. In the 1980s, when great interest is being generated by Kohut's proposal (for example, 1971, 1977) that each person's narcissism is a separate line of development from other aspects of personality structure, intoxicant use is often described as a function of the self-system. This contemporary perspective postulates that by using an intoxicant sufferers from a narcissistic personality disorder attempt to avoid directly expressing their desire to merge with a longed-for, idealized self-object and, in so doing, also avoid reactivating the possibility of a traumatic rejection. Instead, within the self-system, the self is able to function at the high moment of intoxication as the longed-for, idealized self-object. But when intoxication has receded, that intoxicated aspect of the self has a different function in the self-system, more likely appearing to represent the despised, unlovable self. Since it was this debased conceptualization of self that had touched off the search for a merger with an idealized self in the first place, it is logical, according to this theory, that the compulsive desire to reexperience intoxication should recur quickly.

The Observation of Controlled Intoxicant Use:
Additional Evidence for the
Influence of Social Setting

There are many other variations on these psychoanalytically oriented themes; in addition, there are a variety of behavioral-learning theories that offer explanations of addictive behavior patterns. An exposition of these theories is beyond the scope of this chapter. (The interested reader should consult Shaffer and Schneider (1985), Shaffer and Burglass (1981), and Lowinson and Ruiz (1981) for useful entry points into this literature.) Although the forms of expression differ, the purpose of many personality theories is to explain intoxicant problems principally as a function of personality. Paradoxically, little specific writing has appeared that utilizes personality theory to explain controlled use. Doubtless, personality theorists would explain the capacity for control—or the absence of problems with intoxicants—under the same aegis; that is, the capacity for control has been engendered by a coherent early development and positive early relationships with significant others. These developmental conditions would lead to a personality structure that is well defended against the impulses of desolation and rage. Consequently, the internal mechanisms of control are considered to be well equipped to deal with emotional impulses if these should become excessively energized and threaten to get out of hand.

Recently there has been an increased appreciation for the complexities of drug use within the social milieu. Within the last ten years, thinking about drug use exclusively in personality terms has become less common and interactive psychosocial models more prevalent. This development resonates with our position that both personality structure and social milieu must be considered if we are to understand how the process of social learning functions to make controlled use possible.

Relative Ego Autonomy and Average Expectable Environment

The traditional analytic and dynamic models of intoxicant use have not been concerned primarily with the effect of the social setting on the individual but rather with the impact and control exerted by the individual over basic instinctual drives in order to achieve a manageable social existence. These traditional models have continued to conceptualize primitive, biological drives as operating out of a core substratum of the personality that was formed during early development. These perspectives have also emphasized the management of aggressive drives, for example, self-preservation, sexual drives, and preservation of the species. Because these drives are universally transmitted through a family environment and because the personality structures that are developed to control these drives are considered relatively immutable, considerations of the influence of social structure have been given a low priority.

In spite of this history, two constructs of psychoanalytic theory—relative ego autonomy (REA) and average expectable environment (AEE)—which have been useful in other contexts, can be very helpful in explaining how social learning produces limited changes in ego structure and functioning and therefore affects patterns of behavior that include, for the present discussion, intoxicant use and abuse. REA was first conceptualized by Heinz Hartmann (1939) and signifies the capacity of the ego to balance and synthesize the inputs from the instincts with those that arise from the environment, for example, environmental press (Gill & Klein, 1964; Rapaport, 1958; Zinberg, 1975); AEE refers to the physical and social situations in which REA can be delineated and maintained by the individual (Gill & Klein, 1964; Rapaport, 1959, 1960). These concepts have had enormous impact on post-Freudian analytic and dynamic theory.

Since no biological structure or human being can be considered infinitely adaptive, an individual's capacity to adapt can be assumed to function only within a reasonable range of experience. This range is determined after birth by the inputs of the physical and social environment. Individuals with different biological endowments deal with their environmental opportunities differently; they develop different personality structures and adaptive capacities (for example, REA) which function within the range permitted by their environment (for example, AEE).

To illustrate, consider one child growing up in the jungle and another growing up in the city; each will have different skills and capacities. While the jungle child is learning about wild edible plants, the city child will be learning not to touch hot stoves. Although this example is offered qualitatively, the frequency of these behaviors is distinctly observable and, thus, the functional differences between the children quantifiable. Like the constructs of AEE and REA, this example provides a rough indication of the differences and limitations that arise among individuals of different inheritances who live in different chronological, physical, and social environments.

Since the foundation of analytic theory rests on instinct theory or the need of the ego to master the instinctual drives, psychoanalytic theorists have not been stimulated to recognize the importance of the broader physical and social environment in the development of the individual. However, there is another important reason for this failing: Although many theorists have detailed the importance of the child's early years and early relationships, suggesting that the way in which the ego mediates the primitive drives and adapts to the environment is crucially affected by the child's early developmental experiences with parents and significant others, they have not grasped the significant *continuing* influence of the environment on the development and maintenance of REA. The importance of the environmental influence has not been missed by the ego-oriented psychoanalytic theorists; for example, David Rapaport (1958) has suggested that the life changes that occur throughout the developmental process are not limited to the physical situation but also include the social situation. Rapaport considered this social situation to be comprised of the social setting and the prevalent social attitudes. These social forces were considered to threaten REA and continually force the ego to reach a new balance or homeostasis.

Impaired Relative Ego Autonomy: A State of Imbalance

REA may be impaired by conditions that permit only restricted or frightening forms of stimulus nutriment. For example, in stimulus deprivation research the lack of stimuli from the environment fails to balance the emotional drives; the result is a loss of ego autonomy and an increase in primary process, autistic, psychotic-like thoughts (Heron, Bexton & Hebb, 1953; Heron, Doone & Scott, 1956; Lilly, 1956). Similarly, in concentration camps where external conditions maximize the individual's sense of danger and arouse fears and neediness, the primitive drives, instead of acting as guarantors of autonomy from the environment, prompt the individual to surrender to it. It is not surprising that Rapaport used George Orwell's *1984* as a text; this work clinically details how the balance between drives and environmental stimuli, when deliberately upset, can reduce REA and turn individuals into stimulus-response slaves. If human beings are to maintain their sense of identity, values, ideologies, and orderly thought structures, they need to receive constant environmental support for their existing verbal and memory structures.

Relative Ego Autonomy and Heroin Addiction

An understanding of REA with its inherent dependence on the balancing inputs of the id and environment clarifies the mental state and behavior pattern of heroin addicts. Addicts are cut off from many sources of stimulus nutriment. Often a compulsive drug user is alienated from his family and friends; if these relationships do exist, they typically center on acrimonious pleadings to give up drugs. Condemned as a deviant by the larger society, the addict's inputs from the general environment give him an entirely negative view of himself. His only other social setting input consists of the limited litany of his drug-using reference groups: Have you copped? When? Where? Was it good stuff? Did anyone get busted? What do I need to do? What if I get busted? Do you think I will get busted? The addict resides in a relatively stimulus-deprived environment.

The heroin addicts' dependence on the environment is consolidated by the need to continue coherent relationships with the external objects that remain available to their interactive efforts. Thus, suffering from constant doubt about their ability to maintain these relationships, heroin addicts readily accept society's deviant stereotype as their own identity. Essentially this holding on to what remains of the external environment maximizes the ego's autonomy from the id; however, this autonomy is achieved at the cost of impairing the ego's autonomy from the environment by minimizing the input of affective and ideational signals that usually regulate judgment and decision.

Consequently, the heroin addict is caught in an environmental dilemma: His dependence on social support systems is increased by his need to use narcotics, but his access to that support is curtailed by the deviant label society has placed on him. Concurrently, the addicts' drive structures, derived from primitive instincts, are kept at peak tension by the desire for pharmacologic gratification as well as by the fear of being unable to get it, that is, the fear of withdrawal. He is at the mercy of primitive impulses and the overwhelming sense of neediness that invades or, perhaps more accurately, blocks the capacity to perceive and integrate objective reality. Filled with doubts, he gullibly responds to those in the external environment who offer schemes that promise magical succor and continues to seek a drug that will provide relief from this emotional quandary. When REA is upset, the ego tends to seek a new balance or homeostasis. For the heroin addict, this new balance is likely to be inflexible and achieved rather slowly. This balance is established under very difficult conditions: while the input from both the id and the environment is insufficient or distorted, internal drive structures are making variable but insistent demands for drug gratification and, as the clinical evidence from our patients has demonstrated, the ego struggles to retain any level of ego functioning that still remains.

This internal struggle principally accounts for the rigidity that creates problems for therapists who work with narcotic addicts. The patient's new homeostasis of ego functioning cannot easily absorb fresh stimulus information from the environment. In fact, it is difficult for addicted patients to accept input so neutral and sustaining as that of a reasonable therapeutic relationship. Actually, the therapeutic relationship is particularly difficult for the addict in treatment to tolerate because therapy is *intended* to be at variance with the patients' usual relationships and to make their reliance on selective perception, quick repression, projection, and denial more difficult. All of these intrapsychic defenses are used by addicts to avoid coming in contact with those perceptions, affects and ideas that are at variance with their acceptance of themselves as addicts and of the internal state that has been derived with that acceptance.

The psychological state, or the set, of the addict is reminiscent of the regressive state described in our earlier discussion of REA. This state results when the ego is unable to maintain its relative autonomy from either the id or the external environment; the barriers between the ego and the id processes become fluid. Primary process images, ideas, and fantasies rise to consciousness, and interest in magic, belief in animism, generalized, unfounded suspiciousness, and acceptance of extremely childish rhetoric become regressively active in ego functioning. As individuals are forced to rely increasingly on primitive defense mechanisms, their sense of voluntariness and inner control over behavior tend to disappear.

Often, addicts seem to be vaguely aware of their own primitive responses, but cannot tolerate these in consciousness long enough for scrutiny. The addicts' ego struggles to retain its existing capacity to function, no matter how unsatisfactorily; however, the primitive feelings usually seem so real that he is unable to transform them into secondary process thinking. The observed primary process responses are not unlike those of the LSD user in the 1960s, particularly the user whose trip experience has little in common with his previous social and psychological experiences. By the 1970s, however, the changing social setting—the appearance of well-defined social groups knowledgeable about tripping—enabled the user to respond in a secondary, rather than primary, process manner (Zinberg, 1974).

Now that we are beginning to understand the impact of the social setting on the developing organism as an ongoing process, it is not possible to sustain the view that personality and social setting are two independent entities. Just as REA is considered as a relatively stable structure that represents a continually shifting balance between internal forces (which change at different life stages) and an external environment (which is constantly in the process of change), so the relationship between personality and social setting is seen as a relatively stable but continually shifting balance. The changes in that balance may make a specific behavior that was once deviant or a source of disruptive emotional conflict no longer unacceptable or, conversely, behaviors that were once considered innocuous may become unacceptable. In a changing culture with different social attitudes that are internalized and integrated by the ego, evaluations of behaviors must be frequently reexamined in view of these shifting social landscapes.

Average Expectable Environment

Any consideration of REA would be incomplete without including the equally important and complementary construct of AEE. The AEE comprises the consistent, regular relationship between an individual and their social setting that guarantees a coherent series of mental functions free from domination by primitive impulses. This construct makes it possible to coherently consider, from a psychoanalytic perspective, the role of social change, in the development of the subtle complex of self-awareness that is variously called a mature ego, an identity, the self, a sense of self-actualization, or some combination of these.

Although many theorists have considered the early social environment as the singular causal factor in the development of stable personality structures, it is obvious to any social observer that changes in the social setting continue to affect ego development throughout the life cycle. In addition, the environment experienced by infants changes from generation to generation, if not from one decade to the next. For example, consider breast-feeding: during one decade, breast-feeding is popular; in the next, it is less popular. Whether it is in vogue or not contributes markedly to the infant and his or her relationship with the environment.

Traditionally, the issue of how individuals mastered their early primitive drives and longings was sufficiently preoccupying so that the study of social influence on personality development did not receive adequate attention. The partially true assertion that environmental change does *not* contribute to the process of essential personality development has also contributed to this trend. Since there are only a few basic building blocks of the personality, the essential structure is laid down very early. These basic elements of the developing personality include a few fundamental affects (feelings) and predispositions (whether based on genetics or early experience or early introjections, for example, internalizations of significant others). As a result of these fundamental factors, social change has a greater impact on what happens *after* the basic structure of personality has been established than on the original formation of that structure. Essentially, the building blocks of personality are in place. The cornerstones cannot be moved; yet rearrangement of the secondary structure is possible, both on a short-term (consciousness change) and long-term (personality modification) basis. Thus, as a result of genetic predispositions, early development, and social circumstances, each person has available a range of ego functions that can become relatively autonomous. Although this range may be limited, the social setting determines exactly which of these perceptions, discharges, and capacities are most likely to achieve REA. In spite of the differential effects of social learning processes on the various personality structures, a balance always emerges.

Average Expectable Environment and Personality Structure

The history of LSD illustrates the impact of AEE on personality structure. At the beginning of the drug revolution, Becker (1967) made the prediction that, after the subjective effects of the psychedelic became more familiar and users knew what to expect from their use of the drug, their fears would be minimized and consequently any adverse reactions would be less severe and less frequent. Becker's early predictions were correct. Becker did not underestimate the consciousness-changing properties of LSD. He knew that the drug was many times more powerful than marijuana; he also recognized the impact that social learning processes would have to socialize users to the experience. More recently, Bunce (1979) provided empirical evidence for Becker's cultural experience hypothesis. In a phenomenological study of the "high state" (Zinberg, 1974), something which was not so obvious to Becker and others was revealed: When individuals experienced the psychoactive effects of LSD, they would select explanatory constructs out of the range of cognitive and emotional percepts available to them, and their continuing responses to the drug experience would follow these available explanations of their situation. In other words, the boundaries of one's AEE—boundaries that are determined in part by the social learning process—act/react interactively to largely determine one's response to a drug experience. It is likely that this process also operates under most conditions of uncertainty: where the social situation is new and/or unknown and when responses to these events are also new or not yet known.

Average Expectable Environment and the Information Explosion

Recently, Zinberg (1984) noted that in addition to the impact of widespread drug use on personal behavior, our society may be facing a remarkable and powerful change in the process of social learning. The rate of knowledge development is one of the most important factors affecting the AEE. Philosophers of science have pointed out that the rate of growth of knowledge has increased exponentially, as judged by rates of publication, patents, and other indices. Specifically, before 1945, it took approximately one hundred years for the sum of knowledge to double; then, amazingly, it doubled between 1945 and 1960, and again between 1960 and 1970. In the 1980s, the totality of human knowledge is supposed to be doubling at the rate of every twelve years (Zinberg, 1984).

This rapid change means, for one thing, that parents and children do not share the same AEE. Parents born in the 1920s, 1930s, or even the 1950s, often find computers strange and forbidding. By contrast, people born in the 1960s and later regard the computer, whether pocket, desktop, or any other model, as just one more familiar article that they have learned about and use in school and/or at home.

These rapid changes make it more difficult today than ever before for parents and children to share the same AEE. Consequently, much of the learning that takes place is horizontal, that is, intragenerational; this pattern stands in direct contrast to the vertical, that is, intergenerational learning, that has characterized cultures from the beginning of recorded history until the beginning of the knowledge explosion. The peer group has become responsible, in the main, for passing on a variety of social information, for example, about work, relationships, and customs. Most information about drugs, particularly including the sanctions and rituals associated with use, has been transferred through peer groups (Huba, Wingard & Bentler, 1979; Shaffer, Beck & Boothroyd, 1983). The information conveyed varies enormously from one peer group to another, but the horizontal process of information dissemination remains quite consistent.

Implications of a Shifting Average Expectable Environment

Just as the information explosion has influenced the AEE, the converse will likely be responsible for changing the social attitudes toward drug education and prevention. It is probable, for example, that in spite of efforts made by some antidrug organizations to get youngsters to believe and proclaim the prohibitionistic line that all drug use is abuse, familiarity with drugs will cause future generations to make distinctions among drugs and patterns of use that are not being made by contemporary parents or policymakers. As AEE includes parameters for the relationship to drugs, the drug-use learning process will change. Instead of the powerful, exclusive influence of the peer group, for example, drug-use patterns will likely be shared within the family—as is the case with alcohol use now (cf. Shaffer et al., 1983). In fact, presently, these changes seem to be taking place with respect to certain illicit drugs, specifically marijuana.

The Natural History of an Illicit Drug

When an illicit drug is newly introduced to the social setting, its use is considered deviant. Generally, those who seek out new drugs have strong motives for doing so and are therefore considered by the larger social group as misfits or psychologically disturbed. Their drug use is accompanied by high anxiety because they fear society's disapproval, as well as its legal sanction; furthermore, their anxiety is high because they have little knowledge of the drug's effects. When deviant drug use becomes more prevalent and popular, as marijuana use did in the mid-1960s, knowledge about the drug and its effects increases. Slowly misconceptions are corrected. New ones may develop, however—for example, the idea that all marijuana users are peace-loving, or that users become more confident and think of themselves less as deviants.

In the midst of the inevitable controversy and questioning that develops between the first-generation marijuana users and the straight culture, a second generation of users appears. Instead of attempting to break with the straight society, the second-generation user, motived by curiosity or an objective interest in the drug's effect, stimulates a more comprehensive cycle of information acquisition about the drug and its consequences. When this second generation of users supports the arguments of the first generation of user, they are more likely to be heard. They are greater in numbers, more diverse in background, and their motives are less antagonistic and, therefore, more acceptable. Thus, this generation of users has the opportunity to explode many of the stereotypical myths that exist about marijuana use and users.

As the second-generation users develop, the larger society moves away from its formerly rigid position toward marijuana and becomes confused. This confusion motivates nonusers in the social setting—those not motivated by drug hunger or social rebellion—to experiment with the drug. The reports of this subgroup have an even greater effect on the larger social setting than either of the other two groups discussed above. Furthermore, as more diverse groups of people comprise the using population, it becomes more probable that various drug-use styles will work better and cause less difficulty.

In sum, as each generation of users acquires more knowledge about the drug and as this information is disseminated, there is less likelihood that users who have disturbed personalities will predominate. A very few years from now, large numbers of people who are experienced with marijuana will have children entering adolescence; these parents may play a very different role in socializing their children from that played by their own parents.

Advancing Technology and the Inhibition of Informal Social Controls

As the drug technology has advanced, providing an ever-increasing variety and availability of both licit and illicit substances, this situation has inhibited the development of rituals and sanctions like those that accompany the social use of many natural drugs. For example, before Indians use peyote, they all take part in the ritual of preparing the drug. This ritual puts them in the right frame of mind for using the drug, gives them knowledge of the drug, and emphasizes the quality of use, thus providing an opportunity for social learning and the development of social control. In our culture, the responsibility for drug preparation has been transferred to the technological expert or manufacturer; this transfer of preparation has restricted the natural development of social controls. The first-time user can be suddenly confronted with a substance that he or she does not understand and has not handled before; for this substance, rituals, sanctions, or other social controls have not had time to develop and be disseminated and assimilated.

In addition to providing society with new and more powerful drugs that lack built-in social controls, advanced technology has also supplied the means of publicizing the effects of these new drugs. In the 1960s, the various media suddenly introduced the public to the adverse and disastrous effects of a psychedelic trip. The psychedelic experience of a variety of users was telescoped into a few searing media presentations. These presentations gave the impression (which most of the public believed) that these adverse reactions were normal responses to the psychedelic drug use. Those who had personal experience that prevented them from being convinced by the media accounts were forced into a sharply opposing position. Neither one of these reactions to the new patterns of drug use permitted (1) adequate opportunity for social learning about the range of drug responses or how to best cope with them or (2) the development of social sanctions and rituals that might prevent many of the dysfunctional reactions.

The Impact of Social Change on Personality

Most dynamic theorists do not deny that technological change brings about social change. However, they do question the view that social change contributes to continued personality development. Rather, two dominant drives, sex and aggression, are postulated to energize how individuals and society work out ways for those impulses to achieve a degree of discharge under acceptable social circumstances. For example, when alcohol is used to remove inhibitions, society accepts flirtatious and argumentative behavior within certain limits that are subtly but differentially defined by various ethnic groups and social classes. It is peculiar that these same theorists do not apply similar logic to individuals who use marijuana in a controlled way in order to focus attention on a particular event or reduce the boundaries between conscious self and sensation. Both users feel trapped between mixed sensations that pull in various directions, and they find reassurance in the capacity to focus for a time on a socially acceptable discharge or a derivative discharge of a primitive impulse. In both cases, the ego's usual relative autonomy from the id is maintained by its traditional guarantor of stability, the external environment, which determines the acceptability of each form of discharge.

Since the ego has the capacity to discharge primitive affects in a variety of ways and consciousness change is one of those ways, then it follows that consciousness change vis-à-vis intoxicant use is linked to impulse discharge. It is unlikely that interest in intoxicants or consciousness change is instinctual as some have suggested (Weil, 1972). It is more likely, however, that social rituals and ceremonies define acceptable patterns of discharge, concurrently providing social controls for the range and intensity of such discharge. For example, South American Indians have organized and controlled the use of psychedelic drugs around a variety of special occasions. Interestingly, societies such as these have not been able to cope successfully with the introduction of a new, technologically advanced intoxicant—distilled alcohol. Perhaps, for this Indian culture the vehicles for social learning are not sufficiently sophisticated to accommodate this substance or, conversely, the pace of learning with respect to alcohol may be differentially slow.

Conclusion

No society can hold back technological and social changes. New substances, along with new ideas about their use, are continually introduced to the social matrix, and it takes time for society to sort out which of these affect personality development and personal relationships. Not only must the drug and the personal need of the user be taken into account but also the subtleties of history and social circumstance. Zinberg (1984) suggests that Griffith Edwards, director of the intoxicant research center at Maudsley Hospital in England, is perhaps one who understands this complex interaction most clearly (for example, Edwards, 1974). He once remarked, in pointing out the fallacy of trying to separate the specific incident of drug-taking from its social matrix, "One could not hope to understand the English country gentleman's fox-hunting simply by exploring his attitude toward the fox" (G. Edwards, personal communication, 1974).

Finally, the view that intoxicant use depends only on the drug or on a disturbed personality may seem attractive to those who accept the moral condemnation that society has visited on illicit drug use. However, for experts who utilize psychodynamic, psychoanalytic, and social learning theory to further such a perspective is to belittle their own clinical and theoretical aims as well as the capacity of their powerful theories to incorporate social structural variables and the social learning process.

References

Becker, H.S. (1967). History, culture, and subjective experience. An exploration of the social basis of drug-induced experiences. *Journal of Health and Social Behavior*, 8, 163–176.

Bunce, R. (1979). Social and political sources of drug effects: The case of bad trips on psychedelics. *Journal of Drug Issues*, 9 (2), 213–233.

Edwards, G.F. (1974). Drugs, drug dependence, and the concept of plasticity. *Quarterly Journal of Studies on Alcohol*, 35, 176–195.

Gill, M.M. & Klein, G.S. (1964). The structuring of drive and reality: Rapaport's contributions to psycho-analysis and psychology. *International Journal of Psychoanalysis*, 45, 483–498.

Hartmann, H. (1958). *Ego psychology and the problem of adaptation* (D. Rapaport, Trans.) New York: International Universities Press. (Original version published 1939).

Heron, W., Bexton, W.H. & Hebb, D.O. (1953). Cognitive effects of a decreased variation in the sensory environment. *American Psychologist*, 8, 366–372.

Heron, W., Doone, B.K. & Scott, T.H. (1956). Visual disturbances after prolonged perceptual isolation. *Canadian Journal of Psychology*, 10, 13–18.

Huba, J.G., Wingard, J.A. & Bentler, P.M. (1979). Beginning adolescent drug use and peer and adult interaction patterns. *Journal of Consulting and Clinical Psychology*, 47, 255–276.

Kaplan, E.H. & Weider, H. (1974). *Drugs don't take people, people take drugs*. Secaucus, N.J.: Lyle Stuart.

Khantzian, E.J. (1975). Self selection and progression in drug dependence. *Psychiatry Digest*, 36, 19–22. (Also in H. Shaffer & M.E. Burglass (Eds.) (1981). *Classic contributions in the addictions*. New York: Brunner/Mazel.

Khantzian, E.J., Mack, J., & Schatzberg, A.F. (1974). Heroin use as an attempt to cope: Clinical observations. *American Journal of Psychiatry*, 131, 160–164.

Knight, R.P. (1937). Psychodynamics of chronic alcoholics. *Journal of Nervous & Mental Disease*, 9, 538–548.

Kohut, H. (1971). *The analysis of self*. New York: International Universities Press.

Kohut, H. (1977). *The restoration of self*. New York: International Universities Press.

Krystal, H. & Raskin, H.A. (1970). *Drug dependence: Aspects of ego functions*. Detroit: Wayne State University Press.

Lilly, J.C. (1956). Mental effects of reduction of ordinary levels of visual stimuli on intact healthy persons. *Psychiatric Research Reports*, 5, 1–9.

Lowinson, J.H. & Ruiz, P. (Eds.). (1981). *Substance abuse: Clinical problems and perspectives*. Baltimore: Williams & Wilkins.

Orwell, G. (1949). *1984*. New York: Harcourt Press.

Rado, S. (1958). Narcotic bondage. In P.H. Hoch & J. Zubin (Eds.), *Problems of addiction and habituation* (pp. 27–36). New York: Grune & Stratton.

Rapaport, D. (1958). Theory of ego autonomy: A generalization. *Bulletin of the Menninger Clinic*, 22, 13–35.

Rapaport, D. (1959). A historical survey of psychoanalytic ego psychology. In E.H. Erikson (Ed.), *Identity and the life cycle* (Psychological Issues, Monograph 1). New York: International Universities Press.

Rapaport, D. (1960). On the psychoanalytic theory of motivation. In M.R. Jones (Ed.), *The Nebraska symposium on motivation* (pp. 173–247). Lincoln, NB: University of Nebraska Press.

Rosenfeld, H.A. (1965). On drug addiction. In H.A. Rosenfeld (Ed.), *Psychotic States.* New York: International Universities Press.

Shaffer, H., Beck J. & Boothroyd, P. (1983). The primary prevention of smoking onset: An inoculation approach. *Journal of Psychoactive Drugs, 5,* 177–184.

Shaffer, H. & Burglass, M.E. (Eds.). (1981). *Classic contributions in the addictions.* New York: Brunner/Mazel.

Shaffer, H. & Schneider, R. (1985). Trends in behavioral psychology and the addictions. In H. Milkman & H. Shaffer, (Eds.), *The addictions: Multidisciplinary perspectives and treatments.* Lexington, MA: Lexington Books.

Weil, A. (1972). *The natural mind.* Boston: Houghton Mifflin.

Weil, A., Zinberg, N.E. & Nelson, J. (1968). Clinical and psychological effects of marihuana in man. *Science, 162,* 1234–1242.

Wishnie, H. (1974). Opioid addiction: A masked depression. In S. Lesse (Ed.), *Masked depression.* New York: Jason Aronson.

Zinberg, N.E. (1974). *"High" states: A beginning study* (Drug Abuse Council Publication No. SS-3). Washington, D.C.: The Drug Abuse Council. (Also in H. Shaffer & M.E. Burglass (Eds.). (1981). *Classic contributions in the addictions.* New York: Brunner/Mazel.

Zinberg, N.E. (1975). Addiction and ego function. *Psychoanalytic study of the child, 30,* 567–578. (Also in H. Shaffer & M.E. Burglass (Eds.) (1981). *Classic contributions in the addictions.* New York: Brunner/Mazel.)

Zinberg, N.E. (1984). *Drug, set, and setting: The basis for controlled intoxicant use.* New Haven: Yale University Press.

7

Addictive Behavior and the Justice System

Alexander M. Hunter
Robert A. Pudim

The justice system does not handle cases involving addictive behavior well. The reason for this may well be the justice system itself.

The justice system, a wag once observed, is neither a system nor justice. There is some truth to this because the justice system deals primarily with laws and lawbreakers. Justice, according to the dictionary, is the impartial adjustment of conflicting claims or the assignment of merited rewards or punishments. By this definition, sometimes the system metes out justice and sometimes it does not. Divine justice, poetic justice, or even ironic justice are seldom found here.

When it comes to the justice system and how it deals with addictions, there are inconsistencies. Individuals have been released from criminal responsibility for their actions, set loose in the community too soon only to engage in criminal conduct again. At the same time, no justice system that finds defendants guilty while ignoring their mental ability to control their actions can be considered fair and just. To better understand how this dilemma was created, it is necessary to look at various elements of the justice system—the laws, the courts, and the three Js (judges, juries, and jails).

The Laws

At their best, the laws of a state or nation represent the formal controls a society places on an individual's behavior. The informal controls—the attitudes, opinions, and behavior of friends and neighbors exert far more control on an individual's behavior than laws do or even will do, for that matter. Nevertheless, laws tell society in an organized way what is acceptable and unacceptable behavior and spell out penalties for actions the society will not tolerate.

Laws often do not reflect the *actual* impact a set of behaviors has on society. Most often they reflect the impact a particular group of legislators at a specific time *think* they have on society. If a particular group of legislators believes gambling is worse for society than some investment practices, even though both operate on similar laws of chance, then gambling will be declared illegal and investments will be supported by special legislation. The actual impact of each might very well be that the investment practices are as destructive to the savings and credit of people as is gambling.

The men and women who make laws do not always represent those who are best qualified to make such decisions. Like radio talk show hosts and journalists, the people elected to serve in the legislature are expected to be experts on everything. Although legislators come from diverse backgrounds, few, if any, possess real expertise in addictive behaviors. All too often their attitudes are similar to that of one legislator in Colorado who sat on a committee controlling funding for alcoholism at University Hospital. According to the legislator, alcoholism isn't a disease caused by viruses or bacteria. Alcoholism is just a question of willpower and weak individuals who refuse to seek help from God.

In addition to medieval opinions affecting a law's formulation, when hearings are held preliminary to formulating a law, experts are invited to testify and the resulting legislation often will be found to be a mixture of latest research and political expediency. This last reference is an acknowledgment of the effect of available revenues, media attention, and the impact lobbyists have on the precise formulation of a law. Why more money from the taxes paid on alcoholic beverages does not go into alcohol treatment is explained by some of these factors.

Once the legislation is passed and becomes law, it is fixed as if carved in granite. If subsequent research produces findings contradicting the original testimony used to formulate it, the law will not be thrown out or amended. That the law is wrong factually does not make any difference to the individual prosecuted under it. The familiar tag line is "It may not be right, but it's the law. If you don't like it, change it." Prosecutors have little choice. They are required by oath to prosecute lawbreakers. Until the courts declare a law invalid or the legislature repeals it, a law must be upheld.

Finally, laws must be written in a clear and unambiguous manner. This has led to the evalution of the peculiar, but exact, language found in laws. Legal language and definitions must specify accurately the nature of certain antisocial behaviors and the penalties for indulging in them. When the law attempts to be specific about subject matter which is not clearly understood, strange consequences result, particularly if a different terminology is involved. There has been a trend lately to legislate mandatory treatment, court supervised, for certain types of addictive behavior. These laws are being written at the same time heated debates are going on in the therapy field over which types of treatment modalities are useful and which new approaches are effective. It is no wonder that laws are found to be arbitrary, vague, and capricious, particularly in regard to a developing field such as addictions.

The intent of this discussion, seemingly an indictment of legislators and legislatures, is to explain how insensitive or bad laws come to be found on the books. The impressive thing we must keep in mind is how many good laws are written given the obstacles, difficulties, and restraints they encounter as they weave their way through the legislative process.

The Courts

The concept of *diminished capacity* has been around in one form or another for many years. The notion of diminished capacity is connected with the concept of *crime*, and crime is intimately connected with laws.

It is necessary to back up a little, therefore, and discuss the legal definition of crime. A crime is an intentional violation of the criminal law, committed without defense or excuse, and penalized by the state (Tappan, 1947). This definition covers everything from vagrancy, drug and alcohol abuse, blocking driveways, prostitution, theft, gambling, robbery, and homicide. This legal definition is broader than the average person's notion of crime but, at the same time, is narrower and more precise than moral definitions that include references to actions that are sinful, bad, or evil.

A crime, according to law, is an intentional act that violates the prescriptions and proscriptions of the criminal code (as written by the legislature) under conditions in which no legal excuse applies. Indirectly, there is no crime without law (and a state to punish the lawbreaker). There is no crime where an act (that would generally be considered offensive) is justified by the law. There is no crime without intention. There is no crime where the offender is considered incompetent, that is, without capacity or having diminished capacity. It is in dealing with these last two elements of intent and capacity where the justice system and addictive behavior have difficulty.

As a result of our moral history, criminal law is concerned with intentional action. It focuses on an individual being responsible for controlling behavior. It also articulates in a formal, specific manner public morality. Researchers in the addiction field are less interested in the responsibility question and are most concerned about identifying and diagnosing addictive disorders and understanding the complex relationship of genetic, physiological, and environmental causes of addictive disorders. Oliver Wendell Holmes, Jr. (1920) jokingly observed that a good deal of the court's time is spent distinguishing between "stumbling over a dog and kicking it" (p. 316). Accidents should not count as crimes. If "a dog can tell the difference between being kicked and being stumbled over," Justice Holmes (1920, p. 316) observed, so, too, can judges and juries.

The problem is some accidents are defined as the fault of the person involved because he or she was negligent. According to the model used by our courts, a reasonable person ought to use judgment in controlling his or her behavior in order that some accidents will not occur. For example, a reckless driver in an accident is guilty. The driver is assumed to be able to control his or her vehicle and control his or her actions and, therefore, is held accountable for the accident. This set of assumptions has implications in dealing with addictive behavior. The courts try to restrict crime to the intentional breaking of the criminal code. The criminal code can be broken in two ways—impulsively rather than premeditatedly and accidentally rather than intentionally. The first type is treated more kindly than the latter.

If addictive behavior is defined as (1) compulsive or repetitious behavior (or use, if drugs are involved), (2) involving loss of control, and (3) continued repetition despite adverse consequences, then the question of intentional breaking of the criminal code by an addict is an interesting one. The question of accidentally breaking the criminal code drops out as a consideration.

Motivation is usually the key to proving intent, the prosecution arguing one side and the defense the other. *Illegal intent* is that which a person has in mind when he or she does something. It is his or her purpose. It is what he or she wishes to have happen. A *motive*, on the other hand, is that which moves a person to act. A motive *may* be an intention but is not always. Intentions are one of many motivators of action. In short, intention has a narrow focus and motivation is wide and blurred. A junkie may intend to use illicit heroin, but his motive may be to feel better. Intentions may or may not cause a person to do something. A criminal intention, without an action is not a crime.

The criminal laws, however, make the act of using or possessing heroin or cocaine without a physician's prescription illegal. The act of using or possessing other substances such as alcohol, on the other hand, is legal until an individual does something illegal such as driving an automobile.

Motives, it is argued, move individuals with or without intent. Some people in the field of psychology claim motives can be unconscious. Some say they are not. The courts cut through this confusion by saying an intention is reserved for thoughts or for verbalized plans. Intention has no connection with whatever it was that caused the ideas of the offender.

Prosecutors of crimes must show intent, and they do this often by constructing a motive for the crime. Prosecutors bring up reasons why a defendant acted the way he or she did. Good reasons for a crime, unfortunately, are not always the real reasons it happened.

There is one more consideration when deciding whether a crime has occurred. People are liable to the criminal law only if they are mentally competent, regardless of whether they intended to do what they did. This part of criminal law is how the legal meaning of intention is contained in the concept of competence.

Deep in our minds and history is the theory that people should not be punished for actions that are beyond their control. Such actions within or outside our control are connected with definitions of capacity or competence. Unfortunately, what passes for competence at one time or place is considered incompetence in another.

The usual approach is to find a cognitive test for competence. Courts look to the mens rea, the thing in the mind, as definitive of a person's ability to form a criminal intent and as the controller of actions. Until a mind is sufficiently well formed and unless it functions normally, courts must exclude a person from criminal liability. Defendants are not responsible (or are less responsible) for their actions if they were acting under duress, were under the age of mental competence, were mentally handicapped, or were insane.

A person involved in a criminal act because he or she is addicted does not fall into the category of being under age, mentally handicapped, or acting under duress in criminal proceedings. The question of insanity, however, frequently arises. If the offender's capacity to control his or her behavior has been damaged, then the offender is not guilty. Eliminating defects such as senility, idiocy, and full-blown psychosis, the question comes down to whether certain conduct deserves punishment or treatment. Behavior caused by something beyond one's control should not be penalized. This last statement opens up a philosophical can of worms which the courts do not want to touch. The definition of *competent before the law* varies with what we want the law to do. Does law exist to punish, to bring about penitence, to rehabilitate, to restrain, or to create examples from which others can learn? The courts make decisions that touch on one, some, or all of these questions.

It is in the insanity considerations where the definition of addiction has its application because the argument can be made that the offender's capacity to control his or her actions has been affected. To the courts, the place one looks for this diminished capacity is in the mind. Irresistible impulses do not count toward guilt and punishment.

Generally capacity is determined from signs of sanity. *Sanity* refers to soundness, to being whole. A good definition of sanity probably does not exist. Law, which prides itself on the precision of its language and depends heavily on accurate definitions, is in real trouble with this notion of sanity. The psychologists and psychiatrists who are good at defining neurosis, psychosis, and so on have thus far failed to develop an objective, testable definition of sanity that would satisfy the requirements of the justice system. The courts instead have been forced to turn to three ambiguous guidelines—the M'Naghten rule, the irresistible impulse rule, and Durham's rule.

The M'Naghten rule is used in many, but not all, of the states. It was first stated in an English trial of Daniel M'Naghten in 1843 and is "that every man is to be presumed to be sane, and . . . that to establish a defense on the ground of insanity, it must be clearly proved that, at the time of committing the act, the party accused was labouring under such a defect of reason, from disease of the mind, as not to know the nature and quality of the act he was doing, or if he did know it, that he did not know he was doing what was wrong" (Goldstein, 1967, p. 45). There are many legally vague phrases present in the M'Naghten rule. "Disease of the mind," "wrong," and "the nature and quality of the act" are some of the phrases that have been attacked in court. Critics argued that, using M'Naghten's rule, a full-blown psychotic could be found sane and that it has already happened. In *People* v. *Willard* (1907), Willard, who was declared insane in the state of California by reason of alcoholic paranoia, was nevertheless hanged legally as a sane person (Biggs, 1955, p. 218). Knowledge of right and wrong has now come to be regarded as only one test of capacity. Most criminal acts caused by an addiction would be punishable by the M'Naghten test.

The irresistible impulse rule is used in about twenty states. The irresistible impulse rule acknowledges the fact that there are mental states in which cognition is unimpaired but volition is damaged. Some people know right from wrong and still cannot control their actions. The problem here is there are no experts in the field of the mind who can with certainty distinguish between uncontrollable behavior and behavior which is merely uncontrolled. If the definition of addiction is accurate and it is indeed a compulsive act involving loss of control, then the irresistible impulse rule would eliminate addicts from criminal culpability. Unfortunately, with both the defense and prosecution calling in their psychiatric experts, this particular testing field for insanity is filled with legal messes and large, gaping holes (Hakeem, 1958).

Durham's rule came from *Durham* v. *U.S.* (1954). Judge David Bazelon said, "an accused is not criminally responsible if his unlawful act was the product of a mental disease or mental defect" (Kaufman, 1982, p. 18). The rule is that the mind which controls humans is a functional unit in which reason and emotion are blended and that separating knowing from feeling (in M'Naghten's rule) is false to our knowledge of man. Durham's rule seems to get around the M'Naghten shortcomings. It, too, has been labeled as vague because it does not equate mental disease with a psychosis (as defined by psychiatrists). It gives no criterion by which to judge the defendant's capacity, and judges and juries must rely on psychiatric experts (Arthur, 1969; Ash, 1949; Eron, 1966; Goldberg & Werts, 1966). It has been said that Durham's rule has a tendency to regard disapproved deviant behavior such as homosexuality or narcotic addiction as being per se proof of mental disease (Goldberg & Werts, 1966, p. 246). The last step is a step too far for most courts because the criminal act itself has been used as evidence of mental sickness, as has overeating Twinkies been claimed as the cause of criminal acts. Criminal conduct is not insane merely because the crime is extremely bizarre or strange.

The Model Penal Code developed by the American Law Institute (ALI) (1953) and used by Irving Kaufman (1982) in *U.S.* v. *Freeman* (1966), says a person shall not be held accountable for a crime "if at the time of such conduct as a result of mental disease or defect he lacks substantial capacity either to appreciate the criminality of his conduct or to conform his conduct to the requirements of law" (ALI, A53, sec. 4.01). The proposal specifies that "the terms mental disease or defect do not include an abnormality manifested only by repeated criminal or otherwise anti-social conduct" (ALI, 1953, sec. 4.01).

It would absolve from punishment a person who knows what he or she is doing yet is driven to crime by delusions, fears, or compulsions. This test is closer to modern ideas of the mind as a unified entity whose functioning can be impaired in many different ways.

The debate continues in the courts about who should be held responsible for his or her actions. In the United States, only two to four percent of all offenders are classified as having diminished capacity (Wolfgang & Ferracuti, 1967, pp. 201–202). The actual numbers seem higher because trials dealing with this subject receive a large share of media attention.

The various tests of sanity are fallible and never can be perfected. How broadly they are interpreted and if they include addictive behavior depends on society's attitude at a given time. The courts reflect this changing attitude in their decisions. Where the pendulum once swung to shift responsibility from individuals to their environment or to social or psychological factors (Nettler, 1974), the movement is now to hold citizens responsible for much broader ranges of behavior.

Judges, Juries, and Jails

There is a question whether being treated for one's crime because an addictive disease caused it is better than just being convicted and sent to jail. Judges, probation officers, and others tend to recommend longer terms for treatment than for straight incarceration (Cousineau & Veevers, 1972, pp. 257–258). Studies (Wheeler, 1968; Wilson, 1972) indicate that treatment is often used in a punitive manner or considered to be easier than hard jail time and therefore should be longer to make it equal to jail sentences.

Whether this is true or not, the decision of guilty or innocent, sane or insane, by the judge or jury is connected with a set of beliefs which society has about what it wants the law to do and what it believes it does. This set of beliefs has a bearing on who it is willing to excuse from criminal liability or what kind of sentences it expects to be levied on offenders.

Probation officers and corrections authorities also respond to this public attitude. A decade or so ago, society tended to believe addicts were responsible for what they did but that they should be forgiven. Today the swing is to a feeling that addicts are responsible for what they did and should not be let off lightly. Under the somewhat misleading call for law and order, juries and judges are saying to alcoholics, for instance, that they should pay in the coin of the realm or community service for what they did because they made a responsible choice when they chose to drink in the first place. The call is now for a guilty but mentally ill verdict for such cases.

Although many acts of crimes without victims have been removed from the criminal code, this should not be interpreted as enlightened awareness of the cause of these acts. Crimes without victims are often offenses related to addictive behavior such as public drunkenness, drug addiction, attempted suicide, or gambling. Although these acts may no longer be criminal, the consequences of the acts are. Gambling may not be a crime but not paying taxes on winnings or not having a license to gamble is; being high on heroin is not criminal but having heroin is.

It has long been considered a waste of judicial energy to prosecute as a crime what might be regarded as a nuisance or an illness. The "revolving door" alcoholic, the person repeatedly arrested for assault or drunken driving, is not reformed or cured by being jailed nor is he or she a deterrent to other drinkers, yet the public (and, indirectly, the legislature, judges, and juries) continues to call for tougher laws with longer jail sentences rather than detoxification centers. The reality is that the general population does not regard addiction as a disease. Because judges, juries, and jails, along with the courts and laws, lag behind public opinion, the justice system is perceived as being too late with too little by the public and hopelessly antiquated and out of touch by workers in the addiction field.

There are some lessons to be learned. The first is when testifying at legislative hearings, it is necessary to be as concrete and unambiguous as possible. It is better for an expert to leap to a conclusion than a lawmaker. The qualifications and disclaimers careful investigators find necessary tend to be cast aside in the pursuit of writing a law which will not be thrown out by the courts as ambiguous, vague, and capricious.

Second, if addictive behaviors are going to be treated differently in the justice system, then the beliefs and attitudes of the general population must be changed by bringing to the public's attention the latest discoveries and research in the addiction field. It is change in the informal controls society places on individuals which result in change in the formal controls placed on them by the legal system. Clever lawyers and expert witnesses may alter the course of one trial, but changing the informal controls can change the way the entire justice system treats addicts.

Taking these two steps could help the justice system handle cases involving addictive behavior more effectively than it has in the past.

References

American Law-Institute. (1953). Committee report. *Model penal code.* Philadelphia: American Law Institute.

Arthur, A.Z. (1969). Diagnostic testing and new alternatives. *Psychology Bulletin, 72,* 183–192.

Ash, P. (1949). The reliability of psychiatric diagnoses. *Journal of Abnormal and Social Psychology, 44,* 272–277.

Biggs, J., Jr. (1955). *The guilty mind: Psychiatry and the law of homicide.* Baltimore, MD: Johns Hopkins Press

Cousineau, D.F., & Veevers, J.E. (1972). Juvenile justice. In C.L. Boydell, C.F. Grindstaff & P.C. Whitehead (Eds.), *Deviant behavior and societal reaction.* Toronto: Holt, Rinehart & Winston.

Eron, L.D. (1966). *The classification of behavior disorders.* Chicago: Aldine.

Goldberg, L.R. & Werts, C.E. (1966). The reliability of clinicians' judgments: A multitrait-multimethod approach. *Journal of Consulting Psychiatry, 30,* 199–246.

Goldstein, A.S. (1967). *The insanity defense.* New Haven, CT: Yale University Press.

Hakeem, M. (1958). A critique of the psychiatric approach to crime and correction. *Law and Contemporary Problems, 23,* 650–682.

Holmes, O.W., Jr. (1920). In H.J. Laskie (Ed.), *Collected legal papers.* Cambridge, MA: Harvard University Press.

Kaufman, I. (1982, August 8). The insanity plea on trial. *New York Times Magazine,* p. 16.

Nettler, G. (1974). *Explaining crime.* New York: McGraw-Hill.

Tappan, P.W. (1947). Who is the criminal? *American Sociological Review, 12,* 96–102.

Wheeler, S. (1968). Agents of delinquency control: A comparative analysis. In S. Wheeler & H.M. Hughes (Eds.), *Controlling delinquents.* New York: Wiley.

Wilson, J.Q. (1972, Fall). The problem of heroin. *The Public Interest, 29* 3–28.

Wolfgang, M.E. & Ferracuti, F. (1967). *The subculture of violence.* London: Tavistock.

Part II
Treatment Perspectives

8
Testing Hypotheses:
An Approach for the Assessment
of Addictive Behaviors

Howard J. Shaffer
Charles Neuhaus, Jr.

T his chapter will consider the need for a practice theory in the addictions and will apply the concept of hypotheses testing to the assessment and diagnosis of addiction. The purpose of this discussion is to provide a parsimonious means of organizing and verifying clinical information, thus making the assessment procedure both manageable and teachable. Discussed here are the initial steps necessary for the development of a practice theory in the addictions.

Diagnosis and Assessment: Some General Considerations

The assessment and diagnosis of addiction is a difficult task given the conflicting and controversial state of affairs in the field. Unless clinicians are able to recognize and organize the essential clinical information available during the process of assessment, they will be overwhelmed by the quantity of data that seem to be equally relevant or, conversely, select only that data they subjectively deem important.

Complicating matters, the concept of addiction is not categorical. That is, addictive behaviors are not defined by a consensually agreed on set of criteria (Burglass & Shaffer, 1983). The diagnosis and assessment of addictive behaviors can only be made by comparing the behavior(s) in question with other associated behavior patterns. This comparative analysis may include the patterns of use, abuse, or nonuse of psychoactive substances, as well as the intensity of involvement with nonpharmacologic activities. To illustrate, while some individuals may recreationally use certain amounts of a particular substance, others may ingest the same amounts of this drug and, because of their prior experience, social circumstance, and/or profession, be considered addicted. The fundamental factors that comprise addiction—drug, set, and setting—must be examined as an interactive whole (Zinberg, 1984; Zinberg & Shaffer, 1985). The definition of addiction has a commonsense component not unlike the implicit agreement of what is a mountain or season and what is not (Vaillant, 1982). "As with the label, *mountain*, the conceptual validity of *alcoholism* as a diagnosis depends upon a higher order of concept formation than provided by any concrete definition. No single set of criteria will ever be either necessary or sufficient. Like faces or mountains, the whole is always easier to recognize than the parts" (Vaillant, 1982, p. 144).

The absence of a practice theory in the field of addictions contributes still more to the confusion that surrounds the assessment of addictive behavior. Practitioners fail to distinguish between theories of addiction and theories of abstinence or controlled use; further, there is a lack of meaningful integration of theory, research, and practice. Shaffer and Gambino (1979) have suggested that, without a practice theory to guide the activities of clinical work, the practitioner is left to his own ideas about the nature of addiction, the course of treatment, and the goals of treatment. "The development of a practice theory will be most likely achieved when practitioners recognize the need to incorporate their values and goals into explicit and precise theories of practice" (Shaffer & Gambino, 1979, p. 301). While clinical practice has not made full use of the knowledge gained in theory and research, it is equally true that theory and research have been guided little if at all by the needs of, and experiences gained in, practice (Shaffer & Gambino, in press).

Paradigms, Practice, and Assessment

Recently, the concept of paradigm has been applied to the practice of clinical services (Burglass & Shaffer, 1981; Sederer, 1977; Shaffer, 1977; Gambino & Shaffer, 1979; Shaffer & Gambino, 1979, in press; Shaffer & Burglass, 1981; Shaffer & Kauffman, in press) as a miniature world view that shapes a practitioner's understanding of the phenomenon to be assessed and treated. An operating paradigm serves as a template through which the clinician views patients and their problems; this template organizes information and suggests which questions to ask and which data are important, thus generating testable hypotheses. In addition, "while paradigms provide sets of assumptions by which the person interprets experience, paradoxically, they operate so automatically that their proponents do not seriously question or challenge their inadequacies . . . this is the blinding function of paradigms" (Shaffer & Gambino, 1979, p. 300). Thus, practitioners generally do not recognize the extent to which they are committed to viewing the world through a particular perspective.

Clinical observers often find what they are looking for and do not see that which does not interest them. In addition, because of their particular clinical persuasions, therapists often unknowingly communicate their expectations for patient performance; this sequence of events directly influences the clinical setting and whether or not patients will consider certain material important enough to be discussed and examined. For example, psychoanalysts look for and find unconscious material such as unresolved oedipal conflicts and drive/affect defenses, while ignoring reinforcing events that might serve to develop a conditioned response pattern. Social psychologists attend to environmental, cultural, and familial influences while typically disregarding metabolic disturbances.

Likewise, diagnosticians form implicit attitudes, hunches, and observations even before a patient actually presents for evaluation. The available data may or may not support these implicit impressions. For example, if the referral source is a probation officer, a preconceived notion of illegal behavior and/or antisocial personality may color the assessment. Similarly, if the patient stumbles as he enters the office, it may be indicative of a toxic substance, lameness, poor eyesight, or something else. Unless articulated, these impressions risk being ignored or taken as facts, which may or may not be accurate.

Clinicians need to make explicit their rules, observations, assumptions, and goals—all of which are defined by the operating paradigm that provides the context and template for their work (Kuhn, 1970). Only when the paradigm is articulated and thus made observable can its utility be evaluated and its limitations recognized. The following sections of this chapter focus specifically on techniques that require, as well as provide the vehicle for, clinicians to articulate their operating models and the implicit clinical decisions that are associated with these models.

Formulations: The Cornerstones of Diagnosis and Assessment

Utilizing special knowledge, for example, personality theory, cognitive models, and systems theory, the clinician observes behaviors and conceptualizes a working image of the nature of the patient's presenting problem as well as an understanding of the patient as a unique and distinct human being. The clinician gains this understanding through *inferential* and *organizational* processes; these activities are also two of the cornerstones of artistic endeavor, social perception, and impression formation (*cf.* Megargee, 1966; Shaffer & Kauffman, in press).

There are important differences between understanding and organizing impressions about the patient and the patient's problem. These differences are sharpened and clarified by comparing *clinical* and *dynamic* working formulations.

> A working clinical formulation consists of more or less traditional diagnostic judgments about the nature and severity of a patient's psychological condition . . . an initial evaluation is not complete until the therapist has reached three general diagnostic conclusions: (a) whether his patient is suffering primarily a psychotic, characterological, or psychoneurotic disorder; (b) whether the presenting problems are primarily psychogenic in origin or instead related to organic brain dysfunction or some toxic condition that requires medical evaluation; and (c) whether the patient's psychological difficulties are so slight as to not require ongoing psychotherapy or so severe as to call for immediate supportive intervention. (Weiner, 1975, pp. 57–58)

A clinical formulation suggests not only a diagnostic category but also provides the basis of a treatment plan. The clinician needs to determine if treatment is necessary and which type of treatment is appropriate.

A dynamic formulation involves a more complete understanding of the person than a clinical formulation.

> A working dynamic formulation consists of a general impression of what the patient is like as a person and how he got to be that way. Included in this formulation are some fairly clear ideas of the nature of the conflicts the patient is experiencing; the defenses he uses against the anxiety these conflicts produce; his style of coping with social, sexual, and achievement related situations; his attitudes toward significant people in his life and what he perceives their attitudes to be toward him; and how his past and present life experiences have contributed to his becoming distressed and seeking help. (Weiner, 1975, p. 58)

Dynamic formulations are rarely if ever complete, as these are typically reorganized and revised throughout the course of treatment. Taken together these formulations offer a clinicial heuristic for organizing and understanding the clinical vissitudes of both diagnosis and treatment—without emphasizing the traditional diagnostic categories that can be stigmatizing and dehumanizing (Laing, 1967).

Assessment and Prescriptive Treatment

Although armed with (perhaps because of) the body of knowledge extant in the addictions, the practitioner is hard pressed to provide a truly eclectic therapy. Bewildered by the diversity of philosophical positions and theoretical perspectives, the less experienced practitioner, in particular, is apt to retreat to a narrow, restricted model that does not allow for individual patient differences. Since the addictions exist without respect to substance (or behavior) of abuse, age, gender, or diagnosis, it follows that the practice model should be eclectic, calling for *prescriptive* treatment plans that draw on those aspects of theory and practice thought to be useful to a particular client (Burglass & Shaffer, 1981; also see Dimond, Havens & Jones, (1978) for an excellent discussion of eclectic psychotherapy).

Karl Menninger (1963) noted that "Treatment depends upon diagnosis . . . One does not complete a diagnosis and then begin treatment; the diagnostic process is also the start of treatment" (p. 333). If one is to offer a prescriptive, eclectic therapy, the assessment process must be as thorough and as flexible as possible to provide the basis for generating a specific prescription for a particular individual. In order to facilitate the development of a practice model in a field that is presently dominated by implicit rules, values, and ideas, we will now present an assessment model that is readily teachable and learnable. It is essential that information in the addictions become teachable and learnable since these are two characteristics of scientifically accepted fields of inquiry—something that the addictions presently is not. While the following model is not, in fact, a formal practice theory, it is an attempt to make explicit some of the values and assumptions that guide clinical practice.

Assessment and Hypotheses Testing

Recently several authors (Lazare, 1973, 1976, 1979a, 1979b; Renner, 1979; Shaffer & Kauffman, in press) have clarified the process of assessment by offering a multidimensional model based on hypotheses generation and testing. This model proposes that assessment efforts be directed toward the testing of clinical hypotheses generated by biological, sociological, psychodynamic, and behavioral perspectives. Lazare (1973) has noted that during the clinical assessment process a variety of perspectives are implicitly utilized but rarely articulated. He noted that the biological, sociological, psychodynamic, and behavioral models are the most commonly used, unarticulated, clinical perspectives. In the next section of this chapter, each of these viewpoints will be introduced and typical hypotheses offered to illustrate the corresponding clinical perspective.

Testing hypotheses along these four dimensions fosters an approach that successfully (1) reduces the assessment process to manageable proportions; (2) provides a "cognitively economical" (Mischel, 1979) approach for clinical assessment; (3) establishes a model that permits either a narrow or eclectic approach to the diagnostic process (Dimond & Havens, 1975; Dimond, Havens, & Jones, 1978); and (4) facilitates the organization of clinical material fundamental to the assessment of drug abuse and addiction. Consequently, the following discussion of the clinical assessment process and associated various techniques will be conducted from the perspective of Lazare's hypotheses generation and testing model for the conduct of clinical work.

Hypotheses as Partial Psychodynamic Formulations

The concept of hypotheses is essentially analogous to a *partial psychodynamic formulation.* These hypotheses are considered partial formulations "because any one alone is insufficient to provide adequate understanding of any given patient. In the process of bringing these partial formulations to the interview for consideration, they become hypotheses to be tested" (Lazare, 1979a, p. 132). By identifying a variety of hypotheses from each of the four areas presented above, this approach "(1) helps the clinician make efficient use of limited time in attempting to be comprehensive, (2) guards the clinician from coming to premature closure in the collection of data, and (3) provides a stimulus for the exploration of relevant but neglected clinical questions" (Lazare, 1979a, p. 132). In addition, this schema permits the following discussion to focus specifically on hypotheses relevant to drug abuse and addiction. (The reader interested in references explicating a more general hypotheses testing approach to clinical assessment is referred to Lazare (1973, 1976, 1979a, 1979b.)

Before specific hypotheses are illustrated, the following caveat is in order: Although the hypotheses that follow are particularly relevant to addiction, *we are not suggesting that just these hypotheses be tested instead of other more general hypotheses appropriate to comprehensive assessment. Hypotheses associated with addiction should be included for testing within the typical assessment regimen. Substance abuse and addiction disorders cut across all other diagnostic categories and should not be casually disregarded as a possibility during assessment.*

Hypotheses to Be Tested: A Partial Catalogue

The following discussion is a brief review of hypotheses that we have found useful in our assessments of drug-involved patients.

Biological Hypotheses

Biological hypotheses consider psychiatric disorders as the manifestation of a disease process. "For each disease, it is supposed that there eventually will be found a specific cause related to the functional anatomy of the brain" (Lazare, 1979b, p. 4). Identifying and understanding the particular disease process involved determines the clinician's choice of treatment.

Can the patient's problem be understood as a result of drug intoxication or withdrawal? Is the patient evidencing any signs of intoxication, overdose, or withdrawal? When present, these signs require an immediate clinical decision: Does the patient require hospitalization? As noted earlier, "Drug use does not exempt individuals from other psychiatric conditions. . . . For that reason, patients need to be evaluated carefully for evidence of schizophrenia, major affective disorders, or other psychiatric conditions of an organic nature that may require specific medication and treatment" (Renner, 1979, p. 465).

Can the patient's drug use be understood as a manifestation of genetic causes or predispositions? Is there any evidence that the patient comes from a family with a history of addiction? Although there is considerable controversy surrounding the nature-nurture issue, there is evidence to suggest that genetics contribute to the psychological effects produced by various psychoactive substances (Collins, 1985). Regardless of whether the evidence confirms or refutes this hypothesis, careful consideration of this issue will encourage clinicians to distinguish between the attitudes, customs, and social patterns that may be passed down from generation to generation vis à vis family socialization and the biological factors antecedent to substance abuse.

Has drug use altered the patient's neurological/psychological functioning? Is there any evidence (for example, impaired memory, sensorium, capacity for abstraction) that permits the patient's problem to be understood as a function of organic impairment? Such impairment, for example, may be due to the acute effects of (1) intoxication or withdrawal, (2) residual organic deficiencies resulting, perhaps, from long-term use, or (3) complications associated with an attempted suicide. These possible relationships need to be tested and clarified by the diagnostician.

Psychodynamic Hypotheses

Psychodynamic hypotheses focus on the mind and the associated mental, cognitive, and affective processes that influence human behavior. According to this model, "the developmental impasse, the early deprivation, the distortions in early relations, and the confused communication between parent and child lead to the adult neuroses and vulnerabilities to certain stresses" (Lazare, 1979b, p. 4). Psychodynamically oriented therapy is directed toward the resolution of intrapsychic conflict; strengthening the ego; permitting the experience of overwhelming dysphoric affect; learning to understand the meaning of thoughts, feelings, and behaviors.

Can the patient's drug use be understood as an attempt to reduce dysphoria? Wurmser (1974) and Khantzian (1975) have suggested that the specific pharmacologic effects of opiates may serve a progressive effect, whereby regressive, dysphoric states may actually be reversed. Wurmser considered that narcotics may be used adaptively by addicts in order to compensate for defects in affect defense, particularly against feelings of rage, hurt, shame, and loneliness. Khantzian stressed the use of narcotics as a drive defense; he considers that narcotics may act to reverse regressive states by the direct antiaggression action of opiates. Thus, opiates are considered to counteract the disorganizing influences of rage and aggression on the ego (for more information about Khantzian's self-medication hypothesis, see Khantzian & Schneider (1985), in this volume). Both Khantzian and Wurmser suggest that the psychopharmacologic effects of drugs can substitute for defective or nonexistent ego mechanisms of defense; in addition, both theorists consider developmental impairments, severe predisposing psychopathology, and problems in adaptation as central themes in understanding the etiology of addiction. Consequently, it is essential for the clinician to ask and understand what drug use accomplishes intrapsychically for the patient and how the drug attains this end. Khantzian (1975) has considered that drugs may be selected by users specifically for the differential psychopharmacologic effects produced (for example, containment, energy, release of inhibition). Only a thorough drug-use history (including the psychological effects produced) will provide a clue as to the possible role of these psychodynamic issues in drug use, abuse, and addiction. It is vital to understand that the patient's choice of drug (in use) and their drug preference may be different (Hartford, 1978).

Generally, a drug history will reveal a pattern of episodic use—often involving trial and error with a variety of drugs—in a specific social context; gradually such use may escalate to a point perceived by the patient to be out of control and typically is associated with psychological and/or physical dependence. Renner (1979) has adroitly underscored that addicts may have great difficulty acknowledging their underlying psychological difficulties. It may be easier for addicts to present their problems as medical or adverse drug reactions than psychological in nature (for example, depression, rage, low self-esteem). The assesor might consider accepting the existence of some "real" medical problem while explaining that such problems may also be caused or aggravated by psychological stress. After a firm therapeutic alliance has been established and the patient feels reassured that the therapist does not believe that he is worthless and hopeless, it will be possible for him to admit more easily to his psychological difficulties. (Renner, 1979, p. 466)

Can the patient's drug use be understood as compulsive or controlled: Is the patient's problem due to addiction, "chipping," or some intermediate level of controlled use? Zinberg and his colleagues have demonstrated, contrary to popular belief, that not all drug use is compulsive (Harding, Zinberg, Stelmack & Barry, 1980; Zinberg, Harding & Winkeller 1977; Zinberg & Harding, 1982; and Zinberg & Jacobson, 1976). It is possible—perhaps even common—for drug use to be controlled in some fashion (cultural, contextual, religious, etc.); patients may be aware of these controls or they may not. In order to properly address the issue of controlled use, abuse, and addiction, the assessor should attend and probe for evidence that clarifies the extent of compulsive or controlled drug use and the conditions under which these occur—perhaps differentially.

Can the patient's difficulties be understood as antecedent or consequent to drug use? Zinberg's (1975) now classic paper on addiction and ego function cleverly noted that psychopathology or ego deficiencies actually may be a *consequence* of drug use rather than a predisposing factor. During assessment the clinician must clarify and discriminate pre-drug involved behavior patterns from post-involvement patterns. Psychological regression and dysphoria may be the result of hustling for drugs and being involved in an illicit activity instead of some predisposing psychopathy.

Sociological Hypotheses

Lazare (1979b) has written that sociological hypotheses

> focus on the way in which the individual functions in his social system. Symptoms are traced not to conflicts within the mind and not to manifestations of psychiatric disease, but to the relationship of the individual to his manner of functioning in social situations, i.e., in the type and quality of his "connectedness" to the groups which make up his life space. Symptoms may therefore be regarded as an index of social disorder.

Treatment from the sociological perspective consists of interventions designed to change the relationship(s) that exist between patients and their social milieu.

Does the patient's drug use occur in limited or varied environmental contexts? Typically, substances are used within a variety of contextual conditions and not within others. An assessment of these conditions will permit the clinician to understand which social situations encourage, precipitate, or inhibit drug-taking. What do these environments have in common? What are the differences? For example, specific situations have similar characteristics that have been considered to elicit cognitions and/or expectations that may or may not initiate a sequence of drug-taking behavior (Wikler, 1965, 1973). In addition, there are many cultural rituals that tend to control drug use (for example, cocktail party, happy hour, "do not drink before lunch"). These ceremonies tend to restrict potentially disruptive and/or abusive behavior patterns to specified places and times. Is the patient's problem behavior restricted to these sanctioned events or does it tend to generalize—perhaps compulsively—to a wide variety of contexts? If so, perhaps the patient is attempting to alter consciousness and/or mood rather than participate in a ceremony or ritual.

Can the patient's behavior be understood as an attempt to draw attention to a familial problem or difficulty? "Often, a patient's drug use can be seen as a cry for help or an effort at social communication" (Renner, 1979, p. 467). Adolescents may be using drugs as a means of expressing their individuality, rebellion, or hostility toward their parents when channels of communication are limited. Drug use can also be a desperate attempt to communicate to parents (or others) who have been placating or ignoring a young person who is "out of control," experiencing serious psychological distress, and in need of "special" attention (for example, treatment).

Can the patient's drug-use behavior be understood as a response to peer group pressure? Initial drug use often occurs in the company of one's best friend. Using drugs in the context of a social group that has established reasonable limits for such use should not be considered as psychopathology unless there are specific problems that can be identified during assessment. Are the drugs used within the limits established by the reference group or beyond? Are the drugs used and the pattern of use indicative of self-destructive tendencies that are reflected in other patterns of behavior? If so, then perhaps other psychiatric problems are evident; however, "While clinicians cannot condone an individual's participation in illegal activities, it is not appropriate to suggest that such people are in need of psychiatric treatment purely because they choose to use illegal drugs" (Renner, 1979, p. 466).

Behavioral Hypotheses

Behavioral hypotheses are based on the assumption that addictive behavior can be viewed as a set of learned behaviors rather than as a consequence of deep-seated psychological or social trauma or physical illness. The behavioral treatment that emerges from this view involves applying procedures and techniques derived from known principles of learning to modify, reduce, or elimate maladaptive behavior and to foster the acquisition of more adaptive behavior patterns. (See Shaffer & Schneider (1985) for more information about the behavioral perspective; also see Krasnegor (1980) and Callner (1975) for reviews of the behavioral literature in the addictions.)

Can the patient's problems be understood as contingent on the reinforcing properties of the drugs that are or have been used? Does the use of drugs provide (1) primary positive or negative reinforcement, for example, euphoria versus relief from a withdrawal syndrome, or (2) secondary positive or negative reinforcement, typically as a result of classical conditioning and chaining?

Can the patient's problems be understood by clarifying the mediational role that cognitions serve between affects and behaviors? Wikler (1965, 1973) considered the mediating role of cognitions to be an essential assessment area for understanding addictive behavior. Every drug user, abuser, and/or addict has thoughts, feelings, motives, ideas, attributions, etc., that come into play during acquisition, maintenance, and extinction of addictive behavior. Until Wikler clarified the role of cognitive activity, behavioral practitioners were apt to discount or ignore the importance of such internal activity in determining the use/abuse and relapse patterns of substance-involved individuals. (See Shaffer & Schneider (1985) for a discussion of the increasing importance that behavioral psychology places on the cognitive determinants of behavior.)

Some Guides for the Testing and Review of Hypotheses

As noted earlier, the present discussion of drug-related hypotheses does not preclude the necessity for information commonly gathered during traditional psychiatric assessment, for example, childhood and family history, social relationship history, and medical history. In fact, gathering this data further offers the clinician an opportunity for hypotheses generation and testing.

Tactically, the diagnostician should note that "It is neither necessary nor desirable to systematically ask questions about each successive hypothesis" (Lazare, 1979a, p. 138). When direct questioning is necessary to test a specific hypothesis, these questions—or perhaps other strategies—can and should be utilized within the natural flow of the interview (Lazare, 1979a). For example, it is possible to discard the hypothesis that a patient may be suffering from drug withdrawal or intoxication while establishing a purpose for the interview or during the history-taking. Thus, if the patient is fully oriented, does not manifest physical signs, appears in good physical health, appears physically comfortable with concurrent normally paced speech and nonverbal cues (for example, speed of movement, no slurred speech, not ataxic, normal pupils), there is little evidence supporting the hypothesis of drug intoxication or withdrawal. Conversely, when data collected from a number of sources (for example, significant others, laboratory results, physical signs, reported symptoms, history) via several methods (for example, psychological testing, neurological examination, urinalysis, clinical observations) converge in support of a particular hypothesis, the hypothesis can be considered confirmed. To illustrate, when a patient reports a history of Valium use and blackouts, displays slurred speech, ataxia, nystagmus, and responds poorly to tests of memory, the hypothesis of sedative-hypnotic use/abuse is supported or confirmed for further inquiry and/or treatment.

Since few hypotheses are ever confirmed or proved in the scientific sense, multiple sources of consistent data yield *support* for hypotheses. Such support connotes the viability of further inquiry and/or intervention; if the nature of the hypothesis does not require additional investigation, then demonstrated support suggests maintaining the hypothesis until evidence to the contrary is demonstrated.

Lazare (1979a) has suggested that all of the available hypotheses be reviewed at two specific times during the clinical examination: first, when the hypotheses that are generated during the initial ten to fifteen minutes of an assessment fail to make clinical sense of the evidence; and second, five to ten minutes prior to the completion of the interview. The first review provides clinicians with an organized opportunity to (1) generate new ideas, (2) redirect their approach or assessment strategy, and (3) provide a useful dynamic formulation for information that was not relevant to the discarded hypotheses. The second review provides an opportunity to be certain that the clinicial formulation is complete; if the clinician determines that it is not, he or she still has ample opportunity to elicit the information that is necessary to complete such a formulation.

In sum, clinicians need not be overly concerned that a particular hypothesis is not well developed, nor must they personally put every hypothesis to the test. For example, the intuitive sense that a patient's present difficulties are related in some unknown way to a previously undisclosed trauma may provide the basis for further clinical exploration. Similarly, although many clinicians are unequipped to test some specific hypotheses, such as the extent of neurological impairment, they should recognize the need for referral and further evaluation—in addition to or instead of the treatment presently provided. Finally, clinicians may (and we encourage this) develop multidimensional hypotheses. It is not essential that these hypotheses fit neatly into one of the four perspectives discussed above (biologic, psychodynamic, sociologic, or behavioral). To illustrate, whether the hypothesis that a patient's drug use may represent an attempt to manage uncomfortable affects that are only evoked in a family setting is considered psychodynamic or sociological is secondary; of primary importance are the generation, testing, and treatment interventions that follow a positively confirmed formulation. Similarly, clinicians need not always generate particular hypotheses for each of the four perspectives. It is essential, however, that each of the perspectives be considered during the assessment process.

Conclusion

The study of addictions is complicated and perplexing. Peele (1979), (Peele & Brodsky, 1975) has demonstrated that addiction is an experience of human beings and not a property of certain drugs. Szasz (1974) effectively argued "that trying to understand drug addiction by studying drugs makes about as much sense as trying to understand holy water by studying water . . . To understand holy water we must of course examine priests and parishioners, not water; to understand abused and addictive drugs, we must examine doctors and addicts, politicians and populations" (pp. xvii, 17).

The pharmacologic properties and molecular structures of drugs, for example, heroin, tell us as little about addiction as the electronic circuits of a video game reveal about the player's fascination for that activity. In spite of how little pharmacologic effects alone reveal about addictive behaviors, clinicians are required to have a working knowledge of drugs and their biological, psychological, and legal consequences. In addition, practitioners must diligently observe and assess the signs and symptoms of withdrawal and intoxication in order to identify and distinguish the influence of essential biological—including medical complications—and psychodynamic factors (the interested reader should consult Kauffman, Shaffer & Burglass (in press a, in press b) for further biological information and a detailed discussion of these phenomena).

While we can readily agree on what season it is or which protuberance is a mountain (Vaillant, 1982), without the equivalent of thermometers or protractors, such consensual agreement is rare in the addictions. Shaffer and his associates (Gambino & Shaffer, 1979; Shaffer, 1977;

Shaffer & Gambino, 1979; Shaffer & Burglass, 1981; Shaffer & Kauffman, in press; Khantzian & Shaffer, 1981) have described the preparadigmatic nature of the field of addictions and the lack of agreement as to
the causes of addiction as well as the course of proper treatment.
Theorists continue to search for explanations that will satisfy and include a wide variety of perspectives (psychoanalytic, psychosocial,
metabolic, biochemical, behavioral, etc.). These competing orientations
serve to identify different theoretical camps rather than facilitate the
conduct of eclectic, prescriptive clinical practice or the development of
a practice theory.

As a result, contemporary clinicians working in the addictions find
themselves in a field where there are probably as many treatment
models as treatment programs, each with its implicit strategies and expectations. Within each modality (for example, methadone maintenance)
one can find programs espousing various, and sometimes conflicting,
strategies (for example, methadone and psychotherapy—sometimes only
group, sometimes only individual, or perhaps both; methadone only; etc.).
Within a given program, one can find practitioners with different implicit
and/or explicit treatment goals (for example, detoxification versus long-
term maintenance).

These various theoretical orientations and the assessment protocols
applied during evaluation are responsible for (1) determining the focus of
the assessment—including the data that will be determined important
and relevant as well as the data that will be ignored; (2) the system that
will be implemented to organize the data obtained in the assessment; and
(3) the treatment plan and protocol to be utilized.

Generally, clinicians agree that science provides a useful guide to
practice, yet these practitioners often disregard science and apply their
own perspectives and principles to problem identification and solution
(Shaffer & Gambino, 1979; Shaffer & Gambino, in press). The natural
sciences are founded on the concepts of paradigmatic analysis and
hypotheses testing. Theories are advanced and then subjected to the
rigors of the scientific method. The operative theory is valid until dis-
proved. It is arguable whether the practice of social service as a whole,
and the addictions in particular, can be conceptualized in this manner;
nevertheless, if these areas of endeavor are to be accepted within the
realm of science, they must be subject to scientific principles. The
hypotheses testing approach to assessment and diagnosis in the addictions provides clinicians with a vehicle that permits scientific principles
to be accessed, implemented, and evaluated—thus paving the way for
the development of a practice theory. In a preparadigmatic field beset by
chaos, an organized teachable and learnable clinical program replaces
mystery and magic with a practical focus for the conduct of clinical
assessment and intervention.

References

Burglass, M.E. & Shaffer, H. (1981). The natural history of ideas in the addictions. In H. Shaffer & M.E. Burglass (Eds.), *Classic contributions in the addictions.* New York: Brunner/Mazel.

Burglass, M.E. & Shaffer, H. (in press). Diagnosis in the addictions: Conceptual problems. *Advances in Alcohol and Substance Abuse.*

Callner, D.A. (1975). Behavioral treatment approaches to drug abuse: A critical review of the research. *Psychological Bulletin, 82,* 143–164.

Collins, A.C. (1985). Inheriting addictions: A genetic perspective with emphasis on alcohol and nicotine. In H. Milkman & H. Shaffer (Eds.), *The addictions: Multidisciplinary perspectives and treatment.* Lexington, MA: Lexington Books.

Dimond, R.E. & Havens, R.A. (1975). Restructuring psychotherapy: Toward a prescriptive eclecticism. *Professional Psychology, 6,* 193–200.

Dimond, R.E., Havens, R.A. & Jones, A.C. (1978). A conceptual framework for the practice of prescriptive eclecticism in psychotherapy. *American Psychologist, 33,* 239–248.

Gambino, B. & Shaffer, H. (1979). The concept of paradigm and the treatment of addiction. *Professional Psychology, 10,* 207–223.

Harding, W.M., Zinberg, N.E., Stelmack, S.M. & Barry, M. (1980). Formerly-addicted-now-controlled opiate users. *International Journal of the Addictions, 15,* 47–60.

Hartford, R.J. (1978). Drug preferences of multiple drug abusers. *Journal of Consulting and Clinical Psychology, 46,* 908–912.

Kauffman, J., Shaffer, H. & Burglass, M.E. (in press a). A strategy for the biological assessment of addiction. *Advances in Alcohol and Substance Abuse.*

Kauffman, J., Shaffer, H. & Burglass, M.E. (in press b). The clinical assessment and diagnosis of addiction II: The biological basics—drugs and their effects. In T. Bratter & G. Forrest (Eds.), *Alcoholism and substance abuse: Strategies for intervention.* New York: Free Press.

Khantzian, E.J. (1975). Self selection and progression in drug dependence. *Psychiatry Digest, 36,* 19–22. [Also in H. Shaffer & M.E. Burglass (Eds.) (1981). *Classic contributions in the addictions.* New York: Brunner/Mazel.

Khantzian, E.J. & Schneider, R.J. (1985). Addiction, adaptation, and the "drug-of-choice" phenomenon: Clinical perspectives. In H. Milkman & H. Shaffer (Eds.), *The addictions: Multidisciplinary perspectives and treatments.* Lexington, MA: Lexington Books.

Khantzian, E.J. & Shaffer, H.A. (1981). Contemporary psychoanalytic view of addiction theory and treatment. In J. Lowinson & P. Ruiz (Eds.), *Substance abuse: Clinical problems and perspectives* (pp. 465–475). Baltimore: Williams & Wilkins.

Krasnegor, N.A. (1980). Analysis and modification of substance abuse: A behavioral overview. *Behavior Modification, 4,* 35–56.

Kuhn, T.S. (1970). *The structure of scientific revolutions* (2d Ed.). Chicago: University of Chicago Press.

Laing, R.D. (1967). *The politics of experience.* New York: Ballantine.

Lazare, A. (1973). Hidden conceptual models in clinical psychiatry. *New England Journal of Medicine, 288,* 345–351.

Lazare, A. (1976). The psychiatric examination in the walk-in clinic. *Archives of General Psychiatry, 33,* 96–102.

Lazare, A. (1979a). Hypothesis testing in the clinical interview. In A. Lazare (Ed.), *Outpatient psychiatry: Diagnosis and treatment.* Baltimore: Williams & Wilkins.

Lazare, A. (Ed.). (1979b). *Outpatient psychiatry: Diagnosis and treatment.* Baltimore: Williams & Wilkins.

Megargee, E.I. (Ed.). (1966). *Research in clinical assessment.* New York: Harper & Row.

Menninger, K. (1963). *The vital balance: The life process in mental health and illness.* New York: Viking Press.

Mischel, W. (1979). On the interface of cognition and personality: Beyond the person situation debate. *American Psychologist, 34,* 740–754.

Peele, S. (1979). Redefining addiction. 2. The meaning of addiction in our lives. *Journal of Psychedelic Drugs, 11,* 289–297.

Peele, S. & Brodsky, A. (1975). *Love and addiction.* New York: Signet.

Renner, J.A. (1979). Drug abuse. In A. Lazare (Ed.), *Outpatient psychiatry: Diagnosis and treatment.* Baltimore: Williams & Wilkins.

Sederer, L.I. (1977). The importance of seeing psychiatry as more than a science. *Psychiatric Opinion, 14,* 27–29.

Shaffer, H. (1977). Theories of addiction: In search of a paradigm. In H. Shaffer, (Ed.), *Myths and realities: A book about drug issues.* Boston: Zucker Publishing.

Shaffer, H. & Burglass, M.E. (Eds.). (1981). *Classic contributions in the addictions.* New York: Brunner/Mazel.

Shaffer, H. & Gambino, B. (1979). Addiction paradigms II: Theory, research, and practice. *Journal of Psychedelic Drugs, 11,* 207–223.

Shaffer, H. & Gambino, B. (in press). Addiction paradigms III: From theory-research to practice and back. *Advances in Alcohol and Substance Abuse.*

Shaffer, H. & Kauffman, J. (in press). The clinical assessment and diagnosis of addiction. 1. Hypotheses testing. In T. Bratter & G. Forrest (Eds.), *Alcoholism and substance abuse: Strategies for intervention.* New York: Free Press.

Shaffer, H. & Schneider, R. (1985). Trends in behavioral psychology and the addictions. In H. Milkman & H. Shaffer (Eds.), *The addictions: Multidisciplinary perspectives and treatments.* Lexington, MA: Lexington Books.

Szasz, T. (1974). *Ceremonial chemistry: The ritual persecution of drugs, addicts, and pushers.* New York: Anchor Press.

Vaillant, G. (1982). On defining alcholism. *British Journal of Addiction, 77,* 143–144.

Weiner, I.B. (1975). *Principles of psychotherapy.* New York: Wiley.

Wikler, A. (1965). Conditioning factors in opiate addiction and relapse. In D.I. Wilner & G.G. Kassebaum (Eds.), *Narcotics* (pp. 85–100). New York: McGraw-Hill.

Wikler, A. (1973). Dynamics of drug dependence: Implications of a conditioning theory for research and treatment. *Archives of General Psychiatry, 28,* 611–616.

Wurmser, L. (1974). Psychoanalytic considerations of the etiology of compulsive drug use. *Journal of the American Psychoanalytic Association, 22,* 820–843.

Zinberg, N.E (1975). Addiction and ego function. *The Psychoanalytic Study of the Child, 30,* 567–588. [Also in H. Shaffer & M.E. Burglass (Eds.) (1981). *Classic Contributions in the Addictions.* New York: Brunner/Mazel.]

Zinberg, N.E. (1984). *Drug, set, and setting: The basis for controlled intoxicant use.* New Haven: Yale University Press.

Zinberg, N.E. & Harding, W.M. (Eds.). (1982). *Control over intoxicant use: Pharmacological, psychological and social considerations.* New York: Human Science Press.

Zinberg, N.E., Harding, W.M. & Winkeller, M. (1977). A study of social regulatory mechanisms in controlled illicit drug users. *Journal of Drug Issues, 7,* 117–133.

Zinberg, N.E. & Jacobson, R.C. (1976). The natural history of "chipping." *American Journal of Psychiatry, 133,* 37–40.

Zinberg, N.E. & Shaffer, H. (1985). The social psychology of intoxicant use: The interaction of personality and social setting. In H. Milkman & H. Shaffer (Eds.), *The addictions: Multidisciplinary perspectives and treatments.* Lexington, MA: Lexington Books.

9

A Biobehavioral Approach to the Origins and Treatment of Substance Abuse

Thomas J. Crowley

W hat are the factors that contribute to the chances that any given child in the world will grow up to be a substance abuser? Which of the world's children are likely to become abusers of tobacco, heroin, cocaine, or any of the other commonly abused drugs? This chapter reviews the factors which appear to contribute to that risk (see also Crowley, 1972; Crowley & Rhine, 1981) and suggests ways to reduce those factors in order to reduce the risk of relapse in a drug-abusing patient.

The factors that either increase or decrease the risk of drug use may be pictured on a seesaw; some factors push at one end of the seesaw to increase the risk, while others push at the other end of the seesaw and decrease the risk (figure 9–1).

Availability of a drug is a prime factor in increasing the risk of drug abuse. Where there are no drugs, there is no drug abuse. Cocaine and marijuana are now widely abused in our society but were not used twenty years ago; the difference, in part, is the much wider availability of these drugs.

Recognizing the importance of availability, therapists may encourage patients to reduce the availability of drugs in their lives. They can discontinue contact with people who are likely to have drugs and replace those friends with nonusing friends. Similarly, opiate abusers may use naltrexone, a drug which blocks opiates from reaching their sites of action in the brain; even though a user takes an opiate, the opiate is unavailable at its functional brain sites. Addicts' craving for opiates then declines dramatically when they realize that naltrexone has made the drug unavailable to them (Meyer & Mirin, 1979).

Acceptability of a drug in a society increases the risk that a member of that society will become an abuser of that drug. Other users of the drug then are able to teach neophytes the technology of the use, showing them, for example, how to smoke tobacco, drink alcohol, or snort cocaine.

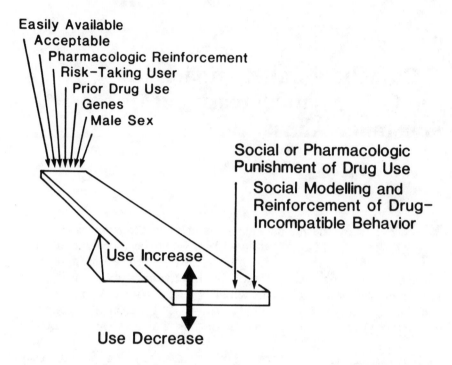

Use Decrease

Note: From "The abuse of alcohol and other drugs," by T.J. Crowley and M.W. Rhine, in *Understanding human behavior in health and illness*, Third Edition, edited by R. Simons and H. Pardes (Baltimore: Williams & Wilkins, 1984). Reprinted with permission of the publisher and © 1984, the Williams & Wilkins Co., Baltimore.

Figure 9–1. Factors That Increase or Decrease the Risk of Drug Use

In addition, other users may reinforce and applaud early efforts at drug use by a neophyte, thus encouraging such use. The new user may gain membership in a group by participating in the use of a drug and may feel social approval and social reinforcement for early attempts at the use of the drug.

If a drug is widely accepted and widely used in a society, a nonuser can learn how to take the drug by observing others and may gain social rewards for becoming a user.

Pharmacologic reinforcement is a major contributor to the continued use of many drugs. The term implies that there is some quality of the drug which drives a user to take the drug with increasing frequency. It is not necessary that the drug make the user feel good; cigarettes do not produce much euphoria, and abusers of many drugs say that the beneficial qualities of the drug on feeling states do not persist after long use. The users of drugs are compelled by some pharmacologic property of the drug to repeat prior use; the drug drives its own further self-administration.

When rats or monkeys are provided with equipment which permits them to inject themselves with drugs, they will vigorously work for injections of alcohol, cocaine, amphetamines, opiates, barbiturates, nicotine, and most of the other drugs which are abused by human beings. This research demonstrates that the tendency for users to repeatedly self-administer a drug derives in part from the properties of the drug and is not entirely dependent on complex psychological or sociological characteristics of users or their environment.

A treatment implication from this factor is found with methadone. This drug reduces pharmacologic reinforcement from opiates through a mechanism of cross-tolerance. Small doses of street heroin become less attractive to a patient treated with methadone because that patient is tolerant to higher doses of opiates. But we have very few other approaches to the problem of pharmacologic reinforcement, and this may contribute to the rather high rate of relapse among substance abusers.

A *risk-taking propensity* may contribute to one's tendency to become a drug abuser. One has to break some of society's rules and strictures in order to abuse drugs. Those who live strictly within society's limits are less likely to experiment with proscribed drugs, and those who never experiment will not get hooked by the pharmacologic reinforcing property of those drugs.

A risk-taking propensity may arise in a variety of ways. For example, adolescents generally tend to be rebellious, and adolescents with troubled home situations are especially likely to rebel and break society's rules. It is clear from studies of adolescent drug abusers that these users have school problems, family problems, and legal problems. Similarly, manic-depressive patients often show indiscretion and a rule-breaking tendency as they become manic. Some cultures may encourage individual risk-taking behavior among members of the culture.

Therapists of drug-abusing patients frequently attend to their patients' risk-taking tendencies, attempting through psychotherapeutic measures to identify and reduce those tendencies.

The experience of *prior drug use* increases the risk of future drug use. When people repeatedly have used drugs in certain circumstances, those circumstances become associated with the drug. When those circumstances arise in the future, they may tend to elicit, through association, further craving for the drug. Friends with whom one has used in the past, troubling circumstances which triggered prior drug-use episodes, and even places and buildings previously associated with drug-use, may initiate a relapse in a now-abstinent drug abuser.

Therapists carefully examine reports of drug craving among their patients, seeking stimuli which trigger these feelings. Recommendations to avoid such stimuli in the future or desensitization to the stimuli may be an important aspect of relapse prevention.

Inborn *genetic characteristics* and *sex* may be potential contributors to a propensity to abuse drugs. For two widely used drugs in our society, alcohol and tobacco, there is evidence of a genetic contribution, and males more frequently become drug abusers than do females. While this evidence is important in determining the risk for substance abuse, it is not relevant to treatment prescriptions at the present time.

At the other end of the seesaw, tending to reduce the risk of drug use, is the presence of *social or pharmacologic punishment* for drug use. Disulfiram (Antabuse) provides a pharmacologic punishment for alcohol use. If one takes disulfiram and then drinks alcohol, one becomes quite ill. The concurrent use of these two drugs is vigorously punished by the illness, and patients tend to discontinue the use of alcohol or to discontinue the use of disulfiram, but they generally do not take the drugs concurrently.

Social punishment also may suppress drug use. The expectation of a vigorous, clear, adverse event (for example, loss of job or loss of spouse) contingent on drug use does deter such use. Of course drug abusers know that adverse consequences may await them if they continue to take drugs, but, in general, these adverse consequences are remote and uncertain. It is the clear, certain consequences (comparable to the disulfiram-alcohol interaction) which effectively deter drug use. Our group has used contingency contracting and frequent urine analyses to assure the delivery of a powerful adverse consequence very quickly after the use of a drug (Crowley, in press). Our data indicate that this kind of social punishment is valuable in reducing drug use, and patients voluntarily enter such contracts to motivate themselves to remain abstinent.

The final factor on our seesaw may be illustrated with an example. A high school coach tells students that they cannot play on his team if they drink alcohol, and he has good sources of information about student drinking. The coach will teach them to play the game, and they will receive important social rewards for playing successfully, but playing becomes incompatible with alcohol drinking under these conditions. Students are forced to choose whether they want the rewards of alcohol or the rewards of playing on the team. Such clear choices appear to reduce drug use. Employee assistance programs use this concept by telling substance abusers that they will lose their jobs if drug-related work deficits persist; continued employment is incompatible with continued drug use. Such programs appear useful in reducing further drug use. These are examples of *social modeling* (the teaching of the behavior) *and social reinforcement* (the rewards for the behavior) *of drug-incompatible behavior* (such as playing on a team or working for a company).

These various factors contribute to the initiation and/or maintenance of drug-taking. Reversing these factors may be important in establishing abstinence in a treatment program. Therapists may find this see-saw concept useful in organizing individualized interventions to assist substance-abusing patients to become abstinent.

References

Crowley, T.J. (1972). The reinforcers for drug abuse: Why people take drugs. *Comprehensive Psychiatry, 13,* 51–62.

Crowley, T.J. (in press). Contingency contracting treatment of drug-abusing physicians, nurses, and dentists. In J. Grabowski, M. Stitzer & J. Henningfield (Eds.), *Behavioral interventions in drug abuse* (National Institute on Drug Abuse Research Monograph). Washington, D.C.: U.S. Government Printing Office.

Crowley, T.J. & Rhine, M.W. (1981). Abuse of alcohol and other drugs. In R. Simons and H. Pardes (Eds.), *Understanding human behavior in health and illness* (Chapter 68). Williams & Wilkins, Baltimore.

Meyer, R.E. & Mirin, S.M. (1979). *The heroin stimulus.* New York: Plenum.

10
The Use of Marijuana and Alcohol by Regular Users of Cocaine: Patterns of Use and Style of Control

Milton E. Burglass

I n the past few years there has been an astonishing increase in the use of cocaine at all levels of American society. Most noticeable, perhaps, has been the broad acceptance of the drug in affluent, successful, and educated circles. Although cocaine-related problems and disabilities are now being recognized with increasing frequency, it is difficult not to conclude that most users manage the drug successfully. Little research attention has been given to the fascinating question of *how* the many noncompulsive users of cocaine manage to control their use of this powerful, compelling, and readily available substance. Whereas one finds numerous studies of factors affecting cocaine use (Gay, 1981; Gay, Sheppard, Inaba & Newmeyer, 1973a, 1973b; Resnick & Schuyten-Resnick, 1976; Siegel, 1977; Siguel, 1977; Spotts & Shontz, 1980; Staats & Poole, 1979; Staats, Poole & Flaming, 1979), these have not specifically explored the successful user's attributions of control.

The traditional objects of inquiry in the addictions have been substances and compulsive users. So long as drug use remained a low baserate behavior, one limited to a narrow segment of society, this concern with pathological use and users was not unreasonable. But changing cultural values and social attitudes now require that substance users be understood not as stereotypes but rather as persons whose particular substance involvement is a multidimensional expression of their individuality (Burglass & Shaffer, in press). Now it is perhaps fitting for the field to take a greater interest in identifying and specifying the dimensions and elements of successful, controlled substance use. Such an approach would be particularly appropriate for drugs like marijuana, alcohol, and cocaine, which are widely and generally responsibly used. Unfortunately, only a few researchers have opted for this approach.

Apsler (1982) used a random household survey to attempt to measure how people control the amounts of substances they use. This study introduced *style of control* as a multidimensional variable in drug-using behavior. Positing five different rules or styles that individuals might apply to determine how much of a substance to use, Apsler found that measures of control style were indeed consistent and that these varied with certain traditional measures of use (perceived degree of dependence and frequency of use).

In the initial phase of an ongoing longitudinal study of forty-four cocaine users, Burglass (1982) found that Apsler's (1982) style of control measure distinguished the thirty-seven controlled and seven compulsive users. Whereas the controlled users characteristically relied on instrumental internal standards ("using until I feel the way I want") to control consumption, the compulsive users tended to employ external ("using as much as is available") or normative internal ("until I feel I should stop") standards. A subsequent study of use patterns and control styles for drugs used before and after the onset of regular cocaine use showed controlled and compulsive users to differ markedly in their choice of drugs, in the amount and frequency of their use, and in their style of control (Burglass, 1983).

Study of Controlled Users

This chapter describes the cohort of thirty-seven controlled users from the ongoing longitudinal study group and reexamines their patterns of use and style of control of marijuana and alcohol. The focus of the chapter is on how these variables changed as a function of regular cocaine use. The primary interest here is not cocaine use per se. Rather, it is learning how ways of using one drug might modify the use and control of another and thereby exploring the dynamic dimensions and elements of successful substance use.

Method

Subjects. The study cohort consisted of thirty-seven controlled users of cocaine (21 female, 16 male), aged eighteen to forty-three years. All were participants in the ongoing longitudinal study begun in 1978. All were originally drawn from the author's private practice of psychiatry and neurology. Their levels of daily use ranged from an estimated 250 mg to 3000 mg inhaled nasally. Duration of cocaine use at the time of entering the study ranged from three to seventy-eight weeks. All subjects were employed or otherwise engaged in career activities. Without exception, each was extraordinarily successful in her or his field of endeavor. None showed evidence of neurological disease, and none met the criteria for a DSM-III Axis I psychiatric diagnosis. (See Burglass, 1983, for the complete sociomedical histories and demographic descriptions of the study population.)

Measures. As participants in the longitudinal study, all subjects underwent extensive medical and psychological testing and examination. All were interviewed at intake by the author for a minimum of four hours. (The complete intake protocol for the longitudinal study can be found in Burglass, 1983.) For the purposes of the present study, each subject also completed a questionnaire on their pattern of use and style of control of marijuana and alcohol. Questionnaire findings are shown in tables 10–1 and 10–2.

Findings

Pattern of Use: Marijuana

Marijuana had been the unequivocal drug of choice for this group prior to their adoption of cocaine for regular use. Interest in marijuana, participation in and identification with the marijuana subculture, and regular use of the drug had been an intimate part of their individual and social identities. They typically reported having smoked daily, both alone and with friends with whom "sharing a joint" had been the ritual expression of an intimately shared consciousness. All but a few associated their discovery and adoption of marijuana with a highly valued, deeply felt process of personal transformation. Most—even those who had been too young to have been conscious participants in the "Woodstock generation"— identified strongly with the ethos of the 1960s. For this group marijuana had been more than just a favored drug; it had been one of the cardinal symbols of an alternative consciousness and life style.

Table 10–1
Pattern of Use of Marijuana and Alcohol before and after Using Cocaine Regularly

Use	Marijuana		Alcohol	
	Before	*After*	*Before*	*After*
Regular	34	6	0	16
Frequent	2	7	3	12
Occasional	1	18	22	5
Rare	0	6	12	4

N = 37

Table 10–2
Style of Control of Marijuana and Alcohol before and after Using Cocaine Regularly

Amount Used	Marijuana		Alcohol	
	Before	*After*	*Before*	*After*
Others are using	6	17	13	4
My usual	4	6	14	2
Feel I should stop	1	0	0	6
Supposed to work	1	1	2	3
Feel like I want	25	13	8	22

$N = 37$

With regular cocaine use, marijuana consumption declined markedly, as did the subjects' interest in smoking as a social activity. As shown in table 10–3, most of the previously regular users became only occasional users. Several subjects attributed this change to loss of contact with (and interest in) their old marijuana-using friends and to an increasingly incompatible set of social, schedule, and performance demands imposed by their rapidly evolving careers. Some lamented this change, experiencing in it the loss of a valued, special aspect of themselves. Others offered as explanations their having "grown up" or having "had to get into the real world sooner or later."

Table 10–3
Marijuana: Changes in Pattern of Use for Females and Males before and after Using Cocaine Regularly

Before		After			
		Regular	*Frequent*	*Occasional*	*Rare*
Regular					
Females	(20)	4	4	11	1
Males	(14)	2	3	6	3
Frequent					
Females	(1)	0	0	0	1
Males	(1)	0	0	1	0
Occasional					
Females	(0)	0	0	0	0
Males	(1)	0	0	0	1
Rare					
Females	(0)	0	0	0	0
Males	(0)	0	0	0	0
Total	(37)	6	7	18	6

Note: Figures in parentheses indicate total, prior to cocaine use.

After experiencing cocaine, subjects began to consider marijuana as inappropriate to their changed circumstances and unsuitable for their current needs. Simply stated, the new circumstances were those of un-bridled success—the new career-related needs were for more energy, enhanced performance, and greater control over motivation. Once pro-ductivity had become an important value, smoking marijuana became counterproductive. Interestingly, nearly all subjects reported that as co-caine use had become regular, they had found marijuana to be increas-ingly soporific, hence counterproductive and unappealing. Although this shift away from marijuana use was more pronounced for women than for men, a few regular users of both sexes continued to use mari-juana as before (table 10–3).

Style of Control: Marijuana

Before cocaine, most subjects had controlled their use of marijuana by internal instrumental means; that is, they had used until attaining a desired feeling state (table 10–4). None had ever viewed the drug as harmful of their use of it as dangerous. Whereas for some the intake of others in a social setting had served as a guide to their own level of use,

Table 10–4
Marijuana: Changes in Style of Control for Females and Males before and after Using Cocaine Regularly

Before		After				
		Others	*Usual*	*Should*	*Supposed*	*Want*
Others are using						
Females	(4)	3	1	0	0	0
Males	(2)	2	0	0	0	0
My usual						
Females	(2)	1	1	0	0	0
Males	(2)	2	0	0	0	0
Feel I should stop						
Females	(0)	0	0	0	0	0
Males	(1)	0	0	0	1	0
Supposed to work						
Females	(1)	0	0	0	0	1
Males	(0)	0	0	0	0	0
Feel like I want						
Females	(14)	8	2	0	0	4
Males	(11)	1	2	0	0	8
Total	(37)	17	6	0	1	13

Note: Figures in parentheses indicate total, prior to cocaine use.

this style of control seemed to have been more a concession to sociability than a consciously chosen method of regulating their own consumption.

Table 10–4 reveals some interesting differences between the sexes. After cocaine use, most women who previously had used an *internal instrumental* control style (for example, smoked to effect) adopted an *external social* control style (using only when, where, and in amounts others were using). The majority of the men, however, continued to use an internal instrumental style of control. Those women and men who before cocaine use had relied on an external social form of control continued to do so afterward.

Pattern of Use: Alcohol

Most subjects had used alcohol very infrequently and in small amounts prior to using cocaine on a regular basis. None had been regular drinkers, and only three reported having been frequent drinkers (table 10–5). Typically, their use of alcohol had been limited to celebrative social occasions which, being highly structured, ritualistic events, were not dedicated to alcohol use. For a detailed analysis of this pattern of alcohol use see Zinberg and Harding (1982) and Maloff, Becker, Fonaroff, and Rodin (1982). All but five subjects reported having actively avoided alcohol because of its undesired effects of sedation, impaired awareness and

Table 10–5
Alcohol: Changes in Pattern of Use for Females and Males before and after Using Cocaine Regularly

		After			
Before		Regular	Frequent	Occasional	Rare
Regular					
Females	(0)	0	0	0	0
Males	(0)	0	0	0	0
Frequent					
Females	(1)	0	0	0	1
Males	(2)	2	0	0	0
Occasional					
Females	(14)	5	5	3	1
Males	(8)	7	1	0	0
Rare					
Females	(6)	2	1	1	2
Males	(6)	0	5	1	0
Total	(37)	16	12	5	4

Note: Figures in parentheses indicate total, prior to cocaine use.

performance, and later physical discomfort (for example, hangover). Most had associated alcohol use with an unenlightened consciousness and a crass life style of which they were highly critical.

Table 10–5 shows the significant change in the pattern of alcohol use that occurred after cocaine became the drug of choice. Most who previously had been occasional or rare drinkers became regular or frequent drinkers. In the main, this group still claimed to dislike alcohol and most people used it preferentially. Yet, they accepted their own ongoing (and in some cases increasing) use of alcohol as an unfortunate but unavoidable part of the cocaine experience. A few reported "getting into" alcohol for its own sake after first using it to titrate excess cocaine effects. All those who were using alcohol regularly or frequently expressed concern about the potential deleterious effects of long-term regular use.

Style of Control: Alcohol

Before regularly using cocaine, most subjects employed an external social style of control for alcohol use (table 10–6), with the amounts being used by those around them typically setting the upper consum-

Table 10–6
Alcohol: Changes in Style of Control for Females and Males before and after Using Cocaine Regularly

Before		Others	Usual	Should	Supposed	Want
				After		
Others are using						
Females	(9)	4	0	1	2	2
Males	(4)	0	0	2	0	2
My usual						
Females	(5)	0	1	0	0	4
Males	(9)	0	1	0	1	7
Feel I should stop						
Females	(0)	0	0	0	0	0
Males	(0)	0	0	0	0	0
Supposed to work						
Females	(2)	0	0	0	0	2
Males	(0)	0	0	0	0	0
Feel like I want						
Females	(5)	0	0	1	0	4
Males	(3)	0	0	2	0	1
Total	(37)	4	2	6	3	22

Note: Figures in parentheses indicate total, prior to cocaine use.

matory limit and their own usual amount the lower limit. Whereas some had used for the desired effect of getting high, they viewed the alcohol high state as an occasionally amusing but unimportant diversion. None seemed to have been using alcohol to cope with internal or external pressures.

After cocaine, most subjects evolved an internal instrumental style of control for alcohol, drinking primarily to take the edge off the cocaine experience. Interestingly, whereas none reported having used an internal regulatory style of control ("until I feel I should stop") for alcohol prior to regular cocaine use, six subjects reported doing so afterward (table 10–6). These same six subjects also expressed serious concerns about the possibly harmful long-term effects of alcohol use as well as fears of becoming caught up with the drug despite their best intentions and precautions.

Conclusion

That cocaine has long been used in conjunction with sedative or opiate drugs is a well-established fact. Depending on when and where one looks for this pattern of combined use, either drug might be primary or secondary. In the study group, cocaine was the predilected drug and directly facilitated the adjunctive compensatory use of alcohol. One interesting question raised by the findings of this study is whether these controlled users of cocaine will continue to use alcohol instrumentally or will eventually get into trouble with it. In a controlled study of polydrug and alcohol use among veterans; Robins, Hesselbrock, Wish, and Helzer (1978) argue that the greater the number of drugs being used, the more likely it is that eventually one will be used compulsively. They further conclude that "there is no such thing as 'the cocaine user'. . . . The single drug with which we associate a user is just the most prominent part of his total drug picture" (p. 86). A very different view is advanced by Zinberg, Harding, and Winkeller (1977), who speculate that "the lessons learned about controlling one illicit drug may be applicable to another" (p. 294). It will be most interesting to monitor the alcohol use of the study cohorts over time. If the analysis of Robins et al. (1978) holds, then a number of subjects will likely progress to problem drinker or even alcoholic status. On the other hand, if Zinberg et al. (1977) are correct, we might expect our subjects to continue to use alcohol noncompulsively. A lesson learned by criminologists from the many ultimately discredited recidivism studies of the 1960s is directly applicable here: The longer one studies a cohort of ex-prisoners or controlled drug users, the higher will be the rate of recidivism or compulsive drug use eventually "demonstrated" (Burglass, 1972).

References

Apsler, R. (1982). Measuring how people control the amounts of substances they use. In N.E. Zinberg & W.M. Harding (Eds.), *Control over intoxicant use. Pharmacological, psychological, and social considerations*. New York: Human Sciences Press.

Burglass, M.E. (1972). *The Thresholds program: A community based intervention in correctional therapeutics*. Cambridge, MA: Correctional Solutions Foundation Press.

Burglass, M.E. (1983). *Cocaine use: Patterns and outcomes*. Cambridge, MA: Corlogical aspects of the dependence syndrome. Paper presented at the Addictive Behaviors Conference, Harvard Medical School, Boston, MA.

Burglass, M.E. (1983) *Cocaine use: Patterns and outcomes*. Cambridge, MA: Correctional Solutions Foundation Press.

Burglass, M.E. & Shaffer, H. (1981). Natural history of ideas in the addictions. In H. Shaffer & M.E. Burglass (Eds.), *Classic contributions in the addictions*. New York: Brunner/Mazel.

Burglass, M.E. & Shaffer, H. (in press). Diagnosis in the addictions I: Conceptual Problems. *Advances in Alcohol and Substance Abuse*.

Gay, G.R. (1981). You've come a long way, baby! Coke time for the new American lady of the eighties. *Journal of Psychoactive Drugs, 13*, 297–318.

Gay, G.R., Sheppard, C.W., Inaba, D.S. & Newmeyer, J.A. (1973). An old girl: Flyin' low, dyin' slow, blinded by snow: Cocaine in perspective. *International Journal of the Addictions, 8*, 1027–1042.

Gay, G.R., Sheppard, C.W., Inaba, D.S. & Newmeyer, J.A. (1973b). Cocaine perspective: Gift from the sun god to the rich man's drug. *Drug Forum, 2*, 409–430.

Maloff, D., Becker, H.S., Fonaroff, A. & Rodin, J. (1982). Informal social controls and their influence on substance use. In N.E. Zinberg & W.M. Harding (Eds.), *Control over intoxicant use: Pharmacological, psychological, and social considerations*. New York: Human Sciences Press.

Resnick, R.B. & Schuyten-Resnick, E. (1976). Clinical aspects of cocaine: Assessment of cocaine abuse behavior in man. In S.J. Mule (Ed.), *Cocaine: Chemical, biological, clinical, social and treatment aspects*. Cleveland, OH: CRC Press.

Robins, L.N., Hesselbrock, M., Wish, E. & Helzer, J.E. (1978). Polydrug and alcohol use by veterans and nonveterans. In D.E. Smith (Ed.), *A multicultural view of drug abuse*. Cambridge, MA: G.K. Hall & Co./Schenkman Publishing.

Siegel, R.K. (1977). Cocaine: Recreational use and intoxication. In R.C. Petersen & R.C. Stillman (Eds.) *Cocaine: 1977* (NIDA Research Monograph No. 13). Washington, D.C.: U.S. Government Printing Office.

Siguel, E. (1977). Characteristics of clients admitted for cocaine abuse. In R.C. Petersen & R.C. Stillman (Eds.), *Cocaine: 1977* (NIDA Research Monograph No. 13). Washington, D.C.: U.S. Government Printing Office.

Spotts, J.V. & Shontz, F.C. (1980). *Cocaine users: A representative case approach*. New York: Free Press.

Staats, G.R. & Poole, E.D. (1979). Changing orientations among cocaine users: Consequences of involvement in community distribution networks. *American Journal of Drug and Alcohol Abuse, 6,* 283–290.

Staats, G.R., Poole, E.D. & Flaming, D. (1979). Regulatory factors affecting cocaine use in a rural area. *British Journal of Addiction, 74,* 391–402.

Zinberg, N.E. & Harding, W.M. (1982). Control and intoxicant use: A theoretical and practical overview. In N.E. Zinberg & W.M. Harding (Eds.), *Control over intoxicant use: Pharmacological, psychological, and social considerations.* New York: Human Sciences Press.

Zinberg, N.E., Harding, W.M. & Winkeller, M. (1977). A study of social regulatory mechanisms in controlled illicit drug users. *Journal of Drug Issues, 7,* 117–133.

11
Addiction, Adaptation, and the "Drug-of-Choice" Phenomenon: Clinical Perspectives

Edward J. Khantzian
Robert J. Schneider

Early attempts to explain compulsive drug use tended to emphasize its erotic aspects (Freud, 1955; Abraham, 1960; Rado, 1933). Many of these and subsequent formulations stressed how individuals attempted to induce a regressive, pleasurable state similar to presumed pleasurable states in earlier phases of development. Although later formulations took into account the relief of tension and distress as a motive for taking drugs (Rado, 1957; Wikler & Rasor, 1953; Fenichel, 1945), surprisingly, there continues to be an emphasis placed on the pleasurable aspects of drug use to explain the compelling nature of drug dependence (Savitt, 1963; Wieder & Kaplan, 1969; Wikler, 1968; Wikler, 1971; Goldstein, 1972).

The work of Glover (1956) was an exception to these trends. He was one of the earlier psychoanalytic investigators who stressed the progressive and adaptive use of drugs. He believed that the addict's involvement with drugs was akin to an obsessive involvement that protected the individual from more regressive, paranoid-sadistic tendencies and psychoses. Glover, however, minimized the psychopharmacologic action of different drugs and emphasized their symbolic meaning to the addict.

More recent psychoanalytic formulations have placed greater emphasis on understanding how an individual's ego organization, including drives and affects, interacts with addictive drugs. Narcotic addicts, for example, seem to depend on the effect of opiates to overcome feelings of dysphoria and ego disorganization associated with rage and aggression—affects and drives that have otherwise been overwhelming for these individuals.

Our own work and that of others have developed Glover's emphasis on the adaptive use of drugs, while incorporating a better appreciation of the psychopharmacologic action of the different drugs (Khantzian, 1974).

Chein, Gerard, Lee & Rosenfeld (1964) affirmed that narcotic addiction was "adaptive and functional" and referred to opiates as effective "tranquilizing ataractic" drugs (p. 14). More recent works by others, stressing the use of drugs in the service of drive and affect defense, represent further specific elaborations on a point of view that considers the use of drugs as a way of coping with one's internal and external environment (Wurmser, 1972; Khantzian, Mack & Schatzberg, 1974; Krystal & Raskin, 1970; Alexander & Hadaway, 1982).

Using clinical examples we would like to review and elaborate in this paper what we believe are some of the psychological vulnerabilities of addicts. We will emphasize how the nature of such vulnerabilities predisposes individuals to find the effects of certain classes of drugs welcome and results in a self-selection or "drug-of-choice" phenomenon.

Vulnerabilities in Self-Care and Need Satisfaction

We have been impressed with two other general characteristics of substance-dependent individuals: (1) vulnerabilities in taking care of and providing for themselves, and (2) special problems in accepting and pursuing their dependency needs.

Beyond the compulsive and driven aspects of drug dependence, we have noticed deficiencies of many addicts in ego structures responsible for self-care and self-protection. High-risk involvements, including the dangers of the drug use and its attendant practices, are evidence of these functional inadequacies. These functions are related to psychological structures or ego capacities that are acquired in early phases of development and are derived from the caring and protective functions originally provided by the parents. They serve to protect against and anticipate harm and danger. Addicts give repeated evidence in their lives, prior to and while addicted, of being impaired in this capacity. Most people would be fearful, apprehensive, or avoid the many aspects and elements of drug involvement that are dangerous. Addicts fail to show worry, caution, or fear, and are vulnerable to the influence of psychological states of disorganization, stress, and/or other regressive influences (Khantzian, 1978, 1980, 1982).

In addition to vulnerabilities in self-care, addicts give evidence of being self-defeating and conflicted in satisfying themselves in the dependency and needful aspects of life. They lack a sense of self-worth, comfort, and nurturance from within and thus remain dependent on others and the environment to maintain a sense of well-being. Nevertheless, they are just as often counterdependent and disavow their needs. As a result, they alternate between seductive and manipulative attitudes to extract satisfaction from the environment and disdainful, aloof postures of independence and self-sufficiency that dismiss the need for others. We have described in more detail elsewhere how these counterdependent and self-sufficient attitudes against ordinary forms of dependency leave addicts susceptible to adopting more extraordinary chemical dependencies to meet their needs and wants (Khantzian, 1978, 1980).

Self-Medication

There is also evidence to suggest that an addict's preferred drug or drugs-of-choice is not chosen arbitrarily or by chance. Although drug-dependent individuals usually have experimented with different classes of drugs, such individuals usually prefer a particular drug because they have found that the particular drug produces subjective effects that are more welcome or necessary. Addicts, who use their drug-of-choice exclusively, often describe other drugs as producing dysphoria (Khantzian, 1975).

Alternatively, some habituated users will "layer" different drugs to modulate affective states or cope with external viscissitudes. This layering pattern is not uncommon among patients on methadone maintenance. For example, a patient's rage and aggression are dampened by methadone but more appropriate methods of dealing with anger are not yet available. When provoked, this individual stifles his anger and adopts an overly passive, withdrawing interpersonal style. This, in turn, results in feelings of frustration, self-depreciation, and impotence. A cocaine "run" then ensues for a period of days or weeks during which valium is used to "mellow out" from the assertiveness and grandiosity fomented by the cocaine. These observations have caused a number of investigators to conclude that such individuals are self-selecting and medicate themselves for underlying psychiatric problems and/or painful, unbearable feeling states (Wieder & Kaplan, 1969; Wurmser, 1972; Khantzian, 1975).

Drug Effects and Adaptive Use

The effects of three major classes of street drugs will be described and a brief clinical illustration of adaptive use (self-medication) by an addict will be presented.

Energizing Drugs

The most popular drugs in this category are amphetamines and cocaine. While these drugs differ in their mechanisms of action and metabolism, they possess similar and well-known energizing properties. From our knowledge of catecholamine metabolism, we know that both drugs produce a relative increase in the availability of monoamines at neuroreceptor sites in the central nervous system which, in part, accounts for the mood elevation with the use of these drugs.

From our clinical experience we know that these drugs take on a compelling quality for many users because they are effective in eliminating the depletion and fatigue states associated with depression. Wieder and Kaplan (1969) found that the use of amphetamines leads to increased feelings of assertiveness, self-esteem, and frustration tolerance. Wurmser (1972) observed that amphetamines help to ameliorate feelings of boredom and emptiness by producing a sense of "aggression mastery, control, invincibility, and grandiosity" by overcoming depression.

These investigators emphasize the importance of psychic and physical energy problems that are commonly observed in depression and chronic depressive states. In the case of depression, "much more energy is expended in the service of denial, guilt, and shame, with the result that the short-term energizing effects of the amphetamines and cocaine give a sense of relief by overcoming painful feelings of helplessness and passivity" (Khantzian, 1975, p. 20).

In general, energizing drugs are used by addicts who have great difficulty managing boredom and depression. Though they may feel overextended and nervous when using these drugs, they avoid the tailspin into despair and hopelessness to which they are prone. Unfortunately, the devastating crash which ensues when these drugs are discontinued is often more intense and profound than the original depression.

Case Illustration 1. John, a patient on methadone maintenance, had a twelve-year history of narcotic addiction. He was stabilized on his methadone dose and maintained a relatively normal life style. He worked steadily as a floor-sander, lived with his girlfriend, and had been off the streets for six months. He was no longer able to work, however, when he broke his wrist in an auto accident. This immediately precipitated financial problems, frustration, boredom, and massive feelings of insecurity. A friend, who owed him money, asked if he could pay him with cocaine. John said he disliked cocaine but accepted it anyway. Soon he was using cocaine regularly (in addition to his methadone dose) and spending time on the streets hustling to maintain his cocaine habit as well as general living expenses. With the help of the energizing properties of cocaine, he became more active and successfully organized drug deals to produce an income. While the dangers and stress which accompanied these activities were disturbing to John, he seemed willing to endure them in exchange for the cocaine effect, which helped to overcome his inertia and depression. At the time he believed cocaine was "keeping me going." Within six weeks his wrist healed. He then was able to return to work, end the cocaine run, and resume his previous life style.

Releasing Drugs

Both alcohol and barbiturates in light to moderate doses have the effect of releasing individuals from inhibitions. For compulsive users the compelling quality of sedative-hypnotic drugs stems from their ability to relieve internal distressful states associated with anxiety and conflict. For some addicted individuals, the anxiety and conflict seem to be related to a neurotic response of inhibitions and defense in opposition to unacceptable impulses. Recent formulations, however, connect the anxiety and conflict to rigid defenses against more primitive and narcissistic longings. Krystal and Raskin (1970), using the work of Jacobson (1964), focus on early phases of development where parental and environmental failures require individuals to split their self and object representations (that is, how they experience themselves in relation to other people). This splitting helps to avoid painful ambivalence by seeing self and others as either all good or all bad. Krystal and Raskin (1970) emphasize the problems that drug-dependent individuals have with ambivalence and how they must deny and rigidly repress aggression and the need for love and forgiveness. They stress that the effects of sedative-hypnotics allow for a brief, and therefore tolerable, integration of these rigidly split self/other representations. The use of sedative-hypnotic drugs is, therefore, less for the purpose of euphoria and more for releasing an individual from dysphoria related to rigid and primitive defenses against painful affects, drives, and related longings (Khantzian, 1975).

Case Illustration 2. Frank, a 26-year-old white male with a ten-year history of drug abuse (primarily narcotics and Valium), had an extensive history of premeditated as well as impulsive violence. As an inpatient he was treated with methadone for six months and had no episodes of violence or loss of control. He had great confidence in the "miracle cure" of methadone when he began outpatient methadone maintenance.

As his life situation began to improve, he had a tendency to develop great expectations for enormous progress in his life. He was inevitably disappointed when everything did not fall his way and he was confronted with the need for work and the acceptance of responsibility for his life. Similarly, with every unfortunate turn of events, Frank painted an overly ominous picture and had difficulty maintaining any hope for the future.

He recently fell in love with a woman whom he immediately idealized. He saw her as a wonderfully caring and understanding person for whom he had nothing but positive feelings. This dreamlike relationship was shattered when his girlfriend left him because he "wouldn't get a job and he was just a junkie." He experienced rage and hurt in reaction to her rejection. He felt he could not cope with these emotions as they were too painful and frightening. He began taking Valium regularly to "fix my feelings." It was only during these periods of low-level chronic intoxication with sedative-hypnotics that he could begin to see both sides of the story and bear the pain of simultaneously loving and hating his former girlfriend.

His splitting, or extreme view of the world, which was prompted by frustration, initially helped him cope but eventually became frightening and difficult to control. Sedative-hypnotics gave him relief from his rigid defense and allowed him to tolerate safely and briefly the ambivalence which otherwise threatened him.

Controlling-Stabilizing Drugs

Throughout our work with narcotic addicts, we often have been impressed with the muting and stabilizing action of narcotics. Early formulations stressed either libidinal factors and/or the pleasurable effects of narcotics to explain the formation and maintenance of addiction to narcotics. While these formulations are useful, we have been more impressed with the specific muting action of narcotics on rage and aggressive drives.

In previous studies (Khantzian et al., 1974) using data from the evaluation and treatment of over two hundred addicts, developmental impairments and deficiencies were revealed in the egos of these narcotic addicts. The deficiencies were reflected in uncontrollable rage, difficulty with impulse control, and dysphoria resulting from their violent feelings and impulses. We were repeatedly impressed with the subjective reports of addicts describing their initial experience with opiates in which they discovered the calming and stabilizing action of the drug. In particular, we observed that "in the course of responding to a carefully taken drug history, patients gave ample descriptions of dysphoric states of bodily tensions and restlessness, anger, rage, violent feelings, and depression that were relieved by heroin and other opiates. With an almost monotonous regularity, the patients used terms such as 'relaxed,' 'mellow,' 'calming,' and emphasized a total body response to describe the effects of opiates when they first began to use such drugs" (Khantzian et al., 1974, p. 65). On the basis of these data, we hypothesized that individuals were predisposed and became addicted to opiates because they discovered the ability of these drugs to supplement and strengthen their fragile egos. The specific and short-term action of narcotics was "to reverse regressive states by attenuating, and making more bearable, painful drives and affects involving aggression, rage, and related depression" (Khantzian, 1975, p. 21).

Narcotics seem to function differently for different people. Most addicts use narcotics to cope with rage and aggression, but some feel it helps with anxiety. Still others use it for both effects or supplement their narcotics with drugs to suit the demands of specific life events. While most narcotic addicts utilize the calming properties of the drug, some rely on its potential to energize by interrupting inertia created by overwhelming affect.

Case Illustration 3. John, a 30-year-old patient on methadone maintenance, had a ten-year history of narcotics addiction. As a union carpenter, he injured his back while on the job and was out of work for six months. Although he was receiving workmen's compensation, he still had financial difficulties. After several weeks of difficulty paying clinic fees, a contract was made spreading his debt over time. At this point, he began expressing his indignation over the fiscal policies of the clinic. He failed to keep his contract arrangement and had a hearing with clinic administrators to review his status. He felt he was treated very poorly during this hearing but typically was unable to reveal these feelings, which subsequently intensified to unmanageable proportions. Nevertheless, he realized he could meet the fee and time deadlines which were established during his hearing. He had no idea why he "just forgot" to make the payment on time the following day. As a result of breaking this final contract, he began using narcotics for a few days. Soon he straightened out his financial problems with the clinic and became noticeably calmer. In reviewing these events, he made it clear that his anger was significantly diminished as a result of the narcotics. The drug allowed him to manage his anger and rationalize (a safer defense) that he was "forced" to resort to narcotics in order to avoid violent behavior, which might have jeopardized his entire treatment.

Discussion

The appeal of drugs resides in the dramatic capacities of these substances to reverse painful emotional states by liberating, muting, or eliminating unmanageable affects which disorganize and disrupt some individuals. The often heard statement that "I was hooked the first time I used the drug" probably stems from a successful attempt at self-medication of longstanding psychological deficits, insufficient coping mechanisms, and uncontrollable (or fear of uncontrollable) affects. However, the adaptive effects of these drugs are short-lived because physical dependence on the drugs sets up artificial drive cycles that have their own associated discomfort/distress.

This more recent self-selection/self-medication view of drug dependency is consistent with the current understanding of various neurotransmitters. These chemicals play a part in, and are responsible for, regulating the central nervous system and, when disturbed or deficient, are associated with psychiatric and psychopathological disturbances.

It seems possible that under normal circumstances, the brain and mind produce chemicals not only in reaction to physical discomfort and pain but also to help maintain optimal feeling and comfort states. Endogenous opiates, for example, might be critical in regulating human aggression. This drive is a vital part of human existence in its controlled forms but can be devastating in its uncontrolled forms. Through further study of the endorphins, we might better understand how they fuel productivity and maintain aggression at optimal levels. Conversely, aberration and dysfunction of endorphin activity might be related to the destructive viscissitudes of human aggression (Khantzian, 1982). Perhaps the delicate interdependence of emotional and chemical processes will defy attempts to sort out cause and effect. Does an initial chemical deficiency result in addiction or vice versa? Alternatively, a chemical deficiency could be psychogenic in origin. Understanding how ego and self-structures interact with chemical regulators may help bridge, or even render unnecessary, the duality of mind and body.

In the meantime, however, it is the guilt and worthlessness felt by the addict for succumbing to drugs which become perhaps the greatest obstacles to recovery. Addicts fail to see their drug use as a misdirected effort to improve themselves. They focus exclusively on the dramatic, maladaptive aspects of prolonged use and become extremely self-punitive. Society's low opinion of them feeds their own poor self-images so that they see themselves as weak, defective, despicable, and even subhuman.

Promoting new coping mechanisms and healthier ego structures is essential for these patients to risk giving up older, reliable methods of coping—even if the old methods regularly backfire. Although the reasons why addicts initially resonate to the use of specific drugs can only be reconstructed, an understanding of how drugs serve addicts in the present is essential to helping them recover.

References

Abraham, K. (1960). The psychological relation between sexuality and alcoholism. In *Selected papers of Karl Abraham* (pp. 80–89). New York: Basic Books.

Alexander, B. & Hadaway, P. (1982). Opiate addiction: The case for an adaptive orientation. *Psychological Bulletin, 92,* (2), 367–381.

Chein, I., Gerard, D.L., Lee, R.S. & Rosenfeld, E. (1964). *The road to H.* New York: Basic Books.

Fenichel, O. (1945). *The psychoanalytical theory of neurosis.* New York: W.W. Norton.

Freud, S. (1955). Three essays on the theory of sexuality. In *The standard edition of the complete psychological works of Sigmund Freud* (Vol. 7, pp. 125–245). London: Hogarth Press. (Original work published in 1905.)

Glover, E. (1956). On the etiology of drug addiction. In *On the early development of mind* (pp. 187–215). New York: International Universities Press.

Goldstein, A. (1972). Heroin addiction and the role of methadone in its treatment. *Archives of General Psychiatry, 26,* 291–297.

Khantzian, E.J. (1974). Opiate addiction: A critique of theory and some implications for treatment. *American Journal of Psychotherapy, 28,* 59–70.

Khantzian, E.J. (1975). Self selectión and progression in drug dependence. *Psychiatry Digest, 36,* 19–22.

Khantzian, E.J. (1978). The ego, the self and opiate addiction: Theoretical and treatment considerations. *International Review of Psychoanalysis, 5,* 189–198.

Khantzian, E.J. (1980). An ego-self theory of substance dependence. In D.J. Lettieri, M. Sayers & H.W. Pearson (Eds.), *Theories on drug abuse: Selected contemporary perspectives.* (National Institute on Drug Abuse Research Monograph No. 30, pp. 29–33). Washington, D.C.: U.S. Government Printing Office.

Khantzian, E.J. (1982). Psychological (structural) vulnerabilities and the specific appeal of narcotics. *Annals of the New York Academy of Sciences, 398,* 24–32.

Khantzian, E.J., Mack, J. & Schatzberg, A. (1974). Heroin use as an attempt to cope: Clinical observations. *American Journal of Psychiatry, 131,* 160–164.

Krystal, H. & Raskin, H.A. (1970). *Drug dependence aspects of ego function.* Detroit: Wayne State University Press.

Rado, S. (1933). The psychoanalysis of pharmacothymia. *Psychoanalytic Quarterly, 2,* 1–23.

Rado, S. (1957). Narcotic bondage: A general theory of dependence on narcotic drugs. *American Journal of Psychiatry, 114,* 165.

Savitt, R.A. (1963). Psychoanalytic studies on addiction: Ego structure in narcotic addiction. *Psychoanalytic Quarterly, 32,* 43–57.

Weider, H. & Kaplan, E. (1969). Drug use in adolescence. *Psychoanalytic Study of the Child, 24,* 399–431.

Wikler, A. (1968). Interaction of physical dependence and classical and operant conditioning in the genesis of relapse. *Research Publications of the Association of Nervous and Mental Disorders, 46,* 280–287.

Wikler, A. (1971). Some implications of conditioning theory for problems of drug abuse. *Behavioral Science, 16,* 92–97.

Wikler, A. & Rasor, R.W. (1953). Psychiatric aspects of drug addiction. *American Journal of Medicine, 14,* 566–570.

Wurmser, L. (1972). Methadone and the craving for narcotics: Observations of patients on methadone maintenance in psychotherapy. *Proceedings of the Fourth National Conference on Methadone Treatment* (pp. 525–528).

12
Treatment of the Chemically Dependent Health Professional

Millicent Buxton
Marty Jessup
Mim J. Landry

C hemical dependency in the health professions was noted as early as the late 1940s in a study by Modlin and Montes (1964), which documented narcotic addiction among thirty physicians over a fifteen-year period. Addicted health care professionals did not fit the stereotype of the average addict. While alcoholics and heroin addicts usually achieve some degree of clandestine peer approval for their addictive behaviors, physicians rarely, if ever, admit, even to colleagues, that they are using (much less addicted to) a controlled substance. Because there is no health professional drug subculture, the addicted nurse or physician is a loner, engaging in a secret activity. It follows that treatment of chemically dependent health professionals differs in fundamental aspects from addiction treatment in the general population.

Scope of the Problem

The American Medical Association estimates that one physician in ten is in some way impaired. The majority of this impairment is due to alcohol or other drug use with about one percent of senility, psychopathology, etc. (Arana, 1982). *Known* alcoholism among physicians is about seven percent, which is about the incidence in the general population (Morse, Martin, Swenson & Niven, 1984). Indeed, the AMA estimates that seven to eight percent of physicians "are now, or will become alcoholics" (Steindler, 1975). Bissell and Jones (1976) and Buchholtz

The Bay Area Taskforce for Impaired Nurses is sponsored by the California Nurses Association and cosponsored by the Haight Ashbury Training and Education Project, a project of the Haight Ashbury Free Medical Clinic. The project is engaged in training, education and research on issues related to chemically dependent nurses. The treatment arm of the project is the San Francisco Support Group for Chemically Dependent Nurses.

(1982), however, estimate that the number of physicians impaired because of alcoholism would be closer to ten percent.

Narcotic addiction among physicians seems to be significantly higher than rates for the general population.

> In 1958 the California State Board of Medical Examiners estimated that in some point in their careers 1 to 2 percent of doctors in that state abused narcotics. In a 25-year period, 0.5% of all physicians licensed in New York State were reported to the Bureau of Narcotic Control as addicts. By contrast, the prevalence of narcotic addiction among American males in the group for 20 to 50 years of age is around one in 1000. (Vaillant, Brighton & McArthur, 1970, p. 365)

Talbott & Benson (1980) at the disabled doctors program in Georgia find that "one of eight physicians in Georgia has been, is, or will be afflicted with the disease of chemical dependency" (p. 56,58), and that twelve to fourteen percent of the physicians in their community, medical society, or hospital staff will have had or will have problems with alcohol and drugs. Verdery (1983) finds chemical dependency among health professionals to be an occupational hazard, with a thirty percent greater chance of developing chemical dependency.

Specific data on nurses and chemical dependency are currently more difficult to obtain than for physicians. Isler (1978) reports that about forty-thousand nurses in the United States are alcoholic. During the one-year period from September 1980 throughout August 1981, the National Council of State Boards of Nursing, with thirty-five states reporting, stated that there were 971 disciplinary proceedings involving nurses. Of these, 649 (sixty-seven percent) "were related to some form of chemical abuse" (Jefferson & Ensor, 1982). Additionally, in a large ten-year survey of anesthesia training programs, which consisted of one-half physician staff and residents and about one-half nurse anesthetists, there were 1.1 percent *confirmed* cases of drug abuse. Interestingly enough, Ward, Ward, and Saidman (1983) noted that "the incidence of abuse was higher in instructors than students," suggesting that increasing age and professional education do not necessarily grant "increasing immunity" (p. 924) against abuse or addiction.

What stands out most clearly with studies that mention either confirmed cases or disciplinary proceedings regarding abuse or addiction is the means of identification of these cases. In both cases, only the most overt and serious behavioral and health problems result in a confirmed case or a disciplinary action. Thus the figures above probably represent primarily late-stage addictive processes.

The authors' estimate of alcohol and other drug dependence among nurses (RNs and LPNs) is a firm eight to ten percent of a total number of

1.7 million nurses in the United States (135,000–170,000). Currently, the American Nurses Association estimates the number of chemically dependent nurses to be as high as 200,000 (Morse et al., 1984). In a recent survey done by the Bay Area Taskforce for Impaired Nurses in San Francisco, all death certificates from the period of January 1980 through June 1983 were reviewed at the Department of Public Health. During this forty-three-month period, the authors found that there were thirty-nine nurse deaths directly attributed to alcoholism or other addictive diseases. Therefore, one nurse died every five weeks in San Francisco County alone. This time-limited survey has far-reaching implications for estimates of current nurse deaths in the United States as a result of addictive diseases. If the incidence of other nurse deaths in large metropolitan cities matches the San Francisco statistics, previous data of one hundred nurse deaths annually (Bissell & Jones, 1976) is far exceeded.

Impaired Physicians

In addition to the stigma of addiction, health care providers also have professional roles, personal expectations, and training that makes their denial of the disease a major barrier in its diagnosis and treatment. Nursing and medical education is historically lacking in any chemical dependency studies. Medical management of the consequences of the disease is usually the only way in which addictive diseases are addressed in an educational setting. For physicians, the role as healer may increase their denial when the disease develops in themselves. An Atlanta surgeon states this clearly, "if somebody had said while I was taking drugs during the daytime 'don't you think you're taking too much?' or 'you might become addicted,' I would have certainly said, 'this can't happen to me, I'm a doctor, I'm too smart, I know what I'm doing' " (Verdery, 1983, p. 10).

Peer Intervention

Peer intervention for chemical dependence has been declared an ethical responsibility on the part of physicians by the AMA and by individual state medical associations. In California, the joint statement of the California Medical Association and the Board of Medical Quality Assurance also reflects this opinion (Council on Mental Health, 1973). Smith (1983) describes the guidelines for peer intervention for physicians who have substance abuse disorders.

1. Three or more people close to the substance-abusing physician who are close enough so that the physician considers the relationship important to his self-image may participate in the intervention. This

would include a spouse, children, employer, clergyman, colleagues, or close friends.

2. The effort should be coordinated by a specially trained intervention counselor. This counselor helps the participants in their own emotional stress regarding the confrontation.

3. The participants present appropriate treatment options to the physician, which have been identified and explored in advance. Denial, as a symptom of addictive disease, is expected and prepared for.

4. The intervention is scheduled at a time that is both a surprise to the physician, and at a time when he is sober.

5. The purpose of the meeting is explained within a context of concern and care, each person reading a prepared list of specific incidents that illustrate the physician's substance abuse problems. These are done in a non-judgmental fashion, limited to observed facts, not suppositions or generalizations.

6. Someone, preferably a trained intervention counselor, would make sure that the meeting does not get sidetracked by the physician. They should enforce the agreement that the physician listen to all of the participants' lists of incidents.

7. When the physician's defenses break because of recognition that he/she does indeed have a serious problem that everyone but themselves have observed, alternative treatment modalities are presented that the physician can choose from.

8. If the physician maintains that he/she can cease their drug-taking behaviors without the benefit of treatment, it should be agreed upon that with the first drink or use of drugs, the physician will enter treatment (p. 24–25).

Treatment programs in an inpatient setting at a hospital are one of the alternatives that should be presented to the physician. Chemical dependency treatment programs effectively provide the beginning of a long-range plan for treatment and recovery strategy. Beginning in an inpatient setting, the physician may come to realize that he or she is a person with addictive disease. He or she may also be introduced to Alcoholics Anonymous, Narcotics Anonymous, Cocaine Anonymous, the Caduceus Club, and International Doctors in Alcoholics Anonymous. The physician may be introduced to the twelve-step process and come to understand that successful lifelong recovery is possible if there is a lifelong commitment. The prognosis for physicians engaged in constructive aftercare is optimistic, and successful recovery figures are reported to be as high as eighty-two percent, (Herrington, Benzer, Jacobson & Hawkins, 1982), eighty-three percent, and even one-hundred percent in a group of regular AA attendees (Morse et al., 1984). Physicians addicted to drugs other than alcohol are reported to have a better prognosis than those addicted to alcohol, and the severity of addiction does not appear related to successful outcome (Morse et al., 1984). This should dispel the popular myth that addiction cannot be successfully treated.

The Chemically Addicted Nurse

The chemically addicted nurse has issues that are specific to her profession. The nurse also is a well-educated helper, and like the physician, he or she is well schooled in managing the pathological consequences of addictive disease but knows little about the disease itself. The nurse may also have a general pharmacologic optimism that reflects trust and reliance on chemicals for their therapeutic value and may believe that he or she is personally immune to chemical addiction. The nurse is keenly aware that certain medications will eliminate or postpone physical and psychic pain. Also, since about ninety-seven percent of nurses are women, many may have children and, in essence, two full-time jobs. For nurses, the opportunities to use chemicals on the job or at home to deal with life stresses are many. Thus the nurse who experiences stress on the job, is pharmaceutically optimistic, has a positive family history of alcoholism or other drug dependency, and has access to psychoactive medication may be at high risk to develop addictive disease.

In a survey initiated by two of the present authors (Buxton & Jessup, 1983), fifty-five percent of the female nurses first self-administered a psychoactive drug working in critical care (ER, ICU, CUU) areas. It was also noted that seventy-five percent of the male nurses first self-administered in critical care areas. Sixty-five percent of the sample reported that another family member had alcoholism or another addictive disease. These statistics again support that addictive disease among nurses is an occupational hazard. In one study, the reasons that nurses gave for their initial use of drugs were physical illness and pain, emotional disturbances, and work pressures (Poplar, 1969). Indeed the chemicals most abused are Demerol® and alcohol (Levin, Preston, Lipscomb & Ross, 1974). Ninety-four percent of the members of the San Francisco Support Group for Chemically Dependent Nurses report Demerol as their primary drug of abuse (Buxton and Jessup, 1983). Additionally, other widely used drugs are the benzodiazepines, including Valium™, and other drugs such as morphine and pentazocine (Talwin®). Barbiturates are occasionally used to replace alcohol in the workplace in order to feel a similar effect while circumventing the detection of alcohol on the breath. Nurses also use amphetamines in combination with central nervous system depressants for performance facilitation and mediation of the depressed effect, respectively.

Identifying the Impaired Nurse

Help for the chemically dependent nurse ideally includes early identification, intervention, and referral to appropriate treatment. Barriers to early identification and treatment generally are lack of education about the disease, institutional cobehavior, and dysfunctional attitudes toward the chemically dependent nurse. Institutional cobehavior is denial of the problem on a large-scale (entire staff) level or among individual colleagues or friends at the workplace. Lack of any policy regarding intervention protocol also is a measure of institutional cobehavior.

Proper identification of the nurse with addictive disease should be centered around observable behaviors and behavior changes. These fall into three areas: personality/behavior changes, job performance changes, and time and attendance changes.

Personality/behavior changes for the alcoholic nurse include increased irritability with patients and colleagues, social isolation, or mood swings. The nurse may become withdrawn and want to work only nights. He or she may take lunches alone and avoid informal staff get-togethers. The alcoholic nurse may have elaborate excuses for certain behaviors, especially appearing late for work. He or she may experience blackouts with memory loss for events, conversations, or phone calls to colleagues. Euphoric recall of events on the floor may also be part of an alcoholic nurse's symptomatology.

Personality/behavior changes for drug-addicted nurses may include extreme and rapid mood swings, irritability with patients or staff followed by extreme calm after taking drugs. They might display an unusually strong interest in controlled substances or the narcotics cabinet. These nurses could consistently have incorrect narcotic counts, show discrepancies between their patient reports and others' patient reports on the need for, or the effect of, medication. They might volunteer to be the med nurse more often than anyone else, wear long sleeves, and have a noticeable incidence of seemingly altered vials.

The job performance changes of the drug or alcohol dependent nurse could include difficulty meeting schedules and deadlines, illogical or sloppy charting, too many medication errors and generally doing the minimum amount of work necessary. Quite often, the nurse with addictive disease will display time and attendance changes such as being increasingly absent from duty without adequate explanation, long lunch hours, sick leave after days off, or calling in to request compensatory time at the beginning of shifts. He or she may be frequently absent from the unit or arrive at work early and/or stay late for no reason. There may be a lavish use of sick leave or consistent lateness.

Intervention for the Impaired Nurse

After thorough consideration of the problem of the involved nurse and of alternatives for solution, the intervener makes the decision to talk with the nurse, express concern firmly and nonjudgmentally, set limits, and suggest concrete steps toward solution. Suggestions are based on the nurse's progression into the disease and the symptoms of the disease as represented by compromised job performance. An intervention should not be conducted with a nurse who is under the influence of drugs or alcohol. The intervention will be much less meaningful, the nurse may not respond as he or she would in a sober state, and it may have to be repeated. If the nurse is under the influence at work, he or she should leave the unit for home and return to meet with the intervener for the intervention within twenty-four hours. Appropriate safety measures for getting the intoxicated nurse home must be observed. All interventions are based on job performance with treatment as the goal. The authors have noted three suicides in the Bay area in relationship to nurses being fired without options for rehire and without referrals for treatment.

This model of intervention is based on the supervisor (intervener) having close, firsthand knowledge of the nursing practice and work style of all staff members. An intervention must be conducted as soon as the supervisor feels concerned for a particular individual. This may be accomplished by early intervention, before there is actually documentation, expressed simply as a statement of concern, noting the reasons for the concern and stating that it is hoped that the nurse will get help or counseling. All interventions may conclude with a referral to available services in the area. These may be written as a list and include Alcoholics Anonymous and Narcotics Anonymous. At the time of early intervention, the nurse is also told that her job performance will continue to be observed. Documentation of all incidents and events relative to this nurse's practice is not initiated.

The interim intervention may follow if the nurse continues to exhibit job shrinkage (diminished work quality). Also the intervener may, indeed, utilize the interim or late intervention for the very first contact with the impaired nurse. Again, this depends on the gravity of the situation. At this time also, secondary incident reports may begin to occur. A secondary incident report documents an error on the part of chemically dependent nurse but does not describe drug or alcohol induced behavior. However, it may be that error occurred as a result of drug or alcohol impairment. Others voicing concern may also begin at this time. The intervener may begin to hear through the hospital grapevine or through formal written incident reports that problems with a particular nurse have occurred. These secondary incident reports and expressions of concern (formal and informal) become part of the constellation of factors in the documentation of the intervener.

During this interim intervention, the job shrinkage is discussed, specific documentation shared with the nurse, and one of the following statements are made: "I am concerned that you may have a health problem" or "I am concerned that you may have a problem with alcohol or drugs." The specificity of the documentation determines which statement the intervener will make. Narcotics charting errors, eyewitness reports of self-administration, or reports of alcohol on the breath with behavior changes are examples of drug-specific documentation. The intervener may then say, "You may have a drug or alcohol problem." The nurse is offered referrals for help (treatment) and informed that if he or she does not seek help and show treatment evidence, there may be consequences which may include termination. All interactions with the nurse should be documented by the intervener and kept in a file separate from the personnel file.

Jefferson and Ensor (1982) have provided a similar model for intervention. They state, however, that intervention may occur when the nurse is under the influence and that careful observation of the nurse's behavior will provide the intervener with additional documentation. They recommend a follow-up meeting with the nurse in twenty-four hours, contingent upon the nurse's sobriety. Jefferson and Ensor (1982) also state that, at the end of the intervention, the nurse and the intervener both sign a memorandum that describes the content of the intervention and that the intervener's immediate supervisor be informed of the events (intervention) as soon as possible. Jefferson and Ensor's guidelines have been the cornerstone of much of the standard intervention techniques in use today for the chemically dependent nurse.

Reporting the nurse to appropriate regulatory agencies will vary according to state nursing practice acts and the intervener's attitude toward the disease. The authors have found that individuals with addictive disease who voluntarily offer themselves for treatment and are compliant with the treatment option may be spared administrative action by the regulatory body. However, individuals who receive intervention, continue to be in denial, and do not respond to the treatment option should be reported to the regulatory body for disciplinary action.

The principles of intervention with the chemically dependent nurse are very similar to those utilized with the chemically dependent physician. There are, however, some special considerations. Intervention for the chemically dependent nurse should be accomplished through intervention protocol developed and implemented by nursing administration. Lacking an employee assistance program, nursing administration must take the responsibility for intervention. The authors' model for intervention is presented in table 12–1.

Appropriate treatment for the chemically dependent nurse is essentially the same as for the physician. A special issue during treatment may be difficulty in accepting the role of patient. Other patients may look on the nurse as the "fallen angel" who has violated the public trust and is therefore worse off than the other addicts in treatment. Some treatment staff may counsel nurses out of the profession, which the authors find inappropriate. It is important for a nurse to be out of an area of chemical access for a period of up to one year. Ultimately returning to his or her specialty is a realistic goal.

The Bay Area Taskforce for Impaired Nurses in San Francisco recommends that a comprehensive and highly structured contract for work reentry is imperative during the first year or two of recovery. The length of contract time differs from nurse to nurse. The purpose of the contract is to afford the employing hospital a measure of security in hiring (or rehiring) a recovering nurse. Through routine screening for drug use, relapse may be identified immediately and intensive treatment resumed. Nurses are afforded a measure of security in that, if there are narcotic

Table 12–1
Model for Intervention with the Chemically Dependent Nurse

Early Intervention
Who:	Identified intervener (head nurse, supervisor)
How:	Confidential conversation
When:	Beginning of problem, notice of job shrinkage, tardiness, sick leave, noticeable behavior changes
What:	Expression of concern (early referral)
	Initiate documentation for further observation

Interim Intervention
Who:	Identified intervener (head nurse, supervisor)
How:	Confidential conversation
When:	Job shrinkage, secondary incident reports, others voicing concerns (formally and informally)
What:	Discuss job shrinkage, documentation accumulated thus far, "I am concerned you may have a health problem or a problem with alcohol/drugs. . ."
	Set limits, make referrals

Late Intervention
Who:	Identified intervener (head nurse, supervisor)
How:	Confidential conversation
When:	Documentation, blatant job shrinkage, obvious behavior changes, eyewitness reports, incident reports
What:	Discuss job shrinkage and documentation
	Referral to treatment
	Set limits: Termination for noncompliancy with treatment along with report to regulatory board

discrepancies on their units, they may indicate sobriety by showing negative toxicology screens. Nurses in recovery will openly desire such a contract and feel secure with one in operation. The components of such a contract are shown in the following list.

No psychoactive drug use

Random urine screening twice weekly, with toxicology and alcohol screens

Weekly nurses group meetings, with the option of open communication with facilitators

AA/NA meetings four times per week

Weekly meetings with supervisor

Participation in recommended aftercare program

Individual psychotherapy (optional)

Antabuse® or Naltrexone (optional)[1]

The guidelines listed are part of a return-to-work contract for the recovering nurse and the hospital or institution he or she is reentering. The contract monitor for the hospital ideally should be the employee assistance counselor. Lacking an EAP program, the contract monitor may be the supervisor of the recovering nurse.

We *strongly* recommend that these guidelines be followed in a very judicious and consistent manner. The superficial appearance of health and sobriety in the recovering nurse is not sufficient to measure the well-being of this nurse. These guidelines are for the protection of the health care consumer, of the institution, as well as the recovering nurse. We recommend that these guidlines be applied through the first year or two. At the end of six months, the contract should be reevaluated by the recovering nurse, the supervisor/EAP counselor, and a chemical dependency treatment provider known to the recovering nurse (Ling & Wesson, 1980).

Peer Support Groups

The emergence of peer support groups has added a very specific and vital form of help and hope for the recovering health professional. Specifically, groups for recovering nurses in California are speaking to the enormous needs for this population. In March 1981, the San Francisco Group for Chemically Dependent Nurses was formed. Since that time, over 250 nurses have attended this group and received legal, treatment and counseling referrals. Presently, there is an average weekly meeting attendance of 40 nurses. Interaction between the newcomers and the nurses with longer times in recovery provides critical role models for the newcomers in attendance. Primary issues discussed in a peer support group for nurses are the basic principles of recovery as they interface with professional issues. For example, returning to work in areas of accessibility, handling colleagues' response to the disease, honesty about recovery, and facing legal consequences are frequently discussed topics. Interventions are often done during such a group to utilize the invaluable experiences of those nurses in recovery. The following list shows some characteristics of impaired nurses from a survey of the 1983 San Francisco Support Group for Chemically Dependent Nurses.

Seventy-eight percent of nurses did not use drugs prior to becoming nurses

Of the female nurses who were terminated from their jobs as nurses, eighty-eight percent were not offered treatment at the time of their termination

One hundred percent of the males who were terminated from their jobs as nurses were not offered treatment at the time of their termination

Sixty-five percent of the nurses state that they have another family member who has addictive disease either actively or in recovery

The average time spent in nursing prior to the self-administration of psychoactive substances was three years

The popularity and potency of peer support groups is evident in that there are thirteen support groups in the state of California addressing the special issues of chemically dependent nurses. There are also many more nationally, such as those in Texas, Ohio, Pennsylvania, New York, New Jersey, Florida, Louisiana, and Iowa, based on the concept of peer assistance.

Legislative Assistance for Impaired Nurses

Currently in the state of California, Assembly Bill 2674 was introduced in the state legislature (February 1984). The purpose of this legislation is to create a diversion program for registered nurses whose competency may be impaired due to the abuse of alcohol, drugs, or mental illness. The key features of the bill would be to identify and rehabilitate nurses who fall into any one of these categories. Article 3.1, section 2770, Chapter 6 of Division 2 of the Business and Professions Code, which serves as an introduction to the proposed legislation on diversion programs, reads as follows:

> 2770. It is the intent of the Legislature that the Board of Registered Nursing seek ways and means to identify and rehabilitate registered nurses whose competency may be impaired due to abuse of alcohol and other drugs, or due to mental illness so that registered nurses so afflicted may be treated and returned to the practice of nursing in a manner which will not endanger the public health and safety. It is also the intent of the Legislature that the Board of Registered Nursing shall implement this legislation by establishing a diversion program as a voluntary alternative to traditional disciplinary actions.

Conclusion

There is a growing movement within the helping professions which acknowledges that addictive disease is an occupational hazard in the health professions. This movement is concerned about addictive disease and the disease process. Addiction is recognized as a treatable disease, and correct treatment requires total abstinence from all psychoactive substances. It is critical to allow the recovering person to return successfully to the world armed with new responses that are healthy in nature and growth oriented. Early intervention based on care and concern for the health of an addicted health professional and treatment is the only appropriate response to this occupational and social problem.

Note

1. Naltrexone is a long-acting narcotic antagonist used in the treatment of opiate-specific addictions. Health professionals who return to work in areas where there is access to opiates have found naltrexone to be an excellent adjunct to a full program of recovery, utilizing the principles of the twelve-step program.

References

Arana, G.W. (1982, May). Treatment and management of the impaired physician. *Hospital Progress*, pp. 60–63.

Bissell, L. & Jones, R.W. (1976). The alcoholic physician: A survey. *The American Journal of Psychiatry, 133,* 1142–1146.

Buchholtz, R.R. (1982, November). The impaired surgeon: Alcoholism. *Surgical Rounds*, pp. 52–61.

Buxton, M. & Jessup, M. (1983). Unpublished survey in the San Francisco Support Group for Chemically Dependent Nurses.

Council on Mental Health. (1973). The sick physician: Impairment by psychiatric disorders, including alcoholism and drug dependence. (A report of the AMA Council on Mental Health, approved by the Board of Trustees and by the House of Delegates, November 1972.) *Journal of the American Medical Association, 233*(6), 684–687.

Herrington, R.E., Benzer, D.G., Jacobson, G.R. & Hawkins, M.K. (1982). Treating substance-use disorders among physicians. *Journal of the American Medical Association, 247*(16), 2253–2257.

Isler, C. (1978). The alcoholic nurse: What we try to deny. *RN, 41,* 48–55.

Jefferson, L.V. & Esnor, B.E. (1982). Help for the helper: Confronting a chemically impaired colleague. *American Journal of Nursing, 82*(4), 574–577.

Levin, D.G., Preston, P.A., Lipscomb, S.G. & Ross, W.F. (1974). A special program for nurse addicts. *American Journal of Nursing, 74*(9), 1672–1673.

Ling, W. & Wesson, D.R. (1980). Naltrexone and its use in treatment of opiate dependent physicians. *California Society for the Treatment of Alcoholism and Other Drug Dependencies News, 7*(4), 1–3.

Modlin, H.C. & Montes, A. (1964). Narcotics addiction in physicians. *The American Journal of Psychiatry, 121,* 358–363.

Morse, R.M., Martin, M.A., Swenson, W.M. & Niven, R.G. (1984). Prognosis of physicians treated for alcoholism and drug dependence. *Journal of the American Medical Association, 251*(6), 743–746.

Poplar, J.F. (1969). Characteristics of nurse addicts. *American Journal of Nursing, 69*(1), 117–119.

Smith, D.E., (1983, September). Intervention techniques for the physician with a substance abuse disorder. *San Francisco Medicine*, pp. 24–25.

Steindler, E.M. (Ed.). (1975). *The impaired physician: An interpretation summary of the AMA conference on "The disabled doctor: Challenge to the profession,"* April 11–12. Chicago: American Medical Association.

Talbott, G.D. & Benson, E.B. (1980). Impaired physicians: The dilemma of identification. *Alcohol and Drug Problems, 68*(6), 56–64.

Vaillant, G.E., Brighton, J.R. & McArthur, C. (1970). Physicians' use of mood-altering drugs: A 20-year follow-up report. *New England Journal of Medicine, 282,* 365–370.

Verdery, V.L. (1983, Winter). "It could never happen to me." *Ridgeview Institute Insight*, p. 10.

Ward, C.F., Ward, G.C., & Saidman, L. (1983). Drug abuse in anesthesia training programs: A survey: 1970 through 1980. *Journal of the American Medical Association, 250*(7), 922–925.

13
Addictive Disease: Concept and Controversy

David E. Smith
Harvey B. Milkman
Stanley G. Sunderwirth

During the past twenty-five years, therapists have found it useful to regard alcoholism as a progressive disease, which, if left untreated, may lead to increasing biological, psychological, or social dysfunction and probable death. Recently, the disease model has been extended to describe compulsive and continued use of a wide spectrum of psychoactive drugs including the currently popular stimulant cocaine. The concept has been criticized because it is said to denigrate personal and social responsibility in the development of addictive behaviors. This chapter explores the broad concept of addictive disease and the controversy that surrounds this perspective.

Scope of the Problem

Substance abuse disorders are one of the major public health problems in the United States. Deaths associated with alcohol abuse and alcoholism now rank third behind heart disease and cancer. Alcoholism as a disease is the country's number one substance abuse disorder, inflicting major economic and health damage on millions of people each year. However, the use and cultural acceptance of other psychoactive substances including illegal drugs are increasing significantly (Smith, in press). For example, in 1962 the National Institute on Drug Abuse estimated that less than four percent of the population had ever used an illegal drug. By 1982, thirty-three percent of Americans age twelve or over had experimented with marijuana, hallucinogenic drugs such as LSD, cocaine, heroin, or prescription pharmaceutical drugs for nonmedical purposes. There are approximately one million narcotic drug abusers and in excess of two million nonnarcotic drug abusers, with stimulant abuse, particularly cocaine, afflicting approximately one million Americans in 1983. Furthermore, the crime-related costs of drug abuse in the year 1982 were placed at a value of ten to twenty billion dollars.

Some patterns of drug experimentation have remained relatively constant in recent years, while others have increased dramatically. Cocaine experimentation doubled between 1979 and 1982. Of particular concern is the experimentation among youth. In 1982, fifty-nine percent of young people had experimented with marijuana and sixteen percent had experimented with cocaine. The experimentation rate with heroin, however, remained constant at approximately one percent. The only subgroup in our society that has shown an increase in the mortality rate in the past two decades has been the sixteen to twenty-four age group. Alcohol and drug related accidents, homicides, and suicides are a major factor in this mortality rate increase.

The Disease Concept

The concept of addictive disease is historically rooted in the perspective first advanced by Jellinek (1960) that alcoholism is a progressive and potentially fatal disorder. Since that time, the disease model for alcoholism has been embraced and promoted by Alcoholics Anonymous, the National Council of Alcoholism, the National Institute on Alcohol Abuse and Alcoholism, and the American Medical Association (Marlatt, 1983). "Alcoholism becomes a disease when loss of voluntary control over alcohol consumption becomes a necessary and sufficient cause for much of an individual's social, psychological, and physical morbidity" (Vaillant, 1983, p. 44). Although there is no universal agreement regarding what constitutes a disease, "biological aberration must be coupled with the social value that what the individual has or does is undesirable in order for there to be sufficient cause to diagnose a disorder" (Sederer, 1985). The marriage of biological disadvantage and negative social judgment is currently examined as it relates to compulsive and continued use of a wide variety of psychoactive substances. In this context, alcoholism is only one of multiple patterns of expression for addictive disease.

As in the case of cancer, addiction is viewed as a primary disease entity with multiple agents linked to its manifest symptoms: alcohol; the sedative hypnotics, including the barbiturates and the benzodiazepines; the opiates and opioids; the central nervous system stimulants including amphetamine and cocaine; and hallucinogens including LSD, PCP, and marijuana. Addictive substances may be used separately or in various combinations. As in other disease processes (for example, diabetes), an individual may have a genetic predisposition for addictive disease, yet may circumvent most of its complications by avoiding the psychoactive substances that trigger its symptoms.

The Biological Basis

The biological basis of drug hunger and compulsive substance abuse is the organism's adaptation to addictive substances. Psychoactive substances affect the rate of neurotransmission in various pathways of the brain. Individuals repetitively ingest substances in order to bring about neurotransmission consistent with a desired feeling state. The sought-after alteration of consciousness differs among addicted individuals and determines an individual's drug of choice. Changes in neurotransmission are homeostatically resisted by the body's biochemistry. They are counteracted by alterations in the level of certain enzymes, which are protein molecules responsible for catalyzing biological reactions. These counteractive influences adjust the rate of neurotransmission so that consciousness alterations are diminished even while substance abuse may continue at the initial level. Consequently, substance abusers must increase the dose of their chosen drug (or drug combination) in order to produce the desired effect. It is the changing level of enzymes which is responsible for tolerance and dependence on substances. Tolerance refers to the requirement of progressively larger amounts of a substance in order to achieve its desired effect or to a diminished effect with regular use of the same dose. Physical dependence is evidenced by withdrawal symptoms that may be defined as "the substance specific syndrome that follows cessation or reduction in intake of a substance that was previously used by the individual to induce a state of intoxication" (American Psychiatric Association, 1980, p. 165). This relationship between enzymes and addiction has been elucidated by Goldstein and Goldstein (1968) as the enzyme expansion theory.

In order to relate addictive disease susceptibility to an inherited trait, one must consider the relationship between enzymes and genetics. Enzymes are synthesized in the body by the schematic process shown in figure 13–1. The enzymes (proteins) are formed from a template of ribo-

PARENTS ⟶ DNA (chromosomes) ⟶ RNA ⟶ PROTEINS (enzymes)

Figure 13–1. Relationship between Enzymes and Genetic Makeup

nucleic acid (RNA), which in turn is formed from a template of the deoxy-ribonucleic acid (DNA), which in turn is embodied in the chromosomes the individual inherits from his or her parents. Thus we can see a direct relationship between enzymes and inheritance. A deficiency (or an excess) of an enzyme or altered (faulty) enzyme can be traced directly to the individual's genetic makeup. If a person inherits faulty genes, these genes may not be able to produce the enzyme necessary to carry out an essential reaction. An example of this is the inability of people with phenylketonuria to convert phenylalanine to tyrosine due to the absence of the enzyme necessary for this conversion.

The inheritance of addictive disease can best be understood using alcoholism as an example. There has been more research on alcoholism than on any other addictive syndrome. A genetic basis for alcoholism has been speculated for over one hundred years. Among the many studies which have been carried out, recent investigations by Cloninger, Bohman, and Sigvardsson (1981) and Bohman, Sigvardsson, and Cloninger (1981) are the most comprehensive. Most of their research was based on adoption studies, which clearly indicate that, regardless of environmental influences, the children of alcoholics are at a greater risk of becoming alcoholics than are the children of nonalcoholics.

To understand the genetic nature of alcoholism, consider the mechanism by which alcohol is metabolized in the liver as shown in figure 13–2. Alcohol (ethanol) is converted to acetaldehyde utilizing the enzyme alcohol dehydrogenase (ADH). The conversion requires a coenzyme, nicotinamide adenine dinucleotide (NAD+). Acetaldehyde is then further oxidized to acetate and finally to carbon dioxide and water. The conversion of acetaldehyde to acetate requires another enzyme known as aldehyde dehydrogenase (ALDH) and the same coenzyme NAD+ needed to convert alcohol to acetaldehyde.

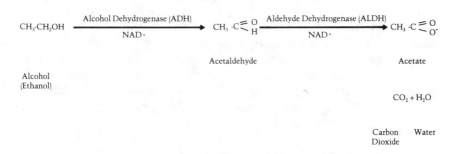

Figure 13–2. Metabolism of Alcohol

Since enzymes (in this case ADH and ALDH) are involved in the metabolism of alcohol, any alteration in the level of these enzymes would change the rate at which alcohol is metabolized. Therefore the alcoholic's inappropriate response to alcohol could be explained on the basis of an inherited altered level of the enzymes ADH or ALDH or both, which are necessary to metabolize alcohol. There have been a number of studies which show that certain individuals at genetic risk to alcoholism metabolize alcohol differently than those individuals reportedly not at risk. For example, Schuckit and Rayses (1979) have shown that the conversion of acetaldehyde into acetate in alcoholics is performed at about half the rate as in the case of nonalcoholics. This explains the well-known fact that in alcoholics there is an accumulation of acetaldehyde. Schuckit and Rayses (1979) also showed that the blood acetaldehyde level was higher in those individuals with a positive family history of alcoholism than in those with a negative family history of alcoholism. Schuckit (1980) also demonstrated that this metabolic abnormality exists prior to heavy drinking. That is, the children of alcoholics who before the experiment had never ingested alcohol were unable to convert acetaldehyde to acetate at the normal speed. The buildup of acetaldehyde, which would be the result of this decreased metabolic rate, would be expected to create severe damage to the liver, since it is primarily acetaldehyde that is responsible for damage to the cells of this organ. We would therefore expect to find a genetic component to alcoholic cirrhosis. Recently, this notion has been substantiated by Hrubec and Omen (1981) using male twin pairs.

Many other metabolic abnormalities of alcoholics have been observed. One example is the formation of the substance 2-3 butandiol produced when alcoholics metabolize or break down alcohol during digestion. This substance is not found in the blood of asymptomatic drinkers. Some researchers have investigated genetic hypotheses by studying differences in alcohol metabolism between races. Schaefer (1978) found that American Indians do not metabolize alcohol as rapidly as Orientals. In addition, Agarwal, Harada, and Goedde (1981) and others have shown that racial differences in sensitivity to alcohol may be related to corresponding differences in levels of the enzyme ALDH. Milan and Ketcham (1981) argue that cultures which have biochemically adapted to alcohol after long periods of exposure (for example, Jewish) have fewer problems with drinking than those with relatively recent history of exposure (for example, Native American).

There is reason to hypothesize that similar genetic influences may be found for compulsive use of other psychoactive substances. Collins (1985) described genetic influences on human and animal reactions to nicotine. Milkman and Sunderwirth (1982) proposed a model of addiction based on changes in enzyme levels, which result from compulsive use of substances or activities (for example, risk taking). It is these alterations in enzyme levels which cause addicts to react differently from nonaddicts to the same experience. This altered response of the individual may be brought about not only by genetic predisposition but also by chronic ingestion of an addictive substance. This does not negate the concept of addictive disease, since there are many diseases that can be related to a genetic predisposition and also can be caused by environmental and behavioral factors. Diabetes, for example, can be inherited or can be environmentally induced.

Diagnosis of Addictive Disease

The diagnosis of addictive disease is facilitated by recognition of the characteristics of substance abuse disorders as described by the American Psychiatric Association (1980). The focus of this diagnostic entity is based on maladaptive behaviors associated with the regular use of psychoactive substances. Drug disorders generally involve a substance-induced toxic effect on the brain due either to intoxication or to drug withdrawal. Diagnostic criteria used to distinguish between non-pathological substance use and substance abuse include:

1. a pattern of pathological drug abuse manifested by intoxication throughout the day
2. inability to reduce intake or stop use
3. repeated attempts to control use with periods of temporary abstinence or restriction of use to certain times of the day
4. continuation of substance abuse despite a serious physical disorder aggravated by the use of the substance
5. the need for regular use of the substance for adequate functioning
6. an episode of complication as a result of intoxication (such as alcoholic blackout or opiate overdose)

The American Psychiatric Association (1980) defines substance dependence as a more severe form of substance abuse because of the requirement of physiologic dependence as demonstrated by tolerance or withdrawal. Characteristics of the withdrawal syndrome vary with the substance. Frequently observed symptoms are anxiety, restlessness, irritability, insomnia, and impaired attention. Although the physical symptoms of substance dependence may indicate a more severe level of addictive disturbance, the phenomenon of addictive disease is viewed as a continuum of disturbed functioning and diagnosis is not predicated on the physical complications of drug dependence.

Compulsive abuse of certain drug groups such as the sedative-hypnotics and narcotic analgetics may produce physical dependency. Compulsive abuse of stimulants such as amphetamine or cocaine, although quite toxic, do not produce a well-defined pattern of physical dependence. They do, however, represent the addictive disease process as the abuser becomes compulsive and continues compulsive use despite adverse health, social, economic, and legal circumstances. Evaluation of the abuse potential of an individual drug is an important aspect in understanding the overall addiction pattern.

Models have been developed where laboratory animals quickly learn to self-administer drugs commonly used for nonmedical purposes. As with humans, whether or not an animal will self-administer a drug depends on a number of factors including the properties of the drug itself, the route of administration, the size of the individual dose, and the time between the work required to obtain a dose and the time of drug self-administration. Drugs such as cocaine, which are more reinforcing when self-administered in animals, tend to have a higher abuse potential in humans. Other drugs, such as chlorpromazine (Thorazine), are never self-administered in animals and appear to have both unappealing properties and very low addiction potential in humans.

Diagnostic evaluation also should focus on impaired occupational or social functioning caused by the pattern of pathological substance abuse. Social relationships can be disturbed by the individual's inability to meet important obligations to family or friends, by displays of erratic and impulsive behavior, and by inappropriate expression of aggressive feelings. Disturbed social interaction is a consequence of intoxicated behavior and personality changes that may be produced by the psychoactive drug. An individual who is abusing substances may also be having legal difficulties because of complications arising from the intoxicated state, for example, car accidents or criminal behavior associated with compulsive drug use and the desire to obtain money in order to purchase drugs.

In order to define legal difficulties arising from compulsive drug use, it is important that one distinguish criminal activity (such as theft) to perpetuate drug intoxication from recreational drug use, which is in conflict with local customs and laws. For example, arrest of an individual who has not compulsively used drugs for simple possession of marijuana is quite different from an indictment for a white collar crime associated with compulsive cocaine use, or for a burglary to support an expensive heroin habit, or for diverting Demerol® (meperidine) from a hospital storeroom for personal use by an addicted health professional.

Occupational functioning can also deteriorate when the substance-abusing individual misses work or school, unable to function effectively because of intoxication or withdrawal. When the substance abuse disorder is severe, the individual's life can be extensively determined by the use of the substance. Physical and psychological functioning may deteriorate markedly. The type of impairment manifested by compulsive abuse is dependent in good part on the drug in question. For example, the opiate addict may be more incapacitated by the life style necessary to obtain the drug than the alcoholic whose addiction has caused severe organ damage.

Tolerance is associated with certain, but not all, patterns of drug abuse. This diagnostic issue is complicated when multiple drugs are used, some of which may manifest cross-tolerance, such as the sedative-hypnotics. An individual may abuse a sedative-hypnotic such as short-acting barbiturate or benzodiazepine and combine these drugs with alcohol, producing mixed addiction. Individuals who abuse drugs in the same group may manifest substantial tolerance yet show gross signs of intoxication to large doses of drug combinations. These individuals are often first seen in an emergency room with overdose or associated dysfunction such as a blackout while driving. These serious consequences may be the first symptom of addictive disease seen by the physician.

Additionally, mixed addiction may result from the alternating use of antagonistic substances such as is seen in the upper-downer cycle. Some individuals use high dosages of stimulants such as amphetamines or cocaine and then use a secondary drug such as alcohol, a short-acting barbiturate, or an opiate to calm the side effects of excessive stimulation. Occasionally dependence and tolerance may start to develop to the secondary depressant drug as well. During detoxification such an individual may experience a complex of symptoms associated with the withdrawal from drugs of different classes.

Withdrawal from dependence on a single drug, from drugs in the same class, or from drugs from different groups requires appropriate medical detoxification procedures to prevent adverse medical sequelae. For example, withdrawal from opiate dependence produces a well-defined abstinence syndrome characterized by gastrointestinal distress, muscle aches, anxiety, insomnia, and narcotics hunger, which rarely is life threatening. In contrast, withdrawal from dependence on the short-acting barbiturates or a barbiturate/alcohol combination may produce life-threatening seizures and require more vigorous medical intervention, perhaps including hospitalization. Further, some withdrawal states may be less debilitating than the actual drug intoxication; for example, the withdrawal from abuse of stimulants such as amphetamine or cocaine primarily involves symptoms of depression and lethargy, whereas high dose intoxication with amphetamine or cocaine may produce a stimulant psychosis characterized by paranoia, ideas of reference, auditory or visual hallucinations, and potentially violent behavior.

Many individuals who develop substance abuse disorders may also have underlying psychopathology such as affective and/or thought disorder. It is important to evaluate an individual with a primary substance abuse disorder to determine if there are other problems such as medical complications or underlying psychopathology. Following detoxification for drug dependence, individuals who have only the primary addictive disease are better managed in an abstinence-oriented treatment approach. However, individuals who have both addictive disease and underlying psychopathology may require psychotropic medication following detoxification and are less suited to abstinence-oriented approaches to treatment.

Treatment

As in most pathological processes, addictive disease is more difficult to recognize or diagnose in its early stages of development. Part of this dilemma stems from the likelihood that a person in an early phase of addiction may have a higher degree of denial vis-à-vis the recognition of his or her dysfunctional life style and consequent suffering. It is in penetration of the defensive use of denial that the concept of addictive disease may have its most potent and beneficial effects. Substance abusers are often more amenable to admitting their disturbance if they are not held morally, spiritually or intellectually responsible for their compulsive patterns of destructive behavior. According to disease theory, substance abusers are not responsible for the symptoms of their disease; they are, however, responsible for their program of recovery. Along with credible diagnosis, a rational intervention approach meets the abuser with a sense of optimism and hope. It is important to stress that recovery—meaning no use—is possible and can be a very positive, life-enhancing process.

The early-addicted person may refute the diagnosis of addictive disease by asserting that the professionally identified disorder simply reflects a moralistic attack on the substance user's values and pattern of living. Early diagnosis of addictive disease may be resisted in the present but may provide the impetus for treatment entry at a later stage in the substance abuse process. As in the example of breast cancer, early problem identification results in more effective treatment, whereas when the disease has metastisized, it is more easily recognized but more problematic to treat. Early diagnosis, based on credible and objective diagnostic criteria, is therefore the initial phase of effective intervention and treatment strategies.

Treatment considerations vary with the specific needs of each addict and drug group of choice. Whereas withdrawal from a combination of alcohol or barbiturate dependence may be life threatening, often requiring hospital detoxification, cocaine withdrawal rarely requires hospital care or adjunctive medication. It is therefore imperative that the specific complications of each type of addictive disturbance must always be addressed by treatment personnel. Smith (1984) provides an extensive review of medical considerations in the treatment of the entire spectrum of substance abuse disorders. Although a detailed account of any particular drug treatment strategy is beyond the scope of this paper, some generic treatment principles are worthy of elaboration.

Diagnosis of addictive disease indicates that drug abstinence is the appropriate treatment goal. Individuals who manifest addictive disease through a particular agent (for example, cocaine) are well advised to abstain from the use of all psychoactive substances. Even a seemingly benign flirtation with marijuana may lead to drug hunger and relapse. It is a common clinical observation that compulsive drug abusers often switch intoxicants only to find that the symptoms of addictive disease resurface through another addictive agent. Drug switching is not an acceptable form of recovery-oriented treatment. Although there will always be a gray area in the diagnosis of addictive disease versus problem drug use, those who have a long history of chronic drug use, with multiple life problems related to substance ingestion, are most likely to fit the disease model. "The exact point at which minimal alcohol abuse (for example, being arrested once for drunk driving) merits the label of alcoholism . . . will always be as uncertain as where in the spectrum yellow becomes green" (Vaillant, 1983), p. 309. The question of treatment aimed at controlled use of substances is beyond the scope of this paper but eloquently discussed by Marlatt (1983) and Emrick, Hanson, and Maytag (1984).

The important ingredients of an abstinence-oriented recovery program may be summed up by attending to the four components which Vaillant (1983) cites as experimentally validated factors in changing an ingrained habit of alcohol dependence. In our model, the generic term *drug* is substituted for Vaillant's specific references to alcohol and drinking: (1) offering the client or patient a nonchemical substitute dependency for drug(s), (2) reminding him or her ritually that even one episode of drug use can lead to pain and relapse, (3) repairing the social and medical damage which has been experienced, and (4) restoring self-esteem.

Depending on the intrapsychic and situational needs of the client, a variety of recovery-oriented self-help groups, including AA, are fundamental to positive treatment outcomes. The relief experience of participating in a group that provides a sense of belonging, reinforces positive self-worth, and provides empathic understanding relative to drug problems may be essential to the recovery process.

In some cases, group support can be bolstered by individual psychotherapy. For other addicts, the only form of treatment which they will entertain is individual psychotherapy. Wurmser (1977) outlines structural and content issues which are germane to individualized treatment efforts. A necessary precondition for effective treatment is a readiness on both sides (client and therapist) for intensive work to occur. In the early phase of abstinence, the therapist may be prepared to respond to crisis situations which necessitate client contact of three to seven times per week. Often, sessions last longer than the traditional hour and telephone availability may be indicated during times of lesser emergency.

The therapy relationship is guided by the therapist's awareness of two basic character structures often found in substance abusers. In the claustrophobic structure, the abuser's predominant fear is engulfment, which may have historical roots in dominating or controlling parental figures. Here the therapist must preserve distance so that the client may trust that he or she will not be robbed of autonomous functioning. In the claustrophilic category, the client's predominant fears are organized around isolation and loneliness. Here, more direct support is needed to counteract the addict's often profound sense of abandonment and despair.

Limit setting is usually a crucial area in addiction-oriented psychotherapy. The client may be faced with the alternative of stopping some form of harmful acting out (for example, substance use) or forfeiting some benefit from therapy (for example, positive recommendation to an employer or probation officer). Each time limit setting occurs, the client has the option to terminate his or her therapy involvement. A useful device for diffusing client resentment is to allow for open communication regarding the client's anger at the therapy-imposed restrictions. In coping with the client's self- or other-directed vengeful feelings, the therapist avoids allowing the client to achieve the unconsciously pursued masochistic triumph, that is, participating in the client's negative self-evaluation or helping to justify fears of betrayal, degradation, and the basic unworth of human relationships. These perceptions, especially when combined with drug hunger, are often the precipitants and rationalizations for relapse.

The experienced addiction therapist recognizes the possibility of moratoriums of passivity where therapeutic progress does not appear to occur. These gaps in overt improvement may endure for months or even years. The client may manifest boredom, interrupted treatment, and long periods of stagnation. To meet the client's self-destructive challenge, the therapist must not be overly invested in progress as a measure of his or her (the therapist's) self-worth. The client should be perceived as having strongly redeeming features and encouraged with an attitude of optimism and hope.

The Controversy

In addition to the formal medical qualities by which alcoholism qualifies as a disease, there are social factors which have enabled widespread public acceptance of this concept. Part of the assimilation of disease theory by the laity may be attributed to a state of cognitive-dissonance resultant from alcohol's status as a legal drug. The underlying public assumption may well be that normal individuals would be unlikely to experience pathological reactions to government taxed (and therefore sanctioned), media promoted, and legally purchased commodities. If alcohol is approved as safe for public consumption, then those who experience alcohol problems may be understood as having a disease. Politically, those who represent interests in the manufacture, distribution, or sale of alcoholic beverages may be inclined to embrace a disease concept. If untoward reactions to alcohol are linked with disease, as, for example, adverse reactions to sugar are associated with diabetes or hypoglycemia, then legislative restriction for those who do not have the disease is unlikely.

Szasz (1974) has been the most outspoken critic of a disease interpretation of drug addiction. His primary concern is that a disease model for substance abuse or other traditional categories of mental illness diminishes the proper distribution of responsibility to both the individual and society. He believes that we scapegoat the drug and the drug user while circumventing the more basic problems in living in our complex societal matrix. Szasz asserts that substance abuse is a culturally relative phenomenon which shows a great deal of historical oscillation. Whereas tobacco smoking in the Ottoman Empire (c. 1650), for example, was punishable by death (Szasz, 1974), it is now widely encouraged by multinational corporate interests. Currently, cigarette and alcohol propaganda are increasingly used in developing countries where health information has not yet reached major segments of the indigenous population. Marlboro and Gauloises, for example, distribute logo-bearing shopping bags and hats to natives in Senegal and other participating African countries. The usually trusting African people may learn to associate particular brand names and symbols with good fortune or personal gain, thereby increasing the likelihood of attraction to potentially harmful substances.

On the individual level, Szasz (1974) argues that the disease model diminishes emphasis on personal responsibility for one's dysfunctional or antisocial behavior. Those who experience problems related to consumption of chemical substances (for example, alcohol) are often excused of legal or ethical responsibility for their actions. Conversely, an unknown number of individuals, who may enjoy the use of other chemicals (for example, marijuana) in an adaptive or recreational manner, may be ritually persecuted or scapegoated as having a dangerous social disease that may contaminate others and will necessarily progress to catastrophic proportions if left untreated.

Critics of the disease model also argue that the concept of addiction as a disease places undue emphasis on medical authority in determining how society should manage what is actually an individual violation of legal, social, or religious norms. Others protest that by designating substance abuse as a disease there is an implied promotion of drug experimentation and use for those who rationalize that they do not have the problem. Zinberg's criticism of the disease model for addiction is that, while the model may have distinct benefit for the treatment of a large population of addicts, it is counterproductive for prevention efforts. Attention is diverted from appropriate social action to overly simplified organic explanations and narrowly conceived biological research quests.

Conclusion

There is a growing body of clinical and research evidence that addiction can be characterized as a disease in that it is a pathological state with characteristic signs and symptoms and a predictable prognosis if the addiction-prone individual continues to use psychoactive drugs. The addictive process is characterized by compulsion, loss of control over the drug, and continued use in spite of adverse consequences. The causation of addictive disease is an interplay between environmental and genetic factors with an early altered response to psychoactive drugs representing a symptom of the disease, particularly in individuals with a high risk genetic profile. Once the individual develops an addictive disease, he or she cannot return to controlled use of the drug. Abstinence and recovery (living a comfortable and responsible life without the use of psychoactive drugs) is presently the most effective long-term treatment for addictive disease.

Although controversy surrounds addictive disease theory and a great deal of research remains to be done, the disease concept is currently regarded by the mainstream of addiction specialists as the best model for understanding and treating a broad spectrum of chronic substance abuse patterns that lead to progressive deterioration of social, economic, or health functions.

References

Agarwal, D.P., Harada, S & Goedde, H.W. (1981). Racial differences in biological sensitivity to ethanol: The role of alcohol dehydrogenase and aldehyde dehydrogenase isozymes. *Alcoholism: Clinical and Experimental Research, 5,* 12–16.

American Psychiatric Association. (1980). *Diagnostic and statistical manual of mental disorders* (3d ed.). Washington, D.C.: Author.

Bohman, M., Sigvardsson, S. & Cloninger, C.R. (1981). Maternal inheritance of alcohol abuse. *Archives of General Psychiatry, 38,* 861–868.

Cloninger, C.R., Bohman, M. & Sigvardsson, S. (1981). Inheritance of alcohol abuse *Archives of General Psychiatry, 38,* 965–969.

Collins, A.C. (1985). A genetic perspective: Inheriting the addictions with emphasis on alcohol and nicotine. In H. Milkman & H. Shaffer (Eds.), *The addictions: Multidisciplinary perspectives and treatments.* Lexington, MA: Lexington Books.

Goldstein, A. & Goldstein D.B. (1968). Enzyme expansion theory of drug tolerance and physical dependence. *Research Publications of the Association for Research in Nervous and Mental Disease, 46,* 265–267.

Hrubec, Z. & Omen, G.S. (1981). Evidence of genetic predisposition to alcoholic cirrhosis and psychosis: Twin concordances for alcoholism and its biological end points by zygosity among male veterans. *Alcoholism: Clinical and Experimental Research, 5,* 207–215.

Jellinek, E.M. (1960). *The disease concept of alcoholism.* New Brunswick, NJ: Hillhouse Press.

Marlatt, G.A. (1983, October). The controlled-drinking controversy: A commentary. *American Psychologist,* pp. 1097–1110.

Milam, J.R. & Ketcham, K. (1981). *Under the influence: A guide to the myths and realities of alcoholism.* Seattle: Madrona.

Milkman, H. & Sunderwirth, S. (1982). Addictive processes. *Journal of Psychoactive Drugs, 14*(3), 177–192.

Schaefer, J.M. (1978). Alcohol metabolism and sensitivity reactions among the Reddis of South India. *Alcoholism: Clinical and Experimental Research, 2,* 61–69.

Schuckit, M. (1980). Alcoholism and genetics: Possible biological mediators. *Biological Psychiatry, 15*(3), 437–447.

Schuckit, M.A. & Rayses, V. (1979). Ethanol ingestion: Differences in blood acetaldehyde concentrations in relatives of alcoholics and controls. *Science, 203,* 54.

Sederer, L. (1985). Diagnosis, conceptual models, and the nature of this volume. In H. Milkman & H. Shaffer (Eds.), *The addictions: Multidisciplinary perspectives and treatments.* Lexington, MA: Lexington Books.

Smith, D.E. (in press). Substance abuse disorders: Drugs and alcohol. In H. Goldman (Ed.), *Lange Textbook on Psychiatry*.

Szasz, T. (1974). *Ceremonial chemistry*. NY: Anchor Press/Doubleday.

Vaillant, G.E. (1983). *The natural history of alcoholism*. Cambridge, MA: Harvard University Press.

Wurmser, L. (1977). Mr. Pecksniff's horse: Psychodynamics in compulsive drug use. In J.D. Blaine & D.A. Julius (Eds.), *Psychodynamics of drug dependence* (National Institute on Drug Abuse Research Monograph No. 12, DHEW Publication No. ADM 77-470, pp. 36–71). Washington, D.C.: U.S. Government Printing Office.

Zinberg, N.E. (1981). Alcohol addiction. In M.H. Bean & N.E. Zinberg (Eds.), *Dynamic approaches to the understanding and treatment of alcoholism*. New York: Free Press.

14
Cognitive-Behavioral Treatment of Problem Drinking

Chad D. Emrick
Joel Hansen
Jeanne C. Maytag

C urrently the alcohol treatment field is dominated by a disease model of alcoholism that had its strongest roots planted in the 1930s. This model has changed little since then despite the wealth of incompatible scientific evidence that has been gathered against it in recent decades (Room, 1980). This body of evidence has shown the disease model to be of limited applicability in explaining comprehensively the etiology and maintenance of alcohol abuse, except in the more extreme cases (Vaillant, 1983). The prevailing model also leads to treatment interventions that are unappealing or inappropriate for a large percentage of individuals abusing alcohol.

A number of alternative theories have been proposed to account for the etiology and maintenance of alcohol disorders. Among them are classic psychoanalytic, psychoanalytic structural, ego psychoanalytic, pharmacodynamic, pharmacologic, bioamine, systems, genetic, and social learning (Pattison, 1984; Saxe, Dougherty, Esty & Fine, 1983). Each theory has its adherents and each, no doubt, describes some part of the complex process that is typically referred to as alcoholism. After summarizing some of the major theories, Pattison concluded that "each [theory] describes only one type of alcoholic or amounts for only one aspect of behavior associated with alcoholism" (p. 92). We are in agreement with this viewpoint.

The purpose of this chapter is to elucidate one theory that has gained adherents largely in the social science field—cognitive-behavioral theory. Our intent is to summarize the contributions that this theory and associated research have made to the understanding of the development, maintenance, and treatment of alcohol problems. We do not believe that the theory necessarily replaces any other that is extant. Nonetheless, we assert that it sheds fresh light on some aspects of the development and maintenance of alcohol disorders, particularly in accounting for variations in alcohol problems across sociocultural groups and across individuals within a particular sociocultural condition. More importantly, the theory suggests potentially efficacious clinical assessment and treatment approaches which may help reduce the vast human suffering caused by abusive drinking.

Theory

Social Factors

Different cultures have widely varying rates of alcohol-related problems. For example, Irish-Catholics are known to have a high rate of alcohol-related social problems whereas traditional Jews have a low rate (Cahalan, 1970). Differences in age, sex, ethnic-religious background, and socioeconomic status are consistently found in large epidemiological studies of alcohol use and related problems. Although such variability could possibly be due to physiological differences between groups, physiological factors do not by themselves appear to be sufficiently explanatory. In contrast, the differences appear to be more "consistently explained in sociocultural terms—in terms of group norms, group cohesiveness, social supports, social controls, etc. . . ." (Braucht, 1983, p. 85).

Laboratory studies of how factors such as group norms influence drinking behavior have shown that modeling is a powerful variable. For example, Caudill and Marlatt (1975) asked heavy social drinking males to participate in a wine tasting task; the amount of wine each subject drank was monitored. Subjects were exposed to one of the following conditions: A confederate who modeled heavy consumption of wine, a confederate who modeled light consumption of wine, or no confederate present. The subjects who were exposed to the heavy drinking confederate drank significantly more than did the subjects exposed to the light drinking confederate or to no confederate. Similar studies using confederates who model either light or heavy drinking have been shown to affect drinking in natural settings (Reid, 1978) and the drinking of alcoholics (Caudill & Lipscomb, 1980). Additional studies have shown male heavy drinkers to be more influenced by modeling than female drinkers or male light drinkers (Lied & Marlatt, 1979; Cooper, Waterhouse & Sobell, 1979). Studies of the impact of the congeniality of the confederate on drinking behavior have generally shown that warm, sociable models influence drinking more than do cold, distant ones (for example, Reid, 1978).

In an especially interesting study, Hendricks, Sobell, and Cooper (1978) attempted to separate the modeling effects of imitation and coaction on drinking behavior. Imitation refers to the passive observation of another's behavior and repeating that behavior at a later time. Coaction requires the simultaneous and interactive performance of a behavior. Hendricks et al. (1978) found that the confederate's amount of drinking affected the subject's drinking only in the coaction task, where both the subject and the confederate tasted wine at the same time. When the subject saw the confederate taste the wine before he did (the imitative condition), drinking was unaffected. George and Marlatt (1983) see these and similar findings as suggesting that when an individual's drinking behavior pattern has already been established "coaction rather than imitation best describes the modeling effects . . . " (p. 125).

The potency of modeling effects from parents can be implied from an investigation by Kandel, Kessler, and Margulies (1978), which found that in eighty-one percent of females where both parents drank hard liquor the children also drank hard liquor. In contrast, only twenty-eight percent of the parents who abstained had children who drank hard liquor. Also, Zucker and his colleagues have consistently found that adolescents with drinking problems, both boys and girls, are more likely to have one or both parents who are heavy drinkers (Zucker & Barron, 1973; Zucker & Devoe, 1975).

Although parental influence may be considerable, a comparison of peer influence and parental influence (Kandel et al., 1978) revealed that peers accounted for about twice as much variance as did parents in predicting age of onset of the use of hard liquor. Also, peer influence is found to increase with age during adolescence (Margulies, Kessler & Kandel, 1977), suggesting that alcohol use is initially more influenced by the family through imitative modeling of parental attitudes and expectations regarding alcohol use but that, as adolescence progresses, peer influence, through coaction, becomes a more potent factor in the development of alcohol use patterns. George and Marlatt (1983) state

> Imitative modeling may be more important to acquisition of an alcohol use pattern, but coactive modeling may be more important to maintenance. During childhood and early adolescence, opportunities for coactive drinking experiences are limited by external restrictions. However, through observation of adult drinkers, for example, parents, youngsters may acquire, store, and later imitate incipient components (for example, cognitive expectations) of their evolving alcohol use patterns. In late adolescence and through adulthood, when drinking is not only acceptable but encouraged, coaction becomes the prepotent source of behavioral information about drinking. Coactive drinking experiences tend to be imbued with a host of social pressures and reinforcers that can propel or retard spontaneous consumption rates. Once an alcohol use pattern becomes established, the individual can conceivably seek coactive drinking experiences that will further strengthen or legitimize the established pattern and associated expectancies. (p. 125)

Perhaps the strongest outcome of modeling is the development of alcohol-related expectancies. The following section addresses such expectancies.

Expectancy

Traditional behaviorism suggests that the actual contingency of an action is what determines the probability of a behavior being emitted. Cognitive-behavior theory, on the other hand, suggests that the *expected* contingency or outcome of a behavior is also a potent factor. People act in accordance with an expected outcome, although *actual* outcome may influence a person's continued acceptance of a particular expectancy (Beck, 1976). As Beck (1976) states, "Man is a practical scientist: He makes observations, sets up hypotheses, checks their validity, and eventually forms generalizations that will later serve as a guide for making rapid judgments of situations" (p. 12). Of course, hypothesis building does not occur in a vacuum; through the process of socialization, hypotheses that are embedded in society's folk wisdom and logic are acquired. Once acquired, individuals test these hypotheses for their validity, and those that are judged to be valid form the basis for generalized expectations.

Generalized expectancies vary widely, from the very specific ("I expect to be satiated after eating a large pizza") to the very broad ("I expect that no one will ever accept me no matter what I do"). Rotter (1966) described and measured a particularly notable generalization, namely, an individual's perceived locus of control over what happens to him or her in life. Those with an external locus of control believe that they have little control over what happens to them, whereas those who have a more internal locus believe that they are able to influence what happens to them directly through their own actions. Such expectancies can greatly influence an individual's thoughts, feelings, and actions.

Behavior is determined not only by an individual's belief that actions will produce a certain effect but also by the belief that the action is within his or her ability to perform it. Bandura (1977) labels this aspect of expectancy as self-efficacy. For example, a woman may believe that walking a tightrope over Niagara Falls will bring her fame yet not attempt to do so since she does not believe that she is capable of the feat. On the other hand, a man may believe that relaxation following a stressful day at work will have a rejuvenating effect and also believe that he is capable of relaxing because he has acquired relaxation skills. Thus, after a difficult day he is likely to engage in relaxation not only because he thinks relaxation will have a positive outcome (an outcome expectation) but also because he thinks of himself as able to relax (an efficacy expectation).

A person's sense of self-efficacy increases as his or her repertoire of coping skills for meeting the demands of the environment increases; however, possession of coping skills does not guarantee self-efficacy. Acquired skills can be inhibited by anxiety or negative thoughts. A socially anxious male may believe, for instance, that he cannot carry on a conversation with someone he has just met despite his ability to do so adequately with people he knows well. Thus, for a sense of self-efficacy to exist, an individual needs to possess not only coping skills for meeting environmental and social demands but also confidence that is built on the belief that he or she is able to execute those skills successfully in the face of situational demands.

With respect to alcohol use, cognitive-behavior theory suggests that people are more likely to abuse alcohol if they lack a sense of self-efficacy yet expect to be able to bring about desired results if they use alcohol. Such alcohol-efficacy expectations (George & Marlatt, 1983, p. 129) derive from (1) experiences in which performance was effective while drinking, (2) observations of others behaving effectively while drinking, (3) encouragement and reinforcement from others for drinking, and (4) reduction of anxiety by alcohol with a resultant expression of coping skills (for example, approaching an attractive person at a party or communicating loving feelings for someone) (George & Marlatt, 1983). With respect to observing others behaving effectively while drinking, Lowery (1980) has documented that television's afternoon soap operas portray alcohol use as generally facilitative of social functioning and helpful in managing negative emotions with few negative consequences from such use. When these portrayals generate beliefs about alcohol's effectiveness and harmlessness, the use of alcohol may be influenced.

Related to alcohol-efficacy expectations are beliefs about the effects alcohol has on the drinker (alcohol-outcome expectancies) (George & Marlatt, 1983, p. 126). Common expecations about alcohol's effects include reduced social anxiety, increased sense of dominance, and increased responsiveness to sexual stimuli. Experimental studies have demonstrated that changes in anxiety, sexual responsiveness, and aggression in response to drinking are more influenced by the drinker's *belief* about how much alcohol he or she has consumed than by alcohol's *actual* effects (George & Marlatt, 1983, p. 129). Beliefs about alcohol's effects are thus thought to exert a significant influence over drinking behavior and may lead to problem drinking. For example, if a man lacks a sense of self-efficacy with respect to expressing himself sexually, he may turn to the excessive use of alcohol because he expects alcohol to produce the desired outcome of enhanced sexual responsiveness.

Consistent with this theorizing, laboratory studies of drinking show that interpersonal stress increases the amount of alcohol that is drunk by problem drinkers but not by social drinkers (Allman, Taylor & Nathan, 1972; Miller, Hersen, Eisler & Hilsman, 1974). Apparently, problem drinkers expect alcohol to provide certain benefits in interpersonally stressful situations that social drinkers do not anticipate. Also, research by McClelland, Davis, Kalin, and Wanner (1972) suggests that men who drink heavily lack a sense of personal power and seek alcohol in order to create a perception of power and control. Their studies have demonstrated that, as men consume larger amounts of alcohol, fantasies of personal power and control emerge.

Of course, such research does not directly test the hypothesis that drinking is mediated by deficits in a sense of self-efficacy, but the findings are certainly supportive of the hypothesis. Direct studies are needed with respect to the influence on drinking behavior of alcohol-related expectancies regarding not only interpersonal stress or feelings of powerlessness but also other negative emotional states such as grief and pain, depression, and chronic stress. Also, research is warranted with regard to expectancies about the effects of alcohol on positive emotional states such as joy, calmness, and excitement. Such research hopefully will be undertaken and lead to a refinement of the expectancy hypothesis.

Cognitive-behavior theory and research are of interest in their own right, yet it is in the application of the theory to the assessment and treatment of the problem drinker that cognitive-behaviorism may have its greatest impact.

Treatment

Assessment

Cognitive-behavior theory and research lead to an emphasis on assessing the expectancies of the alcohol abuser regarding the effects of alcohol on affects, cognitions, and behaviors. For example, examination needs to be made of the individual's *perception* with respect to his or her ability to cope effectively with various situations with and without alcohol. Besides a client's expectancies regarding alcohol effects, assessment needs to explore the client's repertoire of intra- and interpersonal resources for coping effectively with stress, including unpleasant feelings (depression, anxiety, loneliness, anger), biological states (hunger, sexual arousal, tiredness, physical illness, pain, hypoglycemia), social encouragement to drink, and interpersonal events (fights with children, spouse, supervisors, etc.; divorce, separation, death of loved ones). Attention to these aspects of a drinker's life serve to augment the data obtained from a more traditional assessment regarding the type, amount, and frequency of a person's drinking, the actual effects of such drinking on his or her functioning in a variety of life areas, and the degree of physiological dependence that is involved in the disorder.

Assessment of expectancies and resources entails a detailed clinical interview along with some formal psychological evaluation procedures. In the clinical interview, the client is asked very specifically about how alcohol affects mood, thinking, working, socializing, physical pain, hunger, sexual arousal, tiredness, marital and other family relationships, and the like. The purpose of these questions is to arrive at an initial impression regarding the *perceived* effects that alcohol has on the individual. Important information is often obtained, as exemplified in the following case:

Case Illustration 1. A male client in his late thirties requested treatment by one of the authors (Emrick) after having been totally abstinent from alcohol for two years. He reported that he had been living in social isolation after becoming abstinent because he felt very self-conscious in social situations when he was not drinking. Over the course of social drinking, which eventually shifted into a brief period of alcohol dependence, this individual had developed the expectation that he could function effectively in social situations only so long as he had an alcoholic drink at hand. He believed that he did not even need to consume the drink to bring about the confidence needed to perform effectively. Having a drink in his hand was sufficient.

The client sought treatment in order to learn how to drink moderately so that he might resume socializing. Awareness of this client's expectancy regarding the enhancement of social functioning with alcohol led to treatment that was designed to reduce social anxiety through in vivo desensitization. With the reduction of anxiety and the consequent carrying out of all social activities that had previously been seen as impossible without alcohol, the client developed a perception of himself as able to function effectively in social situations while abstinent. Only then was it appropriate to address the issue of whether or not this individual should ever drink again, because no longer did he believe that he needed to drink in order to socialize.

Examination of coping resources is conducted by specific questioning regarding the management of feelings as well as the client's typical responses to various physical states, social situations, and past and current life crises. Such questioning can lead to a discovery of defects and deficiencies in coping resources that will need attention in treatment. A client might report, for example, that she believes she cannot say no when someone offers her a drink in a social situation. Another may report that she used to meditate to relax but that she stopped this behavior years ago and now drinks to relax. A client may be found to suffer from clinical depression in response to which he has drunk to anesthetize the dysphoria. Another may experience panic attacks which have been "treated" with alcohol. A client may report that her marriage is highly conflictual, that she drinks in response to her husband's verbal abuse because she sees herself as being unable to respond otherwise. A client may report that he drinks whenever his pain from an old injury becomes unbearable. Obviously, data such as these give clear direction to the therapist for erecting treatment goals and selecting interventions toward those goals. The following case offers an example:

Case Illustration 2. A male patient in his early forties requested treatment to explore his excessive use of alcohol. Clinical interview revealed that he drank large amounts of alcohol after work, particularly when on assignment out of town. He perceived that alcohol enabled him to shift from placing a considerable amount of stress on himself while on the job to relaxing in the company of others. He believed that alcohol was particularly effective in enabling him to think clearly after a difficult day at work, allowing him to remember experiences that were otherwise not retrievable without alcohol.

Early in treatment his expectations that he could neither relax nor think clearly in the evenings without alcohol were challenged, with the result that he was willing to experiment with alternatives to drinking as a means of relaxing (for example, physical exercise, deep muscle relaxation). Once he stopped drinking he learned that he could relax effectively and have a good memory at his disposal without alcohol. The active ingredient in memory improvement was relaxation, not alcohol. The client was thus freed from an expectation about the impact of alcohol on intellectual functioning through developing alternative skills for managing stress. With these cognitive and behavioral changes, he was able to stop drinking excessively after work.

In addition to the exploration of expectancies and coping skills through clinical interviews, the therapist can use formal assessment instruments to identify issues for treatment. One such instrument is the Alcohol Use Inventory (AUI) (Wanberg, Horn & Foster, 1977). This questionnaire measures the individual's perceptions regarding the effects of alcohol on social and intellectual functioning, affect regulation, and marital interactions. Analysis of specific factors and individual items can illuminate a client's expectancies regarding alcohol effects. The Drinking Profile developed by Marlatt (1976) provides another formal procedure for identifying alcohol expectancies. This profile specifically asks clients to report the effects that alcohol is perceived to have with respect to tension reduction, anger/frustration, anxiety, and self-esteem. Also addressed are intra- and interpersonal stressors that are perceived to trigger the urge to drink. The effects of imitative modeling on the acquisition of drinking behavior are explored by asking the client about the drinking behavior of his or her parents or guardian. Drinking locations and social settings for drinking are explored to identify coactive modeling effects on the client's drinking behavior. Difficulties with affect regulation, interpersonal conflicts, and concerns regarding physical health can be measured using such instruments as the Minnesota Multiphasic Personality Inventory (National Computer Systems, Inc.), the SCL-90 (Derogatis, 1977), or a variety of other assessment instruments. Measurement of an individual's perceptions regarding how much effect he or she has on the world can be made using Rotter's (1966) Internal-External Scale (I-E) and, more pertinent to drinking behavior, the Drinking-Related Locus of Control Scale (Donovan & O'Leary, 1978).

Different treatment approaches can be taken depending on the perceived locus of control. One study (Obitz, 1978) found, for example, that individuals who were willing to take disulfiram scored significantly more in the external direction on Rotter's I-E Scale than were those who did not elect to take the drug. Problems with social assertiveness can be identified and specified using one of any number of self-report instruments (for example, Rathus, 1973). Other measurement procedures can be used when specific problems are suspected, such as the Beck Depression Inventory to measure depression (Beck, Ward, Mendelson, Mock & Erbaugh, 1961) and the Profile of Mood States (McNair, Lorr & Doppleman, 1971) to measure anxiety and other moods. While the list of available measurement procedures is lengthy, the clinician need only select a few which he or she finds most useful in his or her own practice for identifying the cognitive and behavioral correlates of abusive drinking.

Interventions

Once the initial assessment has been completed, the clinician needs to select those cognitive-behavioral strategies which best address the identified problems. Training in social skills and affect regulation can be conducted using well-established behavior therapy procedures. Cognitive variables which are found to underlie and maintain abusive drinking can be corrected using a variety of approaches that have been developed by Marlatt & Gordon (1980), Maultsby (1978), Beck (1976), Low (1950), Ellis (1962), and others. Through such interventions, the client can develop more effective, realistic, and logical responses to internal and external events with the result that he or she gains greater control of emotions and interpersonal situations. Alcohol is then less likely to be sought as a means to induce a state of perceived control or as a way to escape stress through the anesthetic properties of alcohol. With such cognitive and behavioral changes, an important component of the drinking maintenance process is removed with a consequent increase in the probability that the client will be able to stop abusing alcohol.

Nonetheless, should the client abuse alcohol again, he or she can be helped to moderate the destructive potential of the relapse by learning effective cognitive and behavioral responses to the event. Marlatt and his colleagues (see, for example, Marlatt & Gordon, 1980) have been particularly instrumental in developing techniques for teaching clients rational cognitive responses to relapse situations. The techniques that have been developed comprise a significant component of cognitive-behavioral treatment for drinking problems and in our estimation contribute greatly to helping alcohol-abusing clients maintain the gains that are initially made during treatment. In a field that has been plagued by failures to help clients receive long-term, stable benefits (see, for example, Polich, Armor & Braiker, 1980) such a contribution is most welcome.

Conclusion

This chapter has introduced cognitive-behavior theory and its related research. The theory has been found to be helpful in understanding some aspects of the development and maintenance of drinking problems and in devising assessment and treatment strategies. Despite the important contributions of the theory, we realize that it is in some respects still in its infancy. Many hypotheses that derive from it have yet to be adequately tested. For example, at this juncture perceptions regarding the degree of personal control one has over what happens in life have only an *apparent* relationship with the development and maintenance of problem drinking (Marlatt & Donovan, 1982). Also, treatment interventions based on cognitive theory have yet to be refined to the point where the most potent aspects of the treatment can be isolated and the relatively inert components can be eliminated. Nonetheless, the theory appears to offer enough promise for improving our understanding and treatment of problem drinking to merit additional development and empirical testing. Particularly in the face of current treatment methods that have very narrow appeal and generally poor long-term effectiveness (Polich et al., 1980), the investment of financial and human resources in the further development and application of this theory seems clearly warranted.

References

Allman, L.R., Taylor, H.A. & Nathan, P.E. (1972). Group drinking during stress: Effects on drinking behavior, affect, and psychopathology. *American Journal of Psychiatry, 129,* 669–678.

Bandura, A. (1977). Self-efficacy: Toward a unifying theory of behavioral change. *Psychological Review, 84,* 191–215.

Beck, A.T. (1976). *Cognitive therapy and the emotional disorders.* New York: International Universities Press.

Beck, A.T., Ward, C.H., Mendelson, M., Mock, J. & Erbaugh, J. (1961). An inventory for measuring depression. *Archives of General Psychiatry, 4,* 561–571.

Braucht, G.N. (1983). How environments and persons combine to influence problem drinking: Current research issues. In M. Galanter (Ed.), *Recent developments in alcoholism: Vol. 1. Genetics, behavioral treatment, social mediators and prevention, current concepts in diagnosis.* New York: Plenum Press.

Cahalan, D. (1970). *Problem drinkers: A national survey.* San Francisco: Jossey-Bass.

Caudill, B.D. & Lipscomb, T.R. (1980). Modeling influences on alcoholics' rates of alcohol consumption. *Journal of Applied Behavior Analysis, 13,* 355–365.

Caudill, B.D. & Marlatt, G.A. (1975). Modeling influences in social drinking: An experimental analogue. *Journal of Consulting and Clinical Psychology, 43,* 405–415.

Cooper, A.M., Waterhouse, G.J. & Sobell, M.B. (1979). Influence of gender on drinking in a modeling situation. *Journal of Studies on Alcohol, 40,* 562–570.

Derogatis, L.R. (1977). *SCL-90-R Manual.* Boston: Clinical Psychometrics Research Unit, Johns Hopkins University School of Medicine.

Donovan, D.M. & O'Leary, M.R. (1978). The Drinking-Related Locus of Control Scale: Reliability, factor structure and validity. *Journal of Studies on Alcohol, 39,* 759–784.

Ellis, A. (1962). *Reason and emotion in psychotherapy.* New York: Lyle Stuart.

George, W.H. & Marlatt, G.A. (1983). Alcoholism: The evolution of a behavioral perspective. In M. Galanter (Ed.), *Recent developments in alcoholism: Vol. 1. Genetics, behavioral treatment, social mediators and prevention, current concepts in diagnosis.* New York: Plenum Press.

Hendricks, R.D., Sobell, M.B. & Cooper, A.M. (1978). Social influences on human ethanol consumption in an analogue situation. *Addictive Behaviors, 3,* 253–259.

Kandel, D.B., Kessler, R.C. & Margulies, R.Z. (1978). Antecedents of adolescent initiation into stages of drug use: A developmental analysis. In D.B. Kandel (Ed.), *Longitudinal research on drug use: Empirical findings and methodological issues* (pp. 73–99). New York: Wiley.

Lied, E.R. & Marlatt, G.A. (1979). Modeling as a determinant of alcohol consumption: Effect of subject sex and prior drinking history. *Addictive Behaviors, 4,* 47–54.

Low, A.A. (1950). *Mental health through will-training: A system of self-help in psychotherapy as practiced by Recovery, Incorporated.* Boston: Christopher.

Lowery, S.A. (1980). Soap and booze in the afternoon: An analysis of the portrayal of alcohol use in daytime serials. *Journal of Studies on Alcohol, 41,* 829–838.

Margulies, R.Z., Kessler, R.C. & Kandel, D.B. (1977). A longitudinal study of onset of drinking among high-school students. *Journal of Studies on Alcohol, 38,* 897–912.

Marlatt, G.A. (1976). The Drinking Profile: A questionnaire for the behavioral assessment of alcoholism. In E.J. Mash & L.G. Terdal (Eds.), *Behavior-therapy assessment: Diagnosis, design, and evaluation* (pp. 121–137). New York: Springer.

Marlatt, G.A. & Donovan, D.M. (1982). Behavioral psychology approaches to alcoholism. In E.M. Pattison & E. Kaufman (Eds.), *Encyclopedic handbook of alcoholism* (pp. 560–577). New York: Gardner Press.

Marlatt, G.A. & Gordon, J.R. (1980). Determinants of relapse: Implications for the maintenance of behavior change. In P.O. Davidson & S.M. Davidson (Eds.), *Behavioral medicine: Changing health lifestyles* (pp. 410–452). New York: Brunner/Mazel.

Maultsby, M.C., Jr. (1978). *A million dollars for your hangover: The illustrated guide for the new self-help alcoholic treatment method.* Lexington, KY: Rational Self-Help Books.

McClelland, D.C., Davis, W.N., Kalin, R. & Wanner, E. (1972). *The drinking man.* New York: Free Press.

McNair, D.M., Lorr, M. & Doppleman, L.F. (1971). *Profile of Mood States.* San Diego, CA: Educational and Industrial Testing Service.

Miller, P.M., Hersen, M., Eisler, R.M. & Hilsman, G. (1974). Effects of social stress on operant drinking of alcoholics and social drinkers. *Behaviour Research and Therapy, 12,* 67–72.

National Computer Systems, Inc. *Minnesota Multiphasic Personality Inventory.* Interpretative Scoring Systems, P.O. Box 1416, Minneapolis, MN 55440.

Obitz, F.W. (1978). Control orientation and disulfiram. *Journal of Studies on Alcohol, 39,* 1297–1298.

Pattison, E.M. (1984). Types of alcoholism reflective of character disorders. In M.R. Zales (Ed.), *Character pathology: Theory and treatment.* New York: Brunner/Mazel.

Polich, J.M., Armor, D.J. & Braiker, H.B. (1980). *The course of alcoholism: Four years after treatment* (Rept. No. R-2433-NIAAA). Santa Monica, CA: Rand Corporation.

Rathus, S.A. (1973). A 30-item schedule for assessing assertive behavior. *Behavior Therapy, 4,* 398–406.

Reid, J.B. (1978). Study of drinking in natural settings. In G.A. Marlatt & P.E. Nathan (Eds.). *Behavioral approaches to alcoholism* (pp. 58–74). New Brunswick, NJ: Rutgers Center of Alcohol Studies.

Room, R. (1980). Treatment-seeking populations and larger realities. In G. Edwards & M. Grant (Eds.), *Alcoholism treatment in transition* (pp. 205–224). Baltimore: University Park Press.

Rotter, J.B. (1966). Generalized expectancies for internal versus external control of reinforcement. *Psychological Monographs: General and Applied, 80*(1), 1–28.

Saxe, L., Dougherty, D., Esty, K & Fine, M. (1983). *Health technology case study 22: The effectiveness and costs of alcoholism treatment.* Washington, D.C.: U.S. Government Printing Office.

Vaillant, G.E. (1983). *The natural history of alcoholism.* Cambridge, MA: Harvard University Press.

Wanberg, K.W., Horn, J.L. & Foster, F.M. (1977). A differential assessment model for alcoholism: The scales of the Alcohol Use Inventory. *Journal of Studies on Alcohol, 38,* 512–543.

Zucker, R.A. & Barron, F.H. (1973). Parental behaviors associated with problem drinking and antisocial behavior among adolescent males. In M.E. Chafetz (Ed.), *Proceedings of the first annual alcoholism conference of National Institute on Alcohol Abuse and Alcoholism:* Research on alcoholism, clinical problems and special populations (DHEW Publication HSM 73-9074, pp. 276–296). Washington, D.C.: U.S. Government Printing Office.

Zucker, R.A. & DeVoe, C.E. (1975). Life history characteristics associated with problem drinking and antisocial behavior in antisocial girls: A comparison with male findings. In R.D. Wirt, G. Winokur & M. Roff (Eds.), *Life history research in psychopathology* (Vol. 4, pp. 109–134). Minneapolis: University of Minnesota Press.

15
A Multimodality Approach to the Treatment of Addiction

Robert Vaughn Frye

The literature on multimodality programming in the treatment of addictions is meager. Multimodality programming was created in the late 1960s as a response to the factionalism that had developed among different methods of treating opiate addiction. Early multimodality programming consisted of an organized system of clinics with a central intake unit and special support units under one administrative authority (Senay, 1981). Multimodality treatment approaches included services such as detoxification, mental health counseling, group therapy, confrontation therapy, therapeutic communities, methadone maintenance, narcotic antagonists, vocational counseling, social work, and religious counseling (Veterans Administration, 1973).

Recent data imply that addictions are not a phenomenon of the few but one which involves many people (Charlesworth & Dempsey, 1982). These data suggest a need to find alternative treatments in addition to abstinence. A void is created when an individual is asked to give up his addictive resources, whether it be alcohol, licit or illicit drugs, food, gambling, risk taking, etc. Addictions affect survival mechanisms which alter consciousness and are thus highly resistant to change through treatment (Frye, in press). A multimodality treatment approach designed to address the problem of addictions may utilize submodalities or experiential therapies which may provide compensation for the lost addictive resources.

Theories of why humans become addicted are remarkably diverse and problematic (Frye, 1980a, 1980b). A sociobiologic theory of addictive behavior (Frye, 1981a) is comprehensive, interdisciplinary, and grounded in evolutionary theory. It utilizes the concepts of phenotype (observed behavior), genotype (heredity), and environmental factors. This theory postulates that the ability to withhold unpleasant sensations from oneself may permit the individual to take steps to overcome unpleasant stress-producing stimuli. The sociobiologic theory views ad-

The author wishes to acknowledge the research assistance provided by JoAnn Kostman.

dictive behavior as a syndrome based on genetically adaptive behavior patterns, that is, addiction is a social behavior with biological foundations. The behavior alters the individual's perception of stressful situations and promotes behavior change toward objects and circumstances in the environment that are perceived to be threatening (Frye, 1981a).

In the Milkman and Sunderwirth (1982) interdisciplinary addiction model, addiction is defined as self-induced changes in neurotransmission which result in problem behaviors; three addictive types are identified which cluster around excessive needs for arousal, satiation, or fantasy experiences.

Using these two consonant addiction models as a theoretical foundation for treatment planning, a multimodality approach to addiction treatment involves developing programs to assist the client in acquiring skills. These skills involve learning how to cope with stress on affective, cognitive, and behavioral levels (Milkman, 1983).

Affective Modalities

Affective modalities are biopsychological and stimulate a state of altered consciousness. The ability to alter consciousness is a defense mechanism used by vertebrates which augments the organism's evolutionary survival chances under circumstances in which a cold and correct environmental assessment might be sufficiently demoralizing to mean the difference between life and death (Frye, 1980a, in press). It is thought that altered consciousness results from changes in neural/neurochemical mechanisms in the brain brought about by increasing or decreasing neurotransmission (Milkman & Sunderwirth, 1983). Neurotransmission is subject to stimulation or inhibition and appears to be controlled by endogenous chemicals. Addictions appear to alter consciousness by changing levels of neurotransmission. Levels of neurotransmission may may be modified by environmental factors—the totality of physical and social phenomena which surround or affect an individual. Perceived threats to an individual's survival or perceived safety and security are some environmental perceptions which may alter an individual's levels of neurotransmission.

The purpose of affective modalities is to train the client to achieve an affective experience which may alter consciousness and produce feelings, emotions, moods, and temperament. Stress management training may be a congruous modality for this purpose, and the training can involve (1) visual imagery to produce cognitive calming, (2) progressive relaxation to achieve a tension-relaxation contrast, (3) verbal suggestions to achieve deep muscle relaxation, (4) autogenic therapy promoting heaviness and warmth in extremities and calming of the autonomic nervous system, and (5) automated systematic desensitization where the client imagines a hierarchy of anxiety-producing situations under conditions of physical relaxation with the goal of weakening the anxiety responses (Charlesworth & Dempsey, 1982; Chaplin, 1975).

Charismatic group therapy may be another affective modality which may alter consciousness (Galanter, 1978, 1982). Often seen in drug-free therapeutic communities, Alcoholics Anonymous, and religious groups, charismatic therapy may involve totemic objects and rituals with a behavior code. It is associated with a zealous movement, and there is limited differentiation between the care-giver and the recipient. The group members adhere to a consensual belief system, sustain a high level of social cohesiveness, are strongly influenced by behavioral norms, and impute charismatic power to the group or its leadership (Frye, 1981b, in press). The altered states of consciousness produced by charismatic therapy appear to be similar to those seen in the religious conversion experience, and relief from depression and anxiety may be experienced by the charismatic group member (Galanter, 1978).

Meditation is an affective modality associated with a decline in addictive behavior (Aron & Aron, 1980). It usually consists of a sustained effort at thinking, usually of a comtemplative variety. It may involve a mantra or sound pattern as an incantation. The physiologic effects of meditation are opposite to those identified by medicine as being characteristic of the effort to meet the demands of stress (Selye, 1975). Like drug-using behavior, meditation appears to alter the individual's perception of stressful situations and promotes behavior change toward objects and circumstances in the environment that are perceived to be threatening (Frye, 1981a).

A brain wave is the rhythmic fluctuation of voltage between parts of the brain. Alpha brain wave conditioning may be an adjunct affective modality in the treatment of addiction. Clinical research has reported the correlation of alpha activity with subjective states of relaxation, peacefulness, etc. (Kamiya, 1964). The purpose of alpha biofeedback training might be to produce a standard stimulus-response association between alpha control and anxiety reduction; anxiety reduction need not derive from the biofeedback in order to become paired with it. Biofeedback may be useful at an early treatment stage, but later stages must lead to the development of styles of thought and behavior fostering autonomy from existential crutches (Goldberg, Greenwood & Taintor, 1977).

The experiential group marathon is an existential affective modality that can stimulate a state of altered consciousness and consists of a group encounter of extended length, usually twenty-four hours or more.

At the end of a marathon, individuals often feel they have gone through a unique, singular experience that makes them special (Cohen & Rietma, 1980). The individual may report a changed state of consciousness (a peak experience). Active mechanisms in the marathon promoting altered affect might include sleep deprivation, stimulus intensity (sound, light), shared group closeness or cohesion, and emotional release (Frye, Hammer & Burke, 1981; Hoag & Gissen, in press).

Ericksonian psychotherapy is an affective modality that may be used in the treatment of addiction. This modality uses resistance, symptom prescription, paradoxical double binds and strategic interventions with complex embedded metaphors, hypnosis, and strategic use of trance phenomena (Erickson, 1980; Lankton & Lankton, 1983). Neurolinguistic programming is based on Ericksonian techniques and may solicit affective change or altered states of consciousness (Grinder & Bandler, 1982).

Cognitive Modalities

Cognitive modalities include didactic lectures, seminars, workshops, and audiovisual presentations. When individuals receive adequate training in certain skills such as assertiveness, socializing, sexual functioning, or value clarifying, they often change their thinking, behaving, and emoting, and sometimes make themselves less emotionally disturbed (Ellis & Grieger, 1977). Studies have appeared that have demonstrated that skill training has therapeutic effects and such training includes an important cognitive element (Byrne, 1973; Christensen, 1974; Usher, 1974).

Cognitive-behavioral therapy may be used in the multimodality approach to treatment for addiction, and it has proven useful as an alternative and adjunct to traditional approaches. This approach includes assumptions that treatment planning includes the critical element of evaluating how the client perceives the effects of addiction and how the client perceives the reasons for addiction. The treatment planning may then explore alternatives and challenge misconceptions. Specific targets of treatment are identified by the client and therapist so that progress can be objectively measured. A target is defined as a problem area that is related to the addictive behavior (Weiner & Fox, 1982).

Rational emotive therapy (RET) is a cognitive-behavior therapy that assumes everything people do includes very important learning elements. Ellis (1977) wrote that biological inheritance and self- and social-learning tendencies combine to make us human and to provide us with our main goals and satisfactions. We largely control our own destinies, particularly our emotional destinies, by the way we interpret or look at the events that occur in our lives and by the actions that we take. Rational emotive therapy has utilized therapy groups designed for impulsive individuals and has been used to treat addictive behavior such as alcohol abuse (Watkins, 1977).

Behavioral Modalities

Among the techniques available to the behavioral therapist are anxiety-relief responses, assertive behavior facilitation, behavioral rehearsal, conditioned suppression, covert extinction, covert reinforcement, emotive imagery, implosive therapy, replication therapy, self-desensitization, shame aversive therapy, thought stopping, and time out from reinforcement (Chaplin, 1975). Behavioral therapies have been invoked as treatment for addiction utilizing learning principles and techniques. Behavior therapy assumes that disorders such as addiction are learned patterns of behavior that are maladaptive and consequently can best be modified in more adaptive directions through relearning. A direct attack is made on the client's symptoms.

Contingency management is a behavioral therapy in which the behavior is thought to be controlled by its consequences. When the client and clinician arrive at a formal agreement to impose certain contingencies on addictive behavior, the technique is known as *contingency contracting*. Addiction control suggests that for some this technique does alter addictive behavior (Boudin, 1972; Miller, 1975; Hall & Burmaster, 1977).

Aversive therapy is a behavioral modality aimed at reducing the frequency of maladaptive behavior by associating it with aversive stimuli during a conditioning procedure. The use of drugs (Antabuse), electric shock, or other aversive stimuli may become paired with the addictive behavior. The addictive behavior becomes aversive, and the client develops a repugnance for that behavior. Electrical and chemical aversion techniques may be difficult to apply to the typical addicted individual. Covert conditioning or sensitization has gained some acceptance in the treatment of persons addicted to drug using and consists of the use of imagined scenes as aversive and rewarding events (O'Brien & Lorenz, 1979; Callner, 1975; Cautela & Rosensteil, 1975; Chaplin, 1975).

Conclusion

Addicted individuals come from a wide range of social-class, ethnic, and geographical backgrounds; no single program can meet the needs of all addicted persons. In recent years, a better understanding of the need for comprehensive, multimodality programs has evolved (Brill, 1977). There is a need to focus on the individual as well as the addicted behavior.

Because addictions permit individuals to cope by altering stressful environmental assessments and perceptions which may affect survival, successful treatment leading to cessation of addictive behavior must consist of training in other, less destructive ways of coping. As Tiger (1979) has pointed out, humans, being more complicated animals, must have more instincts than others, and "our brains are higher brains, more efficient at diagnosing and ferreting out possible hazards, impediments, problems (moral and factual) and demons and shades with which we can be harassed. It becomes all the more important then that we possess an overriding internal censor of all these mean and depressing thoughts so that we are not immobilized and disconsolate forever" (p. 173).

Addictions may activate the overriding internal censor by causing changes in neurotransmission that promote a feeling of well-being and optimism. Addicts may perceive environmental deficits which need to be filled by satiation; environmental excess which needs to be confronted by arousal; or environmental existential quiescence which needs to be altered by fantasy.

Treatment for addictive behavior may need to consist of a multimodality approach aimed at (1) using cognitive and behavioral modalities to achieve abstinence from the behavior of modification of that behavior, (2) using affective modalities to substitute other behaviors to help fill the void created by abstinence, and (3) using cognitive, behavioral, and affective modalities to provide skill training in altering consciousness to overcome perceived environmental impediments on a long-term basis.

Some modalities and treatment methods briefly reviewed in this chapter are innovative and experimental. O'Brien and Lorenz (1979) wrote that originators of new treatments are usually enthusiastic and report good results, but that controlled studies are necessary to determine efficacy. They recommend that any clinician wanting to try therapies of an experimental nature consider setting up a controlled outcome study if facilities permit.

References

Aron, A. & Aron, E.N. (1980). The transcendental meditation program's effect on addictive behavior. *Addictive Behavior, 7*, 3–12.

Boudin, H.M. (1972). Contingency contracting as a therapeutic tool in the deceleration of amphetamine use. *Behavior Therapy, 3*, 604–608.

Brill, L. (1977). The treatment of drug abuse: Evolution of a perspective. *American Journal of Psychiatry, 134*(2), 157–160.

Byrne, P. (1973). *Stage and sex differences in moral and ego development prior and consequent of independence training.* Unpublished doctoral dissertation, University of Toronto.

Callner, D.A. (1975). Behavioral treatment approaches to drug abuse: A critical review of the research. *Psychological Bulletin, 82*, 143–164.

Cautela, J.R. & Rosensteil, A.K. (1975). The use of covert conditioning in the treatment of drug abuse. *International Journal of the Addictions, 10*, 277–303.

Chaplin, J. (1975). *Dictionary of psychology.* New York: Dell.

Charlesworth, E.A. & Dempsey, G. (1982). Trait anxiety reductions in a substance abuse population trained in stress management. *Journal of Clinical Psychology, 38*(4), 764–768.

Christensen, C. (1974). *Development and field testing of an interpersonal coping skills program.* Toronto: Ontario Institute for Studies in Education.

Cohen, E.S. & Rietma, K. (1980). Utilizing marathon therapy in a drug and alcohol rehabilitation program. *International Journal of Group Psychotherapy, 31*(1), 117–123.

Ellis, A. (1977). Rational-emotive therapy: Research data that supports the clinical and personality hypotheses of R.E.T. and other modes of cognitive-behavior therapy. *The Counseling Psychologist, 7*(1), 2–42.

Ellis, A & Grieger, R. (1977). *Rational-emotive therapy: A handbook of theory and practice.* New York: Springer.

Erickson, M.H. (1980). *The collected papers of Milton H. Erickson on hypnosis.* New York: Irvington.

Frye, R.V. (1980a). The sociobiological paradigm: A new approach to drug-using behavior. *Journal of Psychedelic Drugs, 12*(1), 21–25.

Frye, R.V. (1980b). "Why is sugar sweet?" Drug abuse: A sociobiological approach. In R. Faulkinberry (Ed.), *Drug* (pp. 188–192). Lafayette, LA: Endac Enterprises.

Frye, R.V. (1981a). Drug behavior: An approach from behavioral biology. *Stress, 2*(2), 5–9.

Frye, R.V. (1981b). Sociobiology and the therapeutic community. In A. Schecter, (Ed.), *Drug dependence and alcoholism: Biomedical issues* (pp. 547–559). New York: Plenum.

Frye, R.V. (in press). The therapeutic community: A sociobiologic study. *Journal of Psychoactive Drugs, 16*(1).

Frye, R.V., Hammer, M. & Burke, G. (1981). The confrontation-sensitivity (C-S) group. In A. Schecter, (Ed.), *Drug dependence and alcoholism: Biomedical issues* (pp. 193–199). New York: Plenum.

Galanter, M. (1978). The "relief effect": A sociobiological model for neurotic distress and large-group therapy. *American Journal of Psychiatry, 135*(5), 588–591.

Galanter, M. (1982). Charismatic religious sects and psychiatry: An overview. *American Journal of Psychiatry, 139*(12), 1539–1547.

Goldberg, R.J., Greenwood, J.C. & Taintor, Z. (1977). Alpha conditioning as an adjunct treatment for drug dependence: 2. *International Journal of the Addictions, 12*(1), 195–204.

Grinder, J. & Bandler, R. (1982). *Trans-formations: Neuro-linguistic programming and the structure of hypnosis.* Moab, UT: Real People Press.

Hall, S.M. & Burmaster, S. (1977). Contingency contracting as a therapeutic tool with methadone clients: Six single subject studies. *Behaviour Research and Therapy, 15,* 438–441.

Hoag, J. & Gissen, J.D. (in press). Marathon: A life and death experience. *Journal of Psychoactive Drugs.*

Kamiya, J. (1964). Operant control of the EEG alpha rhythm and some of its reported effects on consciousness. In C. Tart (Ed.), *Altered states of consciousness* (pp. 507–517). New York: Wiley.

Lankton, S. & Lankton, C. (1983). *The answer within: A clinical framework of Ericksonian hypnotherapy.* New York: Brunner/Mazel.

Milkman, H. (1983). *Introduction. Course syllabus for addictions: An interdisciplinary synthesis of concepts and treatments.* Unpublished syllabus. Metropolitan State College, Department of Conferences and Seminars, Denver.

Milkman, H. & Sunderwirth, S. (1982). Addictive processes. *Journal of Psychoactive Drugs, 14*(3), 177–192.

Milkman, H. & Sunderwirth, S. (1983, October). The chemistry of craving. *Psychology Today, 17,* pp. 36–44.

Miller, P.M. (1975). A behavioral intervention program for chronic public drunkenness offenders. *Archives of General Psychiatry, 32,* 915–918.

O'Brien, J.S. & Lorenz, K.Y. (1979). Innovative treatments for drug addiction. In R.L. Dupont, A. Goldstein & J. O'Donnell (Eds.), *Handbook on drug abuse* (pp. 193–201). Washington, D.C.: U.S. Government Printing Office.

Selye, H. (1975). Introduction. In H.H. Bloomfield, M.P. Cain & D.T. Jaffe (Eds.), *TM: Discovering inner energy and overcoming stress.* New York: Delacourte Press.

Senay, E.C. (1981). Multimodality programming in Illinois: Evolution of a public health concept. In J.H. Lowinson & P. Ruiz, (Eds.), *Substance abuse: Clinical problems and perspectives* (pp. 396–402). Baltimore: Williams & Wilkins.

Tiger, L. (1979). *Optimism: The biology of hope.* New York: Simon & Schuster.

Usher, B. (1974). *The teaching and training of interpersonal skills and cognitions in a counselor training program.* Unpublished doctoral dissertation, University of Toronto.

Veterans Administration. (1973). *Professional services.* Washington, D.C.: Department of Medicine and Surgery, Veterans Administration.

Watkins, J.T. (1977). The rational-emotive dynamics of impulsive disorders. In A. Ellis & R. Grieger (Eds.), *Handbook of rational-emotive therapy* (pp. 135–152). New York: Springer.

Weiner, H. & Fox, S. (1982). Cognitive-behavioral therapy with substance abusers. *Social Casework: The Journal of Contemporary Social Work, 63*(9), 564–567.

Part III
Epilogue

16
Diagnosis, Conceptual Models, and the Nature of This Book

Lloyd I. Sederer

There is magic in naming. The act of naming, the assignment of meaning, is the noble mantle we wear on the tip of our tongues. Naming is the act that renders man qualitatively different and separate from other animals.

"And Rumplestiltsken was his name," said the imprisoned queen. In doing so, she freed herself, saved her child, and destroyed that greedy little creature. To treat the wandering womb (hysteria), physicians in the tenth century recited a Latin chant that prohibited, by naming everywhere else, the womb from resting anywhere but within the pelvis (Zilboorg, 1969). The young child who calls for milk rather than uttering a cry to protest his hunger quickly discovers the magic and power of naming.

If naming affords power over the supernatural and mundane, then stripping someone of his name can disempower. When names became numbers in concentration and prisoner of war camps, human identity was stifled, and powerlessness through namelessness was established. Some feminists would argue that a similar event is promulgated on a woman who takes her husband's surname when she marries.

Webster defines diagnosis as "the art or act of identifying a disease from its signs and symptoms" (Gove, 1968). The derivation of diagnosis is from the Greek words *two* and *to know*, which together mean to distinguish or to differentiate. We use the word *diagnosis* as a noun, in naming an illness, and *diagnose* as a verb denoting a process of decision about naming.

Diagnosis is also, from the perspective of this chapter, the central activity of our profession, the organizing principle of our literature and our institutions, and the definer of psychiatric patienthood (Pruyser, 1976). We may wish to consider ourselves like the first umpire who said, "Some are balls and some are strikes, and I call them as they are." Or we may wish to consider ourselves like the second umpire who said, "Some's balls and some's strikes, and I call 'em as I see 'em." We in psychiatry and the social sciences are, however, not a part of a professional world comprised solely of physical facts (umpire number 1) or subjective events (umpire number 2), but, instead, we reside in a world of social realities where definition (diagnosis) has the authority and force of fact. We are a third umpire who states, "Some's balls and some's strikes, but they ain't nothin' till I calls 'em" (Henshel & Silverman, 1975; Kleinman, 1981).

This book about the addictions has been developed in order to define better the problem of addiction from etiological and treatment perspectives. In doing so, and in defining, diagnosing, and fashioning treatment approaches, the content of its chapters determines social reality for those we regard as addicts. This book is the third umpire at home plate in the major league of human disorders entitled addictions.

In this chapter I will first discuss how diagnosis makes a difference and some of the dilemmas diagnosis creates in the field of addictions. I will then examine the biopsychosocial model (the blend of biology, psychology, and sociology inherent to Milkman and Shaffer's integrative approach or interdisciplinary synthesis as described in the introduction) in order to broaden our understanding of the functions and limits of the conceptual framework that underlies all that we see and do in our clinical work.

Diagnosis: Meanings and Dilemmas

What is a disease or a disorder? If applying the concept of a disease to a person defines patienthood, organizes treatment services, and is the basis of payment, and if not applying the concept of a disease to a person denies all the forgoing, we would do well to take a moment to examine some popular notions of disease (Kendell, 1975).

Smith, Milkman, and Sunderwirth (see chapter 13) offer a widely held description of the disease concept in which genetic predisposition interacts with the environment, and control is lost over the consumption of the addictive substance with adverse consequences.

Disease might also be conceived of as suffering. Yet, if disease is suffering, how would we think about the sick who don't complain and the multitude of those who suffer vocally, yet are not sick? Disease could be a lesion, if only all disorders had a palpable or visible pathology. Perhaps disease could be a neat statistical concept in which formulas and clusters determine disorder, though neatness disappears when we consider how these fine tools were fashioned, and by whom. Even if we consider a disorder to be, as has been suggested (Kendell, 1975), the "sum of abnormal phenomena . . . [that] place the affected individual at a biological disadvantage, reducing his chances of survival or procreation. . . ." (p.

14), a highly intelligent offering, we cannot elude the fact that a disease or disorder also acts as a concept that we consider useful for certain specific goals (Sider, 1983b).

Goals, then, or a plan of action, are perhaps what disease and disorder are about. If so, we would then be asking not whether a disorder exists but whether it (the person) should be treated. Zinberg and Shaffer (see chapter 6) address the social psychology of intoxicants and emphasize the critical importance of social setting, not drug substance, in the addictive disorders. The definition of disorder as that which should be treated (or legislated against—see Hunter and Pudim's chapter on legal aspects of addictions) provides a judgment underpinned not by objective facts but by human choice.

Once we encompass social setting, human choice, and *that which should be* in our definition of disease and disorder, we depart from strict science and substance abuse and enter the world of ethics. It is one thing to observe the action of coca extract as used by natives indigenous to the high altitudes of Colombia, South America, or in the recording studios of Columbia Records; it is another matter to define these behaviors as conditions for us to treat (or legally prohibit). I will have more to say about this as we discuss how diagnosis makes a difference.

Diagnosis and the Individual

In medicine, a biological aberration is essential to considering someone diseased, disordered, or ill; it is not, with all due respect to Dr. Sunderwirth (see chapter 2), sufficient. Biological aberration must be coupled with the *social value* that what the individual has or does is undesirable in order for there to be sufficient cause to diagnose a disorder (Parsons, 1951; Szasz, 1961; Veatch, 1973). Biology and social judgment are, therefore, inseparable components of what is denoted as sickness. For those addictions in which a biological aberration is presumed, the same consideration applies. For a biologically based (at least in part) addiction to be considered a disease or a disorder, we would have to apply the social value that this state is undesirable and socially unacceptable. This is how diagnosis impacts on the individual. It is not that the addict has a disease; it is that he has a socially unacceptable disease.

Matters do not stop there. Built onto this conception of disease as an undesirable biological aberration is the obligation to want and to try to get well. What this means is that a set of socially sanctioned professionals are identified to whom the addict should go in order to obtain technically expert help. Shaffer and Neuhaus (see chapter 8) organize the assessment of the addict along hypotheses generating and hypotheses testing lines that lead the clinician to more definitive diagnostic conclusions. Once diagnosed, the addict is urged to pursue treatment, which can be quite varied, as we witness in the section on treatment approaches in this volume. Abstinence may be insisted on or abstinence alternatives (including controlled drinking) developed. Behavior may be examined or personality explored. Biology may be considered preeminent or wedded to a multimodal approach.

What is central to this process is that, once in the hands of experts, the addict is given a careful evaluation which describes a nexus of biological and developmental risk factors and unfortunate social circumstances. As this is done, *judgment* questions about cause and responsibility are raised and often answered and acted on through the treatment rendered. If the addict's disorder is considered to be a biologically determined disease, responsibility and treatment are different from when his disorder is considered one of free will. Is this a biologically determined disease for which the individual has limited responsibility? Or is this a disorder of free will which calls for the development of responsibility in the individual? The addict, through the process of diagnosis, is obligated to seek professional help and, according to the specific judgments rendered by professionals, is either released from or burdened by responsibilities for his disorder.

Matters do not stop there. We are all familiar with the reality that treatment follows diagnosis (Menninger, 1963; Rosenhan, 1973; Szasz, 1965). I think that Carl Rogers was wrong when he opined that therapy was good for all people. For some, and these are more extreme examples, diagnosis and treatment may involve a loss of freedom which can include coerced treatment in employee assistance programs or involuntary hospitalization. Though more subtle, but no less powerful, a subjective loss of personal freedom may occur through whatever erosion of will that the identity of patienthood may foster. Marcel Proust remarked that "for each ailment that doctors cure with medications (as I am told they do occasionally succeed in doing) they produce ten others in healthy individuals by inoculating them with that pathogenic agent a thousand times more virulent than all the microbes—the idea that they are ill." Further, treatments themselves may be toxic, as may be treatment milieus. Finally, the stigma of diagnosis may add insult to injury.

I do not mean to take issue with enforced treatment or to propose that we abandon diagnosis and therapeutics, as some critics suggest, because of the associated unwelcome but inevitable risks. It is ingenuous to consider that any biobehavioral act can be innocuous. The problems associated with diagnosis and its implied therapeutics are not grounds for indicting the entire enterprise but, instead, understanding fully its implications and power in order to attend to the risk/benefit ratio of our work. To retreat into antidiagnosis and to abandon therapeutics would be a return to the dark ages of scientific inquiry. It would be analogous to throwing out our radio because we came across a bad program (Schectman, 1973; Shevrin & Schectman, 1973).

Diagnosis and Society

The withdrawal of the Soviet Union from the World Psychiatric Society after years of internationally based criticism about their abuse of psychiatric theory and therapy is a current and important example of how purposeful misdiagnosis can be harmful to the patient and can undercut the integrity and credibility of a profession (Reich, 1979, 1981). Psychiatric diagnosis, in this instance, had become a tool of the state. Its aim was to categorize medically and rehabilitate social deviance and to eliminate political protest. The transformation of social and political problems into medical ones, in this instance, is obvious, as was the Nazi definition (and disposition) of the Jews. Zinberg and Shaffer (see chapter 6) have already alerted us to the ways in which society (social setting) can determine, in the area of intoxicant abuse, whether and how a disorder will exist.

There are examples of how diagnosis determines social reality (and vice versa) that are not so obvious. In the two examples to follow, we will see how our vision and our values are shaped by our nosology.

The first example contrasts American and French psychiatric nosology. Americans regard diagnosis to be in the service of science. The biopsychosocial model and DSM III (American Psychiatric Association, 1980) are pragmatic, empirical, and operational. In America the aim of science is description and explanation that are valid and reliable. Strikingly different is the metaphysical nature of French psychiatric nosology in which the significance of symptoms is more speculative and existential (Kroll, 1979). Symptoms are weighed by their importance to the equilibrium of an individual's psychic being. Imagine trying to obtain insurance coverage or employee assistance in this country for your psychic being.

The second example is more immediate to this book and involves the ongoing debate between determinism and free will alluded to earlier. Determinism is a doctrine that states that all acts of will result from causes which determine them in a manner that permits no alternative. Free will doctrine imbues the individual with the capacity and the responsibility for choice (Clements, 1983; Sider, 1983a; Thomasma, 1983; Veatch, 1973).

This book offers a theory of addictions as problem behaviors determined by converging vectors of biology, psychology, and sociology. The threat underlying such a potentially deterministic position is that of moral irresponsibility. Are we to consider addictions as biopsychosocially determined events that curtail or eliminate alternative behaviors? Where is the conceptual place for free will theory, for a belief in the dignity of the individual, and in the "virtue of culpability" (Veatch, 1973, p. 66). What place do determinism and free will play in the ideas offered herein and in the everyday concourse of our clinical practices? For which of our patients, and when, do we offer paternalistic treatment for sickness? For which of our patients, and when, do we expect autonomous behavior? We will examine this further in the next section on diagnosis and dollars and later in our review of the prevailing model of this text, the biopsychosocial model.

Diagnosis and Dollars

On October 1, 1983, the federal government began a financial system for Medicare in which hospitals would be reimbursed according to predetermined payments for 467 specific illnesses and procedures. This prospective payment system is known as diagnostic related groups or DRGs. Health and Human Services Secretary Margaret Heckler was quoted (*Boston Globe*, 1983) as regarding "prospective payment for hospitals . . . [as] the most important improvement in the history of the Medicare program" (p. 1), which finances thirty million Americans over age sixty-five and has a cost of 38.5 billion dollars (compared to 3.0 billion sixteen years ago).

If you do not think diagnosis makes a difference, wait until this system of cost control extends beyond Medicare or enters the field of substance abuse. The diagnosis will determine how many days of hospital treatment and what procedures will be reimbursed, and at what rate. Although substance abuse programs are familiar with fixed hospital stays (for example, 28 days) for an alcohol rehabilitation program, the call for diagnosis will be more precise. The third-party scrutiny will be more intense. An important example[1] is provided by those patients who carry dual DSM III Axis I diagnoses of, for example, schizophrenia and alcoholism, or depression and substance abuse. These patients generally cannot tolerate a standard rehabilitation program because of the constraints created by their biological pathology and ego deficits, which must be given priority because they frequently set the rate at which patients recompensate and to what degree they will improve. Accurate diagnosis will, in these patients, determine which treatments need be provided when, how much to expect of the patient, and, further, will substantiate the need for greater prospective payment for this dual DRG.

Diagnosis, Research, and Training

The scientific enterprise of research rests on a descriptive nosology and classification that is clear, precise, valid, and reliable. A language must be developed that can be used by professionals of diverse persuasions in a highly communicable manner. This language, this nosology and classification, is called diagnosis (Feighner, 1979; Frances & Cooper, 1981). Diagnosis is the mother tongue of the profession, without which we could not speak. With no common language, there could be no research, no programs for training novitiates, and no professional texts on the addictions.

Modes of Understanding and the Nature of This Book

Paradigms: Turf, Theory, and Technique

A paradigm is a model or pattern of understanding that "stands for the entire constellation of beliefs, values, techniques . . . shared by the members of a given [scientific] community" (Kuhn, 1970, p. 10). A paradigm provides the "law, theory, application and instrumentation . . . from which spring particular coherent traditions of scientific research . . ." (Kuhn, 1970, p. 10). A paradigm provides the "legitimate problems and methods of a research field for succeeding generations of practitioners . . ." (Kuhn, 1970, p. 11). In essence, a paradigm establishes the profession's turf and articulates its theory and methodology (Lifton, 1976).

Paradigms and Prescriptions

A scientific model becomes a paradigm when it is widely held and unifying for the field at a particular stage in the development of that field. Physics has undergone paradigm shifts from Aristotelian to Newtonian paradigms and then on to principles of relativity and uncertainty. Astronomy moved from Ptolemaic notions to a Copernican vision when the model could not encompass new and contesting data (Sederer, 1977).

Not all scientific fields enjoy the unity of a paradigm. In these preparadigmatic sciences, there exists a set of prescriptions (or notions, conceptions, or trends) with considerable guiding and illuminating power. Further, prescriptions, unlike paradigms, are less enduring and, because they are often oppositional, tend to compete for ideological clout. Preparadigmatic fields are organized around prescriptions and show visible conflict. Change is commonplace, with one prescription occupying theoretical dominance at a given time while others become counterdominant, waiting and vying for their turn at the helm (Watson, 1973). Determinism and free will are familiar examples of competing prescriptions, as are the biological, psychological, and social theories of addictions.

A science without a prevailing paradigm, a science of prescriptions, is fragmented and frustrated in its efforts to establish a research and training tradition. Without conceptual unity, a profession must spend time casting about in search of an organizing conceptual structure. In part, this is the nature of this text, for we are in the preparadigmatic state, trying here to establish a paradigm.

Limits of the Biopsychosocial Model

This text offers us a model meant to embrace a breadth of theoretical positions. In the biopsychosocial model, disease, person, and social situation converge in a manner fully reminiscent of the "Holy Trinity of Destiny," namely heredity, environment, and circumstance, penned by Voltaire some two hundred years ago.

We have before us a paradigm proposal, a conceptual framework that might end divisiveness and fragmentation and provide a heuristic view for the future. Proper diagnosis of biological, psychological, and social substrates for a disorder should prescribe the proper treatment or at least determine the research questions ahead. Unfortunately, this is not the case, as we shall see from recognizing the limits of the biopsychosocial model (Abrams, 1981, 1983).

The first limitation of this model is that it does not provide a method for making a hierarchy of causation. Although biology, person, and circumstance may all have causal explanatory power, how are we to know which cause bears more or less importance? When our causal understanding weighs heavily on biology, our therapeutics follow suit; when our understanding is developmental, our treatment is psychosocial. The biopsychosocial model lends no aid in understanding to what degree which addiction is principally a biological disorder to be helped by drugs specific to neurotransmission. Nor does this model inform us as to which addiction is principally the product of a developmental fault in which the deficiency may be modified by empathic assistance. Do we pursue Khantzian and Schneider's self-medication hypothesis (see chapter 11). Frosch's psychoanalytic understanding (chapter 4), or Collins, Sunderwirth, and Smith's disease concepts (chapters 1, 2, and 13)? The biopsychosocial model offers us breadth but not hierarchy.

A second limitation of biopsychosocial theory resides in mistaking meaning and causation. Freud gave us an invaluable gift in his demonstration that a symptom has meaning. In doing so, however, he took the study of behavior out of "the world of science and placed it into the world of the humanities because a meaning is not the product of causes but the creation of a subject" (Home, 1966, p. 43). When confronted with a binge eater, a cocaine addict, or a compulsive gambler, we can search for biological or learning theory based behavioral causation, or we can seek to understand, for example, the meaning the symptom has for the patient's self-esteem. To explore for meaning is to enter the world and the logic and method of the humanities, which is very different from the logic and method of the sciences. In going from the sciences to the humanities, we replace observation with inference and explanation with interpretation. There are no clear guidelines in the biopsychosocial model for when we are concerned with the meaning of behavior and when we are concerned with its causation. The biopsychosocial model does not tell us when to investigate (or treat) a fact scientifically and when to understand the meaning of an event.

The third, and for this discussion, final limitation of the biopsychosocial model is the problem of treatment staging (Home, 1966, p. 42). It may be possible to discern causes and meanings (through hypotheses testing) and even to weigh their respective importance, yet be left with uncertainty about the sequence of interventions. This problem is well illustrated by the example provided earlier of patients with dual diagnoses of, for example, schizophrenic psychosis and alcohol addiction, or depression and substance abuse. It is my opinion that the more limiting disorder must be treated first (in this case, the schizophrenic psychosis or the depression) for it establishes the rate and distance limiting biological and ego variables. For the dual diagnoses of alcohol addiction and personality disorder, the addiction would have to be treated first. This is my opinion; it is not derivable from the model at hand.

Conclusion

Without a paradigm, we repeatedly confront uncertainty about the legitimate turf of our professional endeavors. Without a paradigm, we have no widely held set of laws to define our beliefs and methods. As we try to apply simultaneously biological, psychological, and social prescriptions, we discover we have no hierarchy of causation and no prescribed sequence for intervention. Finally, the admixture of science and the humanities proposed by the biopsychosocial model exposes us simultaneously to categorically different questions of causation and meaning. Our professional apparatus is an amalgam of technology and ethics. We have one foot in science and the other in the humanities. Our model cannot tell us which foot to lead with. It is not our model that tells us that science is a fine tool but a poor master.

What guides our step, or should, is *not science but the context in which it must reside.* This context is ethical and moral, "that for the sake of which" something exists (Aristotle, 1952, p. 128). A science or technology of addictions must be embedded in considerations of why this science should exist—of the social, moral, and ethical implications of the science. No model can offer that perspective, for this is the domain of values.

This book provides us with a comprehensive and synthetic science and technology of addictions. The work ahead lies not only in perfecting and advancing this science but also in consistently appreciating the ethical and moral context that the science of addictions aims to serve.

Note

1. My thanks to Dr. Nancy Davis for this clinical problem.

References

Abroms, E.M. (1981). Psychiatric serialism. *Comprehensive Psychiatry, 22,* 372–378.

Abroms, E.M. (1983). Beyond electicism. *American Journal of Psychology, 140,* 740–745.

American Psychiatric Association. (1980). *Diagnostic and statistical manual of mental disorders* (3d ed.). Washington, D.C.: Author.

Aristotle (1952). *Posterior Analytics* (Great Books of the Western World, Vol. 8). Chicago: Encyclopedia Britannica Press.

Boston Globe. (1983, September 1). p. 1.

Clements, C.D. (1983). Common psychiatric problems and uncommon ethical solutions. *Psychiatric Annals, 13*(4), 289–309.

Feighner, J.P. (1979). Nosology: A voice for a systematic data-oriented approach. *American Journal of Psychology, 136,* 1173–1174.

Frances, A. & Cooper, A.M. (1981). Descriptive and dynamic psychiatry: A perspective on DSM III. *American Journal of Psychology, 138,* 1198–1202.

Gove, P.B. (1968). *Websters third new international dictionary of the English language. Unabridged.* Springfield, MA: G. & C. Merriam.

Henshel, R.L. & Silverman, R.A. (1975). *Perception in criminology.* New York: Columbia University Press.

Home, H.J. (1966). The concept of mind. *International Journal of Psycho-Analysis, 47,* 42–49.

Kendell, R.E. (1975). *The role of diagnosis in psychiatry.* Oxford: Blackwell Scientific Publications.

Kleinman, A. (1981). Summary of the social labeling paradigm. In C. Eisdorfer, D. Cohen, A. Kleinman & P. Maxim (Eds.), *Models for clinical psychopathology* (pp. 53–57). New York: Spectrum.

Kuhn, T.S. (1970). *The structure of scientific revolutions* (2d ed.). Chicago: University of Chicago Press.

Lifton, R.J. (1976). *The life of the self.* New York: Simon & Schuster.

Menninger, K.A. [with Mayman, M. & Pruyser, P.] (1963). *The vital balance: The life process in mental health and illness.* New York: Viking.

Parsons, T. (1951). *The social system.* New York: Free Press.

Pruyser, P.W. (1976). Introduction to diagnosis and the difference it makes. *Bulletin of the Menninger Clinic, 4*(5), 411–416.

Reich, W. (1979, May 13). Grigorenko gets a second opinion. *New York Times,* sec. 6, p. 18.

Reich, W. (1981). Psychiatric diagnosis as an ethical problem. In S. Bloch & P. Chodoff (Eds.), *Psychiatric Ethics.* New York: Oxford University Press.

Rosenhan, D.L. (1973). On being sane in insane places. *Science, 179*(4070), 250–258.

Schectmen, F. (1973). On being misinformed by misleading arguments. *Bulletin of the Menninger Clinic, 37*(5), 523–525.

Sederer, L.I. (1977). The importance of seeing psychiatry as more than a science. *Psychiatric Opinion, 14*(4), 27, 46–47.

Shevrin, H. & Schectman, F. (1973). The diagnostic process in psychiatric evaluations. *Bulletin of the Menninger Clinic, 37*(5), 451–494.

Sider, R.C. (1983a). Ethics for psychiatry. *Psychiatric Annals, 13*(4), 285–288.

Sider, R.C. (1983b). Mental health norms and ethical practice. *Psychiatric Annals, 13*(4), 306.

Szasz, T.S. (1961). *The myth of mental illness.* New York: Harper & Row.

Szasz, T.S. (1965). *Psychiatric justice.* New York: Collier.

Thomasma, D.C. (1983, Spring). Limitations of the autonomy model for the doctor-patient relationship. *Pharos,* pp. 2–5.

Veatch, R.M. (1973). The medical model: Its nature and problems. *Hastings Center Studies, 1*(3), 59–76.

Watson, R.I. (1973). Psychology: A prescriptive science. In M. Henle, J. Jaynes & J.J. Sullivan (Eds.), *Historical conceptions of psychology* (pp. 13–28). New York: Springer.

Zilboorg, G. (1969). *A history of medical psychology.* New York: W.W. Norton.

Index

List of Contributors

Milton E. Burglass, M.D.
Instructor of Psychiatry
Department of Psychiatry
Harvard Medical School
at The Cambridge Hospital

Millicent E. Buxton, B.A.
Cofounder, Codirector
Bay Area Taskforce for Impaired
  Nurses
Information Coordinator, Haight-
  Ashbury Free Medical Clinic
San Francisco, California

Allan C. Collins, Ph.D.
Professor of Pharmacology
Institute for Behavioral Genetics
University of Colorado
Boulder, Colorado

Thomas J. Crowley, M.D.
Professor of Psychiatry
University of Colorado
School of Medicine
Denver, Colorado

Chad D. Emrick, Ph.D.
Past President, Society of
  Psychologists in Addictive
  Behavior
Codirector, Abstinence Alter-
  natives
Denver, Colorado

Robert Freedman, M.D.
Associate Professor of Psychiatry
  and Pharmacology
University of Colorado Health
  Sciences Center
Denver, Colorado

William A. Frosch, M.D.
Professor of Psychiatry
Cornell Medical College
New York, New York

Robert Vaughn Frye, M.S.
Chief, Drug Dependence Treat-
  ment Programs
Denver Veterans Administration
  Medical Center
Denver, Colorado

Joel Hansen, M.S.
Department of Psychology
Colorado State University
Fort Collins, Colorado

Alexander M. Hunter
District Attorney
Boulder County, Colorado

Marty Jessup, R.N., M.S.
Codirector
Bay Area Taskforce for Impaired
  Nurses
San Francisco, California

Edward J. Khantzian, M.D.
Associate Professor of Psychiatry
Harvard Medical School
at The Cambridge Hospital

Mim J. Landry, B.A.
Research Assistant
Bay Area Taskforce for Impaired
  Nurses
San Francisco, California

Jeanne C. Maytag, Ph.D.
Abstinence Alternatives
Denver, Colorado

Harvey B. Milkman, Ph.D.
Professor of Psychology,
  Department of Psychology
Metropolitan State College
Denver, Colorado

Charles Neuhaus, Jr., M.Ed.
Coordinator of Outpatient
  Services
North Charles Institute for the
  Addictions
Department of Psychiatry,
  The Cambridge Hospital

Robert A. Pudim, M.S.
Office of the District Attorney
Boulder County, Colorado

Robert J. Schneider, M.Ed.
Drug Treatment Specialist
North Charles Institute for the
  Addictions
Department of Psychiatry,
  The Cambridge Hospital

Lloyd I. Sederer, M.D.
Associate Chief, Department of
  Psychiatry
Harvard Medical School
at Mount Auburn Hospital

Howard J. Shaffer, Ph.D.
Assistant Professor,
  Department of Psychiatry
Harvard Medical School
at The Cambridge Hospital

David E. Smith, M.D.
Founder and Director, Haight-
  Ashbury Free Medical Clinic
San Francisco, California

Stanley G. Sunderwirth, Ph.D.
Professor of Chemistry and Vice-
  President for Academic Affairs
Metropolitan State College
Denver, Colorado

Norman E. Zinberg, M.D.
Clinical Professor of Psychiatry
Harvard Medical School
at The Cambridge Hospital

About the Editors

Harvey B. Milkman received a B.S. degree in psychology in 1966 from City College of New York. In 1974 he received a Ph.D. in clinical psychology from Michigan State University. From 1969 to 1972 he conducted research with William A. Frosch at Bellevue Psychiatric Hospital in New York City on the drug abusers' chosen drug. In 1974 Dr. Milkman joined the faculty at Metropolitan State College, where he is currently a professor in the department of psychology.

Dr. Milkman has published extensively on the psychology of addiction. A recent contribution to the field was his chapter in Leopold Bellak's *The Broad Scope of Ego Function Assessment* (1984). Dr. Milkman was the director of a national conference titled *The Addictions: An Interdisciplinary Synthesis of Concepts and Treatments* which was held in Denver, Colorado on October 27 to 28, 1983.

Howard J. Shaffer received a B.A. degree with honors in psychology from the University of New Hampshire, followed by an M.S. and a Ph.D. in psychology from the University of Miami. Presently, Dr. Shaffer is an assistant professor of psychology in the department of psychiatry at Harvard Medical School and The Cambridge Hospital. In addition, he is chief psychologist at the North Charles Institute for the Addictions and coordinator of psychiatric education for the department of psychiatry at The Cambridge Hospital.

Dr. Shaffer edited several books: *Classic Contributions in the Addictions*, with Dr. Burglass, published by Brunner/Mazel; *The Addictive Behaviors*, with Dr. Stimmel, published by the Haworth Press; and *Myths and Realities: A Book about Drug Issues*.